D0495642

Geoffrey Moorhouse is 'one of the best writers of our time' (Byron Rogers, *The Times*), 'a brillant historian' (Dirk Bogarde, *Daily Telegraph*) and 'a writer whose gifts are beyond category' (Jan Morris, *Independent on Sunday*). He is the author of twenty books, which have won prizes and been translated into several languages. In 1982 he was elected a Fellow of the Royal Society of Literature and in 2006 he became Hon DLitt of the University of Warwick. His *To the Frontier* won the Thomas Cook Award for the best travel book of its year in 1984. He has recently concentrated on Tudor history, notably with *The Pilgrimage of Grace* and, in 2005, *Great Harry's Navy*. He lives in a hill village in North Yorkshire.

By Geoffrey Moorhouse

THE LAST OFFICE

1539 and the Dissolution of a Monastery

GEOFFREY MOORHOUSE

PHOENIX

A PHOENIX PAPERBACK

First published in Great Britain in 2008
by Weidenfeld & Nicolson
This paperback edition published in 2009
by Phoenix,
an imprint of Orion Books Ltd,
Orion House, 5 Upper St Martin's Lane,
London, WC2H 9EA

An Hachette UK company

1 3 5 7 9 10 8 6 4 2

Copyright © Geoffrey Moorhouse 2008

The right of Geoffrey Moorhouse to be identified as the author
of this work has been asserted by him in accordance with the
Copyright, Designs and Patents Act 1988.

All rights reserved. No part of this publication may be
reproduced, stored in a retrieval system, or transmitted,
in any form or by any means, electronic, mechanical,
photocopying, recording or otherwise, without the prior
permission of the copyright owner.

A CIP catalogue record for this book
is available from the British Library.

ISBN 978-0-7538-2575-4

Typeset by Input Data Services Ltd, Bridgwater, Somerset

Printed and bound in the UK
by CPI Mackays, Chatham ME5 8TD

The Orion Publishing Group's policy is to use papers
that are natural, renewable and recyclable products and
made from wood grown in sustainable forests. The logging
and manufacturing processes are expected to conform to
the environmental regulations of the country of origin.

www.orionbooks.co.uk

To Michael and Jenny, with love and thanks;
and to Susan, who was at the heart of it

'Grey towers of Durham! ...
Well yet I love thy mixed and massive piles,
Half church of God, half castle 'gainst the Scot;
And long to roam these venerable aisles,
With records stored of deeds long since forgot'

SIR WALTER SCOTT, *Harold the Dauntless*, Canto III

CONTENTS

✠

ILLUSTRATIONS

✠

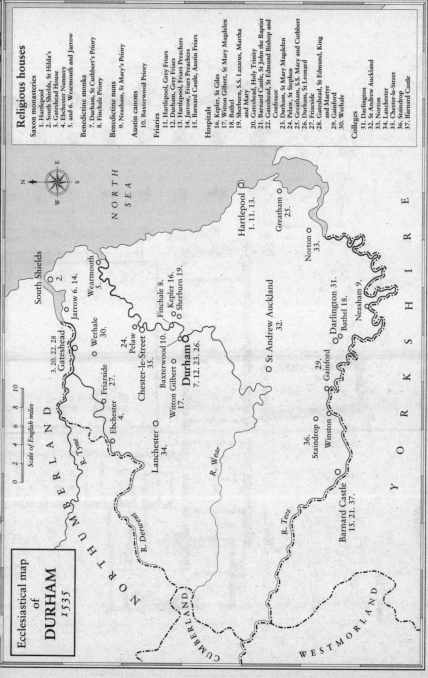

Ecclesiastical map
of
DURHAM
1535

Religious houses

Saxon monasteries
1. Hartlepool
2. South Shields, St Hilda's
3. Gateshead House
4. Ebchester Nunnery
5. and 6. Wearmouth and Jarrow

Benedictine monks
7. Durham, St Cuthbert's Priory
8. Finchale Priory

Benedictine nuns
9. Neasham, St Mary's Priory

Austin canons
10. Baxterwood Priory

Friaries
11. Hartlepool, Grey Friars
12. Durham, Grey Friars
13. Hartlepool, Friars Preachers
14. Jarrow, Friars Preachers
15. Barnard Castle, Austin Friars

Hospitals
16. Kepler, St Giles
17. Witton Gilbert, St Mary Magdelen
18. Bathel
19. Sherburn, S.S. Lazarus, Martha and Mary
20. Gateshead, Holy Trinity
21. Barnard Castle, St John the Baptist
22. Gateshead, St Edmund Bishop and Confessor
23. Durham, St Mary Magdelen
24. Pelaw, St Stephen
25. Greatham, S.S. Mary and Cuthbert
26. Durham, St Leonard
27. Friarside
28. Gateshead, St Edmund, King and Martyr
29. Gainford
30. Werhale

Colleges
31. Darlington
32. St Andrew Auckland
33. Norton
34. Lanchester
35. Chester-le-Street
36. Staindrop
37. Barnard Castle

Scale of English miles
0 2 4 6 8 10

NORTH SEA

NORTHUMBERLAND

South Shields
2.
Jarrow 6. 14.
Wearmouth 5.
Gateshead 3. 20. 22. 28
Werhale 30.
Pelaw 24.
Friarside 27.
Ebchester 4.
Chester-le-Street 35.
Baxterwood 10.
Witton Gilbert 17.
Lanchester 34.
Durham 7. 12. 23. 26.
Finchale 8.
Kepler 16.
Sherburn 19.

Hartlepool 1. 11. 13.
Greatham 25.
Norton 33.

St Andrew Auckland 32.
Darlington 31.
Bathel 18.
Gainford 29.
Neasham 9.

Staindrop 36.
Winston
Barnard Castle 15. 21. 37.

R. Tyne
R. Derwent
R. Wear
R. Tees

CUMBERLAND

WESTMORLAND

YORKSHIRE

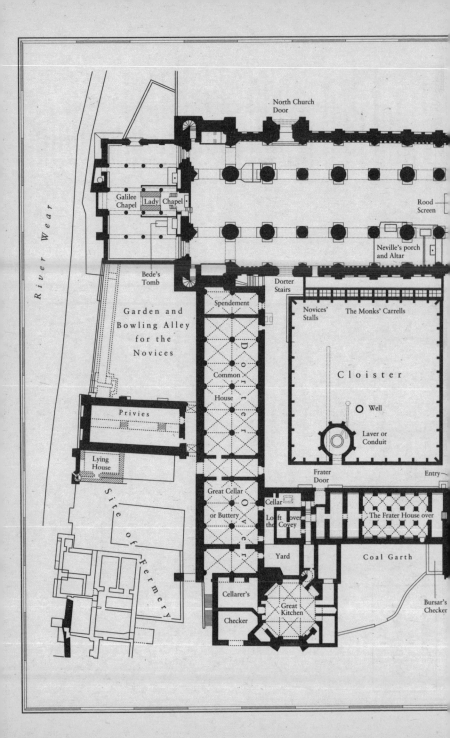

North Church Door

Galilee Chapel

Lady Chapel

Rood Screen

Neville's porch and Altar

Bede's Tomb

Dorter Stairs

Garden and Bowling Alley for the Novices

Spendement

Novices' Stalls

The Monks' Carrells

D o r t e r

Common House

C l o i s t e r

Well

Privies

Laver or Conduit

Lying House

S i t e   o f   F e r m e r y

R i v e r   W e a r

Frater Door

Entry

Great Cellar or Buttery

O v e r

Cellar

Loft over the Covey

The Frater House over

Yard

Coal Garth

Cellarer's

Great Kitchen

Bursar's Checker

Checker

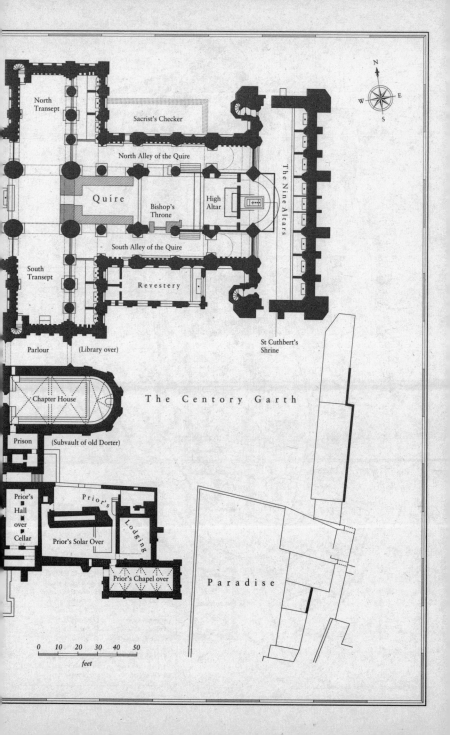

North
Transept

Sacrist's Checker

North Alley of the Quire

Quire

Bishop's
Throne

High
Altar

The Nine Altars

South Alley of the Quire

South
Transept

Revestery

Parlour   (Library over)

St Cuthbert's
Shrine

Chapter House

The Century Garth

Prison   (Subvault of old Dorter)

Prior's
Hall
over
Cellar

Prior's

Lodging

Prior's Solar Over

Prior's Chapel over

Paradise

0   10   20   30   40   50
feet

N
W   E
S

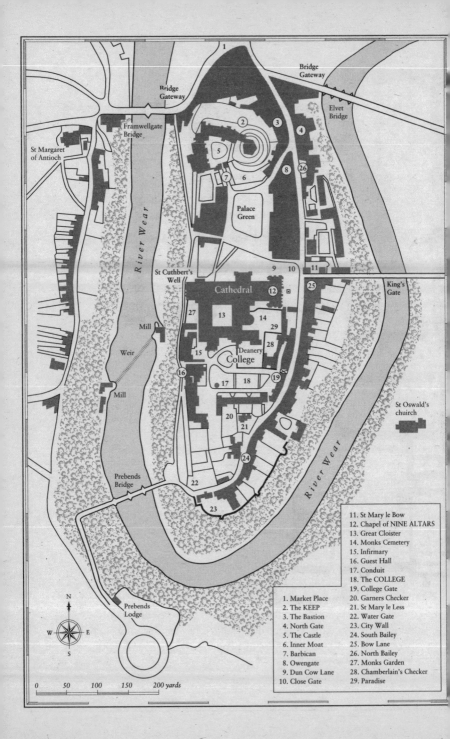

St Margaret
of Antioch

Bridge
Gateway

Framwellgate
Bridge

Bridge
Gateway

Elvet
Bridge

River Wear

St Cuthbert's
Well

Palace
Green

King's
Gate

Cathedral

St Oswald's
chuirch

Mill

Weir

Deanery
College

Mill

River Wear

Prebends
Bridge

Prebends
Lodge

N
W   E
S

0   50   100   150   200 yards

11. St Mary le Bow
12. Chapel of NINE ALTARS
13. Great Cloister
14. Monks Cemetery
15. Infirmary
16. Guest Hall
17. Conduit
18. The COLLEGE
19. College Gate
20. Garners Checker
21. St Mary le Less
22. Water Gate
23. City Wall
24. South Bailey
25. Bow Lane
26. North Bailey
27. Monks Garden
28. Chamberlain's Checker
29. Paradise

1. Market Place
2. The KEEP
3. The Bastion
4. North Gate
5. The Castle
6. Inner Moat
7. Barbican
8. Owengate
9. Dun Cow Lane
10. Close Gate

FOREWORD

✠

The Dissolution of the Monasteries was one of the great catalytic events in our past. It was at the crux of that turning point in English ecclesiastical history which was occasioned by Henry VIII's breach with Rome after two Popes (Clement VII and Paul III) had refused to let him divorce Katherine of Aragon and make Anne Boleyn his Queen in her place. The quarrel between the King and the papacy gave birth not only to the Church of England but also to the other manifestations of the Reformation that would gradually evolve (in some cases directly) from Anglicanism. With some 650 religious houses of one sort and another in England and Wales, the monasteries were a conspicuous presence in the Roman Catholic life of this country, a focal point of faith in all its varied expressions, for a great area surrounding each convent. The faithful civilian populace in these hinterlands was fortified by the knowledge that the monks and other professed religious (of both genders) were perpetually engaged in prayer on their behalf. They were deeply attracted to the idea of pilgrimage to shrines of which the monasteries and other convents were the principal guardians. They believed that they gained merit in the eyes of their Maker by sustaining religious communities with their alms and other donations.

But there were two sides to that coin and the monks themselves supported their local populations in a number of very tangible ways, quite apart from any spiritual benefits that might be conferred as a result of intercession and remembrance. They afforded shelter to weary travellers and sanctuary to the oppressed. They were landlords, and on them depended large numbers of people for their dwellings and the mite of ground from which a subsistence could be scraped. They employed people to work for them, by acting as household servants, farm labourers, skilled craftsmen. They grew crops and bred animals, and what was surplus to their own requirements they sold in their local market places. Because they ate a great deal of seafood, especially during Lent and at other penitential periods, they were important patrons of the nearest fisheries. The monasteries were thus a very considerable factor in the economic life of the nation; and when Henry dismantled them, he deprived his poorer subjects appreciably.

This is not, however, another book about the Dissolution of the Monasteries *per se*, though the Dissolution provides the background and the tension running through much of Part Two. This is, rather, an attempt to convey what life was like in a typical English monastery before the Dissolution began in 1536, and how that life and that presence were transformed by the political and ecclesiastical events for which Henry VIII was responsible. It is about a community of men vowed to a singular way of life that had been established for centuries before they themselves were professed from the novitiate. It is about what happened to them, individually and collectively, as a result of the Dissolution. It is about the evolution that followed a particular date in the sixteenth century, after which nothing was quite the same again for these monks. It is about the transition of the Benedictine Durham Priory into the Anglican Durham Cathedral that we know today, it is about the cult of St Cuthbert, which motivated almost all that happened here for centuries, and it is about the relationship between the monks and the Prince Bishops of Durham, who were among the most powerful and substantial overlords in the nation. Durham Cathedral has been voted (in a BBC poll) the nation's best-loved building, and has been crowned with a more important accolade as one of Britain's first World Heritage Sites. Nikolaus Pevsner declared roundly that 'Durham is one of the great experiences of Europe to the eyes of those who appreciate architecture, and to the minds of those who understand architecture'. He thought the grouping of Cathedral, monastery and Castle on a rock above the River Wear could only be compared to similar configurations at Avignon, above the Rhône, and Prague, above the Vltava. But, magnificent as the architecture and its riparian setting is, there are many other stirring things to be said about and experienced in Durham Cathedral. The narrative that follows is intended, in its own fashion, as a tribute to them all.

I am considerably indebted to a great number of people for various kinds of assistance in writing this book. By far my biggest debt is to the Dean of Durham, the Very Revd Michael Sadgrove, and to Jenny Sadgrove, who is a theologian (and much else) in her own right. It was he who presented me with the idea in the first place; it was the wife and husband who then proceeded to house and fuel me repeatedly across the couple of years when I was engaged in research at Durham, with a generosity that exceeded even their own already high standards. I am also most grateful to Canon Rosalind Brown who, when all the Deanery beds were reclaimed by their rightful owners in an unexpected convergence of Sadgroves from the uttermost ends of the earth on one occasion, offered me shelter and much kindness for the best part of a week. Generous hospitality and great scholarship have always gone hand in hand in Durham and I have received both to a humbling degree from two of the University's most distinguished medievalists, Patrick Mussett and Alan Piper, who effectively placed their life's work in my hands and told me to use it as I wished; Pat Mussett, in addition, took the weight off my now distinctly inadequate Latin and translated some documents for me, while Alan Piper steered me carefully in the right direction when I was investigating the Durham muniments. Other scholars who have helped me in various ways are David Hunt, David Rollason, Andrew Gray and Michael Stansfield, and I thank them all most warmly; as I do John Warren, for introducing me to the splendours of Durham Castle, and Professor Maurice Tucker, Master of University College, who entertained me royally there. Within the Cathedral community my very best thanks go to Lilian Groves, who has shared with me her unrivalled knowledge of the building and its history, and her wealth of experience in working there. I'm also most grateful for the help I received from Norman Emery, the Cathedral Archaeologist, from Brian Crosby, of the Friends Office, and from Anne Heywood, the Chapter Steward; and I could not have been treated with more cheerfully patient assistance than I was by Joan Williams and Catherine Turner of the Dean and Chapter Library, where a great deal of my research was carried out. Outside Durham, I have once again had the benefit of all possible help from Jacqueline Whiteside and her colleagues in Lancaster University Library, whose collections of *Letters and Papers*, various other state papers and a number of learned journals have been an important source of material for three of my books now. But none of this would have happened without the generous backing (yet again) of my publisher, Ion Trewin. Once again I've had the superb backup of Linden Lawson; and, for the first time, of Bea Hemming, who has ensured that every stage of the production went smoothly, which past experience has taught me takes some doing. My thanks to them both.

Finally, I owe a very special debt of gratitude to four people who have sustained me through the writing of *The Last Office* in a quite different way from any of the above. They are my children, Kalyacitta, Andrew and Michael, whose love and support have long been my principal prop and stay; which has now been joined by that of Susan Bassnett, to whom this book is partly dedicated.

PART I

✠

I

TENEBRAE

✠

'And so, being all assembled in the one place, let them say Compline. And when they come out of Compline, let there be no further permission for anyone to say anything. Severe punishment shall be accorded to anyone who is found to infringe this rule of silence, unless speech be made necessary by the arrival of guests or the abbot give someone an order. But, even so, this speaking itself should be done with the utmost gravity and the most becoming restraint.'

RULE OF ST BENEDICT, CHAPTER 42

The monks came into their Priory church of Our Lady and St Cuthbert at six of the clock that evening, three at a time, fifty-four of them all told, some stepping confidently to their stalls, others shuffling carefully with the awkwardness of old age.[1] Each moved as men will who know that they have all the time in the world ahead of them, though every head was bowed in submission to whatever was inevitable, under its cowl. The black Benedictine monks of Durham had in this fashion marked the ending of each day for well over four hundred years, ever

---

[1] The figure is to some small extent speculative, because not all the surviving records of individual Durham monks towards the middle of the sixteenth century are complete; but there is no reason to suppose that there were many more or fewer than fifty-four of them in the Priory at this time. Others were located elsewhere in its dependent cells and in the Oxford college which the monastery supported: perhaps seventy Durham Benedictines overall. Numbers in the community fluctuated over the years, with fifty-nine or sixty *c.* 1483 rising to seventy-four in 1532, which was augmented by eight new monks three years later, then a slight fall before the end of the decade.

since a Norman Bishop, William of St Calais, had installed them high above the river here in 1083; just as each day had begun with the singing of Mattins, the first of the diurnal offices which Benedict himself had ordained, at midnight, when only monks and watchmen and villains were astir. Between Compline and Mattins, the monastic community enjoyed its longest period of unbroken rest.

The church would have been in darkness by now at this turn of the year, had it not been for the candle flames guttering and swaying upon its altars and along its quire. In their wavering glow the vivid colours of paint upon stone, which everywhere brightened the pillars and the walls in the light of day, were dulled and indistinct, and dissolved mysteriously in the encompassing gloom. The massive piers supporting the galleries, triforium and clerestory rising to the roof, and the great arches with their zig-zagging chevrons at each stage, were visible only in their lower courses before they disappeared into the looming emptiness above. Their strange individuality, with deeply incised or graphic decorations (chevrons again, or lozenges for the most part) set upon the huge Norman drums, or plain fluted columns which soared out of sight, and their overpowering strength, were only hinted at in what could be glimpsed at this hour of the winter's day. Nothing could be seen of the sensational stone vaulting upholding the roof, which ran from one end to the other of this tremendous church, and which nobody in the whole of Christendom had ever achieved until it was accomplished in this place. The intricate Gothic screen behind the high altar, dazzling in its virtuosity, with 107 gaudied and gilded figures of kings and queens and saints and divines and benefactors in alabaster, standing each in its own niche, would likewise have been invisible had it not been warmed by the glow of its own candlelight. For over one hundred and fifty years it had been a thing to marvel at, not least because it had been made in London, its various parts then being shipped in crates to the River Tyne and brought from Newcastle to Durham on wagons drawn by oxen. Such a thing had been unheard of before 1380, when one of the Priory's great patrons, John Lord Neville, paid for it to commemorate his generosity.

During the day, the whole length of the building was fulgent with the sunlight shining through the stained window glass, whose scarlets and ambers and sapphires and viridians and purples, and subtler tones in between from every part of the spectrum, dappled in consequence the painted stones to produce an effect that could make the eyes ache with its confusing rhapsody. But when darkness fell, all colour was drained out of the stones and everything was muted, obscure, impenetrable; and just a little lonely. The church then seemed to be waiting for something that would bring it to life again after its hours of watchfulness.

Before entering the quire at this cold hour, the monks had been refreshed with drink in their refectory and had then gathered in the chapter house, along the east side of the cloister, whose pillars were capped with dragons and atlantes and foliate scrolls in almost pagan display, and which was said to be the finest such chamber ever built by the Normans in England.[2] There one of them had read to his brethren for a little while some edifying spiritual text, which might be from John Cassian one night, from St Augustine the next, from some other Father of the Church on the night following; echoing the reading which took place each morning as the religious working day began, when an excerpt from Benedict's Rule was intoned in the same place, to remind the monks whose children they were, and what exacting standards they were expected to maintain. Before Compline, the Prior of Durham, Dan Hugh Whitehead,[3] who had held his great office through twenty increasingly anxious years, had closed this preamble with the ritualised invocation *'Adiutorium nostrum in nomine domini'* ('Our help is in the name of the Lord'), to which his brethren had replied *'Qui fecit celum et terram'* ('Who hath made heaven and earth'). Then they had fallen in behind him and proceeded to their last act of worship for that day. This was the night of Wednesday 31 December 1539.

The evening was cold enough to produce a mist around the monks

---

[2] The atlantes, male counterparts to caryatids, recalled the Greek god Atlas and were found nowhere else in England but Durham, being much more at home in northern Italy and in the south of France.
[3] All Benedictine monks had an abbreviated prefix to their names, denoting *Dompnus* (Master) which was usually rendered as Dom, though in Durham the usage was as often as not Dan. Benedictine nuns were Dame.

as they sang the office and uttered their prayers; for their breath, in the frosty air of the old year, was released in small clouds which punctuated the stalls of the quire. They began with a moment of private and silent prayer and then, at a signal from the Prior, they recited the *Confiteor*, the general confession, followed by an absolution from Hugh Whitehead, a middle-aged man who would soon be elderly, having been a Durham monk for forty years. Three of his brethren had been professed even longer than he, however. Thomas Holburn had been a Benedictine since about 1488 and had been present at the election of Whitehead's predecessor, Thomas Castell, in 1494; now, after occupying several senior positions in the Priory's hierarchy, and after serving as sub-Prior of the dependent Finchale Priory just a few miles downstream from Durham, he was living out the last few years of his life as one of the monastery's sages, quietly awaiting his turn to meet his Maker. Richard Herrington, once the Bursar of Durham College, Oxford, later Steward of the Prior's Household, later still Master of Farne before becoming Feretrar, sub-Prior and then Master of Wearmouth, had been professed about 1491 and was likewise contemplating his end in penitence and faith. As was John Swalwell, who became a Durham Benedictine two years after Herrington and four before Whitehead, another who had filled many of the senior monastic roles, including Master of the important dependency at Jarrow, which he had relinquished only two years ago. Swalwell's elder brother Thomas had only just died and was buried in the monks' last resting place in the century garth behind the chapter house, after a lifetime of monastic scholarship and bibliophilia, in which he had reorganised the archives according to a system which would still be thought serviceable nearly six hundred years later.[4]

There were many much younger monks in the quire for the last office of the old year: Thomas Foster, Roger Rawe, John Sotheran and Richard Foster, all of whom had been professed only for three years and had celebrated their first Masses within the past twelve months;

---

[4] Thomas Swalwell was, according to Alan Piper, whose great scholarship has been tapped to provide the basis for these references, 'a man of exceptionally broad interests and considerable vigour, sustained into old age'.

and John Fishburn, Miles Swalwell, John Blyth, Richard Dennis, Robert Chilton, none of whom had yet reached their first decade as monks. And then there were the men who had sung this office in this church since the turn of the century or a few years after, who included the senior members of the community's well-defined hierarchy, with important responsibilities in the ordering of its affairs: the obedientiaries and their immediate subordinates.

Stephen Marley, the sub-Prior, and therefore Hugh Whitehead's deputy when the older man was away from the monastery, had been Prior of Stamford from 1530 to 1533, before returning to the mother house as Chamberlain and Feretrar: in the first role he supervised the clothing of the monks and the provision of their bedsheets, in the second he kept the keys of St Cuthbert's shrine and its priceless contents; while, as sub-Prior, it was also his duty 'to go every night as a privy watch before midnight and after midnight to every monk's chamber and to call at his chamber door by his name, to see that none of them should be lacking or stolen forth to go about any kind of vice or naughtiness'. Should he, too, be absent or indisposed, then his responsibilities were transferred to the Third Prior at Durham, who was William Wylam, monk here since 1513, sometime Chamberlain and Feretrar, a seminal position in this monastery. Robert Bennett, who had joined the community in 1509, was the Bursar, the chief accounting officer for the Priory's main estates, therefore a key figure in its economic life, though not so much as the Terrar, who was the principal land agent. In charge of its victuals, of feeding everyone from the most awkward novice to the most honoured guest, was Roger Middleham the Cellarer, who had been professed in 1522, and whose principal aide was John Duckett, the Refectorer.

John Porter, who had been Granator and Chamberlain in his time, was now the Sacrist, the obedientiary charged with ensuring that the church was always provided with whatever was necessary to the proper ordering of its offices, its Masses, all its communal acts of worship, which meant that among other things he kept a tun of wine nearby for the Communion services, and ensured that there was always a plentiful supply of candles made of pure wax, which was thought more appropriate to liturgical purposes than tallow, because it was the

innocent product of flowers and bees, rather than something manu-
factured from slaughtered animals. He worked in collaboration with
William Maurice who, as the Prior's chaplain, was in charge of Hugh
Whitehead's large private household and its necessities, as well as all
services which took place in the Prior's private chapel. And then there
was William Forster who, as Granator, supervised the storage and
movement of wheat and other grains that daily arrived from the
monastery's hinterland and were then transferred to the monastic mills
lying down below on the riverbank, including the grain needed to
produce the beer that the monks drank in some quantity.[5] There was
also Henry Brown, the Communar, who supervised the common- or
warming-house beneath the dormitory, where the monks took their
recreation (they also had a garden and a bowling-alley at the back),
and made sure that in winter there was always a good fire burning in
there, with a hogshead of wine handy nearby, to keep holy men warm
on bitter days; he also organised the annual feast between Martinmas
and Christmas, when the Prior and his brethren banqueted on 'figs
and raisins, ale and cakes, and thereof no superfluity or excess, but a
scholastical and moderate congratulation among themselves'. It had
been held only two weeks ago to mark *O Sapientia* (Oh Wisdom!),
which was the opening phrase in one of the great Advent anthems
sung on that day.

Thomas Hawkwell, twelve years a Durham Benedictine and only
just beginning his incorporation into the hierarchy, had been until six
months ago Master of the Galilee, the chapel whose doorway at the
west end of the church was so distant from the quire that not even its
outline could be discerned in this evening's darkness now. Some said,
people who had travelled far across the known world and seen many
strange and marvellous things, that the Galilee and its zig-zagged
columns, its decorated walls, put them in mind of the great Alhambra
citadel of the Saracens in Granada. As its guardian, the Master supervised all the rituals that took place in there, beneath the delicate

---

[5] Ale was also used to wash the organ pipes, which in time appeared to have been
varnished as a result. The riverside mills were for grinding corn in the Middle Ages
and the Tudor years.

murals – of a king, a bishop, a Crucifixion and martyred apostles – which had been painted by pious men in the twelfth century and since: the rituals were invariably associated with the Venerable Bede, the monk-historian from Jarrow, whose shrine had been an object of pilgrimage since 1375. Singing the office with him this night was Richard Crosbie, professed in the community about 1513 and now the Master of the Novices, providing guidance to half a dozen young men, who had been admitted to the Priory when they were eighteen years old for seven years of intensive study before they took their final Benedictine vows. 'And if the Master did see that any of them were apt to learning and did apply his book & had a pregnant wit withal, then the Master did let the Prior have Intelligence, then straight way after he was sent to Oxford to school and there did learn to study Divinity, and the residue of ye novices was kept at their books till they could understand their service and ye scriptures, then at the foresaid year's end they did sing their first mass.'

After the *Confiteor*, the monks repeated some antiphons they had already intoned at Vespers three hours earlier – *Deus in adiutorium, Gloria patri* and *Alleluya* – before chanting the three psalms appointed for this office: the 4th, *Cum invocarem* ('Hear me when I call, O God'), the 90th, *Qui habitat* ('Whoso dwelleth under the defence of the most High') and the 133rd, *Ecce nunc* ('Behold now, praise the Lord') with the pause between verses coming at the caesura, in the traditional monastic fashion, rather than at the metrical line-ending as in secular recitation.[6] The old men's voices trembled with age, but the others sang lustily in great Latin periods, which rose and fell then rose again up to the invisible roof of the quire and along the clerestory, from which, quite possibly, a jackdaw might be watching the all but motion-less activity; for the birds had a habit of sometimes flying into the church at dusk before its doors were closed, and having to remain there until the doors were opened again before the singing of a Chapter Mass at 9.30 a.m.; after which the daily meeting of the full Chapter, the entire community, took place in the chapter house for the excerpt

---

[6] The entire Psalter of 150 psalms was completed at the various offices in the course of every week.

from the Rule, the spiritual reading, a discussion of business and, from time to time, the abasement of some wretched soul who had admitted a grievous fault before his assembled brethren.[7] And those voices were, without exception, singing their well-accustomed Latin in the even more familiar accents of the English North. All monasteries drew their strength and their manpower from their surrounding areas and in Durham's case the monks were generally born within thirty or forty miles of the city. The majority of them came from the middling classes whose substance was in trade and other forms of commerce, though not at a level that produced great wealth. Many had dependants who were grateful to see out their lives in the Priory's almshouses: John Duckett's mother Cristabella had finished up in the Almoner's infirmary some years earlier. Hugh Whitehead's family had deep roots at Monkwearmouth, where St Benedict Biscop had founded a monastery in 674, before also raising the one at Jarrow eight years later.[8]

Every one of these cowled figures had come to his vocation in the same way, entering the novitiate at an age when other young men were securely settled into an apprenticeship or backbreaking toil on the land or – in a few adventurous cases – embarking on a life of uncertainty with the possibility of great prosperity and honour, or of desperate hazard which might end in untimely death. The young monk looked forward only to the solemn prospect of eternity with the most enormous ambition of all, to attain certain salvation at the right hand of God Himself. His was to be the way of perpetual prayer and penitence, of endless worship, of study and contemplation leavened with hard labour in the interests of his community. And when he had

---

[7] The traditional Benedictine horarium for the winter months started with Nocturns at 3 a.m., followed by Mattins at 6 a.m., Prime at 6.45 a.m., Terce at 8 a.m., Sext at noon, None at 1.30 p.m., Vespers at 4.15 p.m. and Compline at 6.15 p.m. At Durham by the sixteenth century, this had been modified into Mattins at midnight, a Chapter Mass at 9.30, High Mass at 10 a.m., Vespers at 3 p.m. and Compline at 6 p.m.
[8] Biscop was a scholar and an aesthete, who brought many books and works of art to the North from his five visits to Rome, thus beginning an attachment to learning in the region that would see Bede become England's first great historian at Jarrow, and still flourished – as it continues to do today – in sixteenth-century Durham.

passed through the rigorously careful hands of Richard Crosbie, and was thought a fit and proper person to remain with the community until the day he died, he was invited to vow himself to the Benedictine way for the rest of his life. Deliberately, his preparation had been strewn with impediments, most particularly the high standards of literacy and scholastic aptitude expected of him in Durham: St Benedict's own injunction when he composed his Rule was that 'When anyone newly cometh to be a monk, let him not be granted an easy admittance; but, as the apostle saith: *Test the spirits, to see whether they come from God.*' But in Durham they far exceeded Benedict's own expectations of novices, which allowed that some might not even be literate when they were professed. A Benedictine was generally expected to commit himself to an explicitly threefold vow of poverty, obedience and chastity, but in Durham the commitment was made as 'I, brother M, priest or deacon, promise before God and His saints my stability, and conversion of my habits, and obedience, according to the Rule of St Benedict, in this monastery which has been built in honour of St Mary ever Virgin and St Cuthbert the bishop in the presence of Dom N.'[9]

The new monk's name and profession might then be entered in the *Liber Vitae*, the great Book of Life, which lay upon the high altar beside 'a marvellous fair book which had the Epistles and Gospels in it... which book had on the outside of the covering the picture of our saviour Christ, all of silver of goldsmiths' work ... [and] did serve for the pax in the Mass'. The *Liber Vitae* had been compiled in the ninth century, listing the names of more than three thousand people associated with the early Church in Northumbria, all inscribed in either silver or gold; but in time, contemporary monks were included in the volume in the order of their professions and therefore of their

---

[9] St Benedict's Rule was composed over several years of the sixth century and was probably completed not long before his death at Monte Cassino in *c.* 550. It envisaged a novitiate lasting for twelve months, whereas Durham's was seven times as long as that. Benedict never defined *stabilitas* and scholars ever since have been trying to decide whether it meant a commitment to remain in the same monastery and not move elsewhere, or to perseverance in the monastic life.

seniority.[10] The members of this community, however, no longer attached the same importance as their predecessors to their names being entered in the book, and were content to be recorded on slips of paper which were kept in a cupboard supervised by William Wylam; during the past twenty years, forty-seven men had been professed as monks of Durham, but most of their names had not been recorded, and those that were sometimes didn't appear until many years after they had joined the community: Cuthbert Heighington, intoning the office this night with his brethren, as he had done for some thirty years now, was not entered in the *Liber* until 1531. There was, nevertheless, something compellingly potent in the ancient volume lying on the altar, full of their communal past and their spiritual forefathers, a visible link with the origins of this anchorhold, and one that was hallowed anew each day as the priest celebrating the High Mass laid his hand briefly on the *Liber Vitae* in his intercessions for the living and the dead.

And when a monk's vocation had run its course, when his end was close at hand, he was taken from his chamber in the dormitory 'with all his appurtenances and furniture' and for his closing days was tended in the infirmary, which stood high above the river at the Priory's western extremity, 'where he might have both fire & more convenient keeping, for that they were allowed no fire in the Dorter'. The Prior's chaplain stayed with the dying monk until his last moment; and when that had passed, a barber was summoned to remove his nightshirt and wash him, to put on his socks and his boots, and to clothe him again in his black habit and cowl before he was carried from the infirmary and laid overnight in the adjacent room known starkly as the Dead Man's Chamber, where he was locked in before the key was returned to the custody of the Prior. When night fell, he was moved yet again into an adjoining chapel dedicated to St Andrew, where he remained until eight the next morning, watched over by two of his brethren,

[10] By 1539, monastic names filled twenty-eight of the *Liber Vitae*'s sixty-five pages, beginning with the sixty-seven names entered in *c.* 1100. The book is now lodged in the British Library, the oldest volume of its kind to have survived from Anglo-Saxon England.

'either in kindred or kindness the nearest unto him ... sitting all night on their knees at the dead corpse's feet'.[11] The body was then borne to the chapter house, where the Prior and the whole community said the Mattins of the Dead before each prayed individually for the repose of their dead brother. No one else was allowed near the chamber while this ritual was being enacted, for it was a very private time in the life of the Priory, as it would be in any grieving family that had just lost one of its own. When this was done, the corpse was carried to the sanctuary garth and there buried with 'a chalice of wax laid upon his breast', and with his last winding sheet held over the grave by four of his brethren while the earth was shovelled in; the sheet was then given to the barber in return for his good offices.

The Benedictine monk's whole life had been a preparation for that moment, and for what came after: nothing else was thought to hold the slightest significance for him when set beside that surpassing verity.

As the darkness thickened around the quire on this last day of the year, Compline ran its course towards its everlasting end. The monks sang the hymn *Christe qui lux* ('Christ Who is the light'), after which the fourteenth chapter of the Book of the Prophet Jeremiah was read, beginning at the verse which affirms and asks *Tu autem in nobis es domine et nomen tuum sanctum invocatum est super nos ne derelinquas nos domine deus noster* ('Yet thou, O Lord art in the midst of us, and we are called by Thy name; leave us not'). The monks gave their thanks for this, *Deo gratias*, then uttered the response that was threaded through all their liturgies – *Kyrie eleison, Christe eleison, Kyrie eleison* ('Lord have mercy'). They said more prayers: *Pater noster* in silence, followed by the Creed, as it was handed down to the Church by devout men gathered in Nicaea twelve centuries before; and when they reached the penultimate phrase expressing belief in the Resurrection of the body, and broke their silence with an audible *Et vitam eternam. Amen* in chorus, so great was their harmony, perfected over the many years in which they had said this office together, that they spoke in unison as if with one voice, not even a syllable discordantly out of step with the others. Their Prior blessed them, after which the monks left the

---

[11] 'Sitting on the knees' was a very localised expression in Durham for kneeling.

places they had occupied from the start of the office and, standing between the two rows of stalls in the quire, chanted the *Trina oratio*, the seven great penitential psalms which all asked for mercy – 'O Lord, rebuke me not in thy indignation ... I will confess my sins unto the Lord... Put me not to rebuke O Lord in thine anger ... Have mercy upon me O God after thy great goodness... Hear my prayer O Lord, and let my crying come unto thee ... Out of the deep have I called unto thee O Lord... Hear me, O Lord, and that soon, for my spirit waxeth faint'.

There was a final Amen, then Compline was done, and the monks left their church to brood upon itself and its place in the divine order of things; and in the darkness above, the stray jackdaw might have watched their going with some wonder at the well-ordered ways of such men. As each monk reached the dormitory and proceeded to his own small cell, he was sprinkled with holy water. And the great silence began, while the night candles guttered and swayed in the place they had just left. The last office was over for another day, another year.

With it also ended an era 460 years long. For King Henry VIII had embarked on a deliberate separation of the Church in England from its parent in Rome, and the monasteries had become a particular target for his zeal for reform, as well as a replenishment of wealth for his almost empty exchequer. Nothing in the life of the Durham Bene-dictines, after Compline on that last day of 1539, would ever be the same again.

II

THE REASON WHY

✠

'As soon as the signal for the Divine Office has been heard, let them abandon what they have in hand and assemble with the greatest speed, yet soberly, so that no occasion be given for levity. Let nothing, therefore, be put before the work of God.'

RULE OF ST BENEDICT, CHAPTER 43

Everything in Durham – the city, its Castle, its Priory – owed its existence to one outstanding topographical fact: the site on which everything had first been built was effectively impregnable. The River Wear flowed past in an extended and narrow loop whose two sides were separated by a peninsula of land on which both Priory and Castle stood, together with the market place and several streets, and which was a mere 250 yards wide where it was attached to its surroundings. The sides of the peninsula were very steep, and from the western walls of the Priory the view of the water below was all but vertical and distant enough to disturb anyone with a disposition to vertigo; hostile forces attacking the site from any direction would have the odds stacked against them right from the start. One other thing commended the river to inhabitants: the Wear was not navigable as far as Durham or even for several more miles downstream, which meant that although this would have regrettable and long-term consequences for the city's commerce, it also guaranteed immunity from Viking longships.

Invading Scots and Danes were the most notorious predators from an early date in the settlement's history, but always they had to travel across country; and it was because of their menace that fortifications were thrown up to augment natural defences provided by the lie of the land. The Normans were the biggest fortifiers of all, as well as the most impressive church builders, and had built their Durham Castle in 1072, twenty years before the foundation stone was laid for the adjacent Priory church by St William of Calais. With a towering keep and curtain walls protecting its courtyards and linking its other parts, it looked mightier than it actually was because, unlike the Priory, it was not built upon solid bedrock, and would need regular maintenance in the centuries ahead. Its appearance, however, was something of a deterrent in itself and, efficiently manned, the Castle was well founded enough to resist all attackers: it never would be taken by an enemy.

Walls had already been built when the Scots laid siege to Durham in 1006 but were repulsed with heavy casualties; whereupon four women washed the heads of the dead, which were then impaled on poles round the perimeter. In 1313 the Scots torched the outskirts of the city and came back again two years later, having been emboldened in the meantime by their victory over the English at Bannockburn. This time they attacked one of the Priory's landholdings out at Beaurepaire, where Prior Geoffrey of Burdon happened to be at the time; who, stout fellow that he was, leapt into the saddle and galloped back to Durham to raise the alarm, while the invaders looted the monastic premises and made off with their booty to Chester-le-Street.[1] Most memorable of all, however, was the encounter which became local legend as the Battle of Neville's Cross just outside the city in 1346, when the Archbishop of York led an army of 16,000 which comprehensively defeated the Scots and captured their King David, Robert the Bruce's son, who then spent the next eleven years in an English prison. The monks of Durham had watched the battle rage from the top of the Priory church's tower and, when the Scots began to retreat, sang the *Te Deum* so loudly that the armies below could hear it clearly, to the great encouragement of the Archbishop's men. A result of these incursions over a long period of time was that a deep-rooted prejudice

---

[1] Beaurepaire eventually became the pit village of Bearpark and its surroundings, where coal-mining flourished until late in the twentieth century on an incline above a tributary of the Wear, two and a half miles to the north-west of Durham.

against the Scots was still manifest in sixteenth-century Durham even though itinerant Scottish tradesmen were to be found in the city by the end of the fifteenth. But as late as 1448, the fullers and the cord-wainers were forbidden by their guilds to employ anyone from north of the Border, and swingeing fines were imposed upon weavers and shoemakers who also infringed such ordinances.

There had been a settlement in this place in prehistoric times, and the *Anglo-Saxon Chronicles* recorded the consecration of a bishop in 762, while the outreach of Elvet, where the river flowed along its gorge past the eastern side of the peninsula opposite, was almost certainly Christianised some time before then. But the moment that would change Durham's nature and powerfully influence all its future history did not come until 995, when the body of St Cuthbert arrived on the peninsula and was forever afterwards associated with a church made of timber there, and its successors. Durham then, according to the monk Symeon, who was the Priory's Precentor before his death in 1129, 'although naturally strong, was not easily habitable; for the whole space, with the sole exception of a moderate-sized plain in the midst was covered with a very dense wood. This had been kept under cultivation, having been regularly ploughed and sown'.

Cuthbert was born *c.* 635 and, although we know nothing for sure about his parentage or birthplace, he probably came from freeman stock or even minor nobility, reputedly a high-spirited, agile child who sounds as though he might have been the ringleader among his peers. When he was eight, however, two incidents (according to the hagiography) evidently marked him for life. In the first he was observed in horseplay with his fellows by a three-year-old, who chided him in the following terms: 'Oh holy Bishop and priest Cuthbert, these unnatural tricks done to show off your agility are not befitting to you or your high office.' In the second, a little later, he suffered some mishap which left him with a swollen knee and a very lame foot; and, while he was recuperating in the fresh air, a stranger in white robes, riding 'a magnificently caparisoned horse', approached and asked for the usual courtesies afforded a guest, but was told that the child could not oblige because of his injury. The stranger then examined the knee, recommended a hot poultice ('You must cook wheat flour with milk, and anoint your knee with it while it is hot') and went on his way; at which 'the boy obeyed his command, perceiving that he was an angel of God'. Cuthbert applied the poultice, cured his leg, 'And from that time, as he revealed to men who can be fully trusted, whenever he prayed to the Lord in the times of his greatest distress, he was never denied the help of angels'.

This was the visionary beginning of vocation, which in many different forms has started every saint in the Christian calendar on his or her path to holiness. In Cuthbert's case the next step was taken when he was a shepherd in the Lammermuir Hills of the Scottish Border country and had a vision of Aidan, Bishop of the church at Lindisfarne, being carried to heaven by bands of angels; whereupon Cuthbert (according to Bede, writing *c.* 721) 'forthwith delivered to their owners the sheep which he was tending and decided to seek a monastery'.[2] So in 651 he joined the abbey of Melrose and after some years there, he travelled south to assist in the foundation of a new monastery at Ripon, where he became guestmaster. This was at a time when the English Church's future, particularly its allegiance to either the Irish (Celtic) or the Roman tradition, was being fiercely debated, an issue that was settled in Rome's favour at the Synod of Whitby in 664. The Roman faction was led by Wilfrid, the Benedictine Abbot of Ripon, and although Cuthbert himself would accept the imminent Whitby decision, his own Abbot and other Melrose dissidents indicated that they would not, so that all were ejected from the Yorkshire monastery, returning to their home in the Borders where, in the year of the Synod, Cuthbert was made Prior.

He was now acquiring a reputation as a caring pastor who would travel great distances to succour people living in remote places, and he was uncommonly attracted to a nocturnal prayer life after the communal worship of the house had ended for the day. He also developed a taste for taking himself off to remote and bleak places for periods

---

[2] Bede's text, *Vita Sancti Cuthberti*, drew heavily on the earlier work, which was almost certainly written by a Lindisfarne monk and is known as 'The Anonymous Life' – 'But', as one commentator puts it, 'it is amusing to notice how carefully he avoids using the same words and phrases.' Popular historians have been doing much the same thing ever since, in whatever field they work.

of solitude. And he continued to have visions, which could disturb onlookers. Bede records an occasion when he was dining out, and

> When they had taken their seats at the table at meal-time, the venerable father Cuthbert suddenly turned his mind from the carnal banquet to contemplate spiritual things. The limbs of his body relaxed and lost their function, the colour of his face changed, and his eyes were fixed against their wont as if in amazement, while the knife he was holding fell to the table ... But when she [Aelfflaed, the Abbess of Whitby] adjured him and importuned him more earnestly to reveal his vision, he said 'I have seen the soul of a certain holy man being carried by the hands of angels to the joys of the heavenly kingdom' ... Then it was clear to all how manifold was the spirit of prophecy in the breast of the holy man, who could not only see the secret removal of the soul in the present, but could also foresee what would be told him by others in the future.

After some years at Melrose, he moved to Lindisfarne as Prior, evidently at his Bishop's urging, and at first this was not an easy transition. 'Within the monastery he had to persuade the brothers to accept a monastic rule rather than their traditional customs, and this aroused bitterness': these customs originated in the old Irish Church and involved many variants from the Roman practice, including a different form of tonsure and a different date for Easter. This discord may or may not have had a bearing on his decision to shift from the community, with his superior's blessing, and that of his brethren, to a small island south-west of Lindisfarne (now known by his name), and then even more distantly to the Farne Islands, in order to live the eremitical life of solitude in earnest, where Aidan had once been when conducting retreats. Cuthbert built himself 'with angelic aid' an oratory there and a cell, and a wall surrounding both that was so high 'that the pious inhabitant could see nothing except the sky from his dwelling, thus restraining both the lust of the eyes and of the thoughts and lifting the whole bent of his mind to higher things'. There he began to battle with demons, as most hermits have throughout time, 'but when the soldier of Christ entered, armed with the "helmet of salvation, the shield of faith, and the sword of the spirit which is the word of God, all the fiery darts of the wicked one" were quenched and the wicked foe himself was driven far away together with the whole crowd of his satellites'.

Cuthbert did not find the solitude he had hoped for on the Inner Farne, because his reputation as a holy man had grown so much that people were constantly pestering him in their own search for spiritual sustenance. They included the high-born as well as the lowly, among them King Oswiu of Northumbria's daughter, who also happened to be Abbess of Whitby; and it was she who was instrumental in the next, somewhat confused episode of Cuthbert's progress in the Northumbrian Church. Largely at her instigation, he was elected Bishop of Hexham and accepted the position reluctantly, but almost immediately was translated to the see of Lindisfarne instead. He had thus put himself in the irreconcilable position of a man whose whole life had been a movement towards solitude and extreme abstinence, temperamentally disinclined to find his way to salvation in community and certainly unable to countenance self-indulgence, but who was now obliged to become a social and sociable person as *episcopus*. Bishops were expected to hobnob with their peers and their betters, as well as to offer lowlier souls succour, and had indulgences thrust upon them, even if these were no more than a bejewelled pectoral cross and other episcopal baubles. As Bishop, Cuthbert travelled across his diocese with a retinue of priests and acolytes, he accepted gifts (as he was entreated to) from the gratefully devout, he rode a horse instead of walking with a staff to support faltering steps, and he was even known now to drink a cup of wine if he was feeling exhausted or unwell. This was no longer an ascetic existence.

It was obviously the tension caused by this contrary way of life that led him, after only two years as Bishop, to resign the appointment; and, besides, he could feel his time running out. He, 'knowing in his spirit that the day of his departure was at hand, threw aside the burden of his pastoral care and determined to return to the strife of a hermit's life which he loved so well, and that as soon as possible, so that the flame of his old contrition might consume more easily the implanted thorns of worldly care'. He spent the Christmas of 686 with his brethren on Lindisfarne and afterwards returned to solitude on the Farne, 'so that, freed from outside anxieties, he might await the day of his death, or rather of his entrance to the heavenly life, in the undisturbed practice of prayers and psalm-singing'. In the depths of winter, this now ailing man of fifty-one crossed several miles of one of the roughest seas round the English coast to an anchorhold that was frequently battered by the waves and howling wind during storms, often hidden from the rest of the world by fog banks, and regularly cut off from the land by weather which would have made it suicidal to attempt a passage: all that to reach a habitat natural only to seabirds and seals. This would have been an heroic effort by an active man at the height of his physical powers. In a contemplative monk within sight of his grave it was nothing less than an act of hallowed lunacy.[3]

Almost three months later, on 20 March 687, Cuthbert died on Farne in the presence of the monk Felgild, who had been sent from Lindisfarne to tend him during his final hours. His brethren had tried to persuade him to rejoin them so that he could be looked after properly, but he had refused because 'I think that it will be more convenient for you also that I rest here, because of the influx of all sorts of fugitives and blameworthy men, who may perhaps flee to my body because, whatever sort of man I am, a rumour has nevertheless gone out that I am a servant of Christ. Therefore you will too often have to plead with those in worldly power on behalf of such men, and will have to bear much difficulty on account of the presence of my body.' The monks on Lindisfarne had for several days been keeping watch for Felgild's signal and, when it came, the brother whose turn it was to keep vigil on a headland near the abbey lit two torches which could be seen by the community some distance away. Then he ran to join them, where they had started singing Psalm 60, *Deus repulisti nos* ('Lord, thou has cast us out, and scattered us abroad').

They ignored Cuthbert's request to be left on Farne, and brought

---

[3] It has lately been suggested (in a sermon in Durham Cathedral on 5 November 2006, by Canon Dr David Brown) that 'Cuthbert's retreat to the Farne may have been an act of cowardice, representing a failure to carry through properly his duties as a bishop'.

his body back to Lindisfarne for burial, where it would remain for more than two hundred years, increasingly an object of veneration by pilgrims, much encouraged by the monks, who disinterred it eleven years after it had been sealed into a stone sarcophagus in their abbey church of St Peter, and transferred it to a wooden coffin standing above ground, where it would more obviously stimulate devotion. The coffin had been made of six oak planks and all its panels were richly decorated, the lid showing Christ in majesty with his four attendant Evangelists, the Virgin and Child at one end, the twelve Apostles along one of the sides, and archangels depicted on the other.[4] The transfer meant that the corpse was exposed after more than a decade underground, during which it ought to have been reduced to a skeleton, but to their astonishment the monks found that it had merely become mummified. As Bede records it, 'opening the sepulchre, they found the body intact and whole, as if it were still alive, and the joints of the limbs flexible, and much more like a sleeping than a dead man. Moreover, all his garments, in which he had been clothed, were not only undefiled but seemed to be perfectly new and wondrously bright.'

Cuthbert had always been associated with miracles. He had been credited with calming stormy seas by the power of his prayer, and with preventing a fire from destroying a house by the same means; he had brought forth water in an arid land and had turned water into wine; he had changed the course of a battle without even being there and he had willed an eagle to bring him food when he ran out of sustenance on a journey. He cured people of their various maladies in proportions that can only be described as Biblical: he drove a demon from a reeve's wife before he had even set eyes on her, he healed the Abbess of Whitby and one of her nuns by means of his girdle, he revived a dying servant who was at death's door, a boy who was dying of a plague, and another who was brought to him during one of his episcopal progresses; he cured a girl of pains in the head and side and, as a final invocation of supernatural power when he was dying himself, he brought his gifts

---

[4] What's left of the coffin can be inspected in the Treasury of Durham Cathedral. The Apostles all hold books but only St Paul has a beard and St Peter is obvious because he is holding the keys to the kingdom of heaven.

to bear on one of his own monks and put an end to the man's chronic diarrhoea; there were many more miraculous healings in addition to these.

And now, long after he should himself have decomposed, he had defied all the precedents of the natural world and revealed himself as a man incorrupt as well as incorruptible. It was not at all remarkable, therefore, that a cult of St Cuthbert should immediately begin, and that this should grip the imagination and the spiritual devotion of the English North as nothing else ever would.[5] Eventually, it could be asserted with some confidence that 'more English churches were dedicated to St Cuthbert than to any other native English saint, with the possible exception of Thomas Becket'; Cuthbert's shrine in the Priory church at Durham was unrivalled in its popularity by any competitor in England north of East Anglia, where particular devotion was made to Our Lady of Walsingham. Such was the enthusiasm for this seer, this thaumaturge, that within thirty or forty years of his death, three different biographies of him had been written; and the monks of Durham were still copying Bede's *Life* in 1528.

It took Cuthbert's body well over one hundred years to get from Lindisfarne to Durham. When Danish raiders advanced on the holy island in 875, the monks shouldered his coffin and set off in search of a safer anchorhold, taking with them also the illuminated volume of Gospels which would forever be associated with Lindisfarne, one of the greatest of all works of medieval art, which almost certainly had been specially created in order to celebrate Cuthbert and glorify his shrine. They had a mind to take the body to Ireland, where it would be beyond the reach of the Danes – and some of the monks, in any case, had never been at ease with the Roman ways – and headed west in order to find a ship that would serve their purpose. They sailed from the River Derwent in Cumbria but were driven back by a tempest, took the hint, and began to retrace their steps to Northumbria. Eight

---

[5] St Cuthbert's remains were not, of course, the only ones to be found mummified long after death in this country; those of Edward the Confessor, Edward I and Charles I were likewise preserved by unusual geological and/or atmospheric conditions. There were others.

years after leaving home, they found what they had been looking for at Chester-le-Street, which the Romans had once fortified beside the Wear, and there they settled for another century until rumour of a further Danish invasion decided them to move on again. This time they journeyed as far south as Ripon but lingered there only a few months before going back to the land which exerted a pull that no other could match. And thus, in 995, they approached the Durham peninsula. Symeon was to record what happened next: 'the vehicle on which the shrine containing the holy body was deposited, could not be induced to advance any further'. A crowd arrived and added their own weight to that of the strangers, but 'the shrine containing the uncorrupted body continued where it was, as firmly fixed as if it were a mountain'. This was clearly a sign from the saint himself: Dunholm, the hill on an island, was where he was meant to be.

The brethren built a timber church round him, which served for three years until it was succeeded by an improved and larger version made of stone: the Alba Ecclesia, which was consecrated by Bishop Aldhun in 998, a cruciform structure which had one tower at its west end and another over the crossing, both of them topped with bronze pinnacles.[6] And this was both the monastic church and the Bishop's cathedral until the Norman invasion of England, which in Durham caused such panic that Bishop Aethelwin and his monks fled to the sanctuary of Lindisfarne, taking their saint with them, after seventy-five years on the peninsula; but only for a few weeks, until 'when Lent was nigh and tranquillity had been restored, they carried the holy body back to Durham; and the church having been solemnly reconciled, they entered it with lauds upon the eighth of the calends of April [25 February], and restored the body to its own proper-resting place'. It would never leave Durham again.

Bishop Walcher of Lorraine, installed in the see by the Conqueror himself, replaced the White Church with a grander version *c.* 1070,

---

[6] The White Church's interior was decorated with sculptures – crossheads bearing the images of winged figures, a Crucifixion, a lion grappling with a serpent, and other quadrupeds – which may have been incorporated as rubble into the subsequent Norman church.

preparatory to bringing Benedictine monks to Wearside, and thereby putting an end to a monastic strain which still bore traces, emotionally at least, of the Irish origins of the Church in the English North, which Whitby in 664 had repudiated. Walcher, however, was done to death in 1080 by a mob on Tyneside in reprisal for a murder committed by one of his officials; and so the task of establishing Benedictine discipline in Durham's monastery was left to another Norman, William, who had once been a secular priest in Rouen before joining the abbey of St Calais in Maine, from which he became the Abbot of St Vincent in nearby Le Mans. And he, drawing on his acquaintance with the great abbeys of northern France, also took the step which was to transform the skyline of Durham from English provinciality into something utterly unimaginable by eleventh-century Northumbrians. Here was something massive and magnetic, timeless and unforgettable, operatic in its stony grandeur, its towering outline a sign of faith and hope, a promise of eternity. The building of the new Cathedral was accomplished in the astonishingly short time of forty years: the foundation stone was laid on 11 August 1093, the work continued under William's successor, Rannulph Flambard, and the structure was finished by Geoffrey Rufus in 1133, though the Galilee and other additions were built throughout the following century. And Durham's whole ethos, its position among English towns and cities, was transformed by what went on in those years, both by the new buildings, their significance, and what they enshrined. The Cathedral and its attendant Priory became one of the country's principal centres of devotion, which affected everything around it, from the way the local community saw itself to the workings of its economy and its status in the national order of things.

The Normans did not at first share the high opinion of St Cuthbert that was axiomatic among Northumbrians by the eleventh century, when he had long since become the focal point of the region's identity. They were so sceptical of the claims made on his behalf that in 1104 the coffin was reopened for a second, a third and a fourth time between 24 and 28 August of that year so that a succession of dignitaries, including Prior Turgot and Bishop Flambard, could check the truth of the legend for themselves. Yet again, the body was incorrupt, as it had been by then for 417 years, which convinced even the Normans that they had something very special on their hands; and from that moment onwards they encouraged devotion at the shrine of St Cuthbert as much as any native Northumbrian could have wished.

Pilgrimage to Durham intensified as a result. People travelled the length of England to prostrate themselves before Cuthbert's shrine, to leave tokens of their devotion there, to be blessed by the monastic priests, and to thrill at their brief proximity not only to the saint himself but to numerous relics associated with him, which included a front tooth and a filament of hair from his head which was said to be impervious to flame (placed on a censer of glowing coals 'it could not be consumed thereby, but it grew white, and glittered like gold in the fire') and which Bede said was used for miraculous cures in the eighth century. Royalty was periodically to be found among the visitors: Henry VI came in 1448, Richard III in 1483, Margaret Tudor (Henry VIII's elder sister) in 1503; even the Scottish King David I paused at Durham *c.* 1113 on his way home from marriage to the widow of an English earl.[7] People came from even further afield, among them a twelfth-century clerk from Bergen, 'two penitents who had traversed the whole of Christendom', and the Italian Aeneas Sylvius, who would become Pope Pius II in 1458, but who three years earlier had been sent on a secret mission to the court of James I in Scotland, and was so miserably sea-sick on the journey north that he prudently decided to return overland, with the pair of palfreys James had presented him with, and 'some money and a jewel for his mother'.

Apart from the incorrupt body itself, however, hidden from view in its oak coffin within the elaborate shrine in which this was set behind the high altar, nothing was more potent than St Cuthbert's Banner, which was certainly in evidence by *c.* 1160. This was a huge sheet of

---

[7] It has been estimated that although most devotees came from Northumbria, a fifth of all pilgrims in the twelfth century had journeyed at least 140 miles, and one man had come 150 miles. These were considerable distances in the Middle Ages. The habit of pilgrimage began to wane during the sixteenth century – donations at the shrine in the 1530s were no more than one-sixth of what had been given in the fifteenth century – but Cuthbert's cult would always be a powerful factor in the distinctive nature of the North.

white and crimson velvet, richly embroidered in gold and silk, with St Cuthbert's pectoral cross depicted in the centre, supported on the cross-bar of a long stave with little bells attached, so big and heavy that although only one man was charged with carrying it – thrust into a leather socket in the white belt he wore round his waist – on ceremonial and other occasions, four other men and the official shrine-keeper's clerk 'with his surplice on' were always alongside him in case a gust of wind or a false step caused him to lose control.[8] The banner was taken in procession round the Cathedral on the feast of St Cuthbert – of which there were two, on 20 March and 4 September – and on other major days in the calendar, after which it was restored to its position beside the shrine. But it was also used as a powerful talisman in time of conflict, invariably with the Scots, who had it brandished in their faces several times on the battlefield, where it was housed each night in a special tent, together with its attendants. Most recently, it had been taken by the Duke of Norfolk to fight at Flodden Field in 1513, when the Scots were annihilated, their James IV and most of his nobility killed by the English, who believed that the presence of the banner among them meant that their victory had been sanctioned by St Cuthbert himself.

The pilgrims brought gifts which might be pitifully token from some impoverished believer, strangely exotic from some well-travelled zealot, or staggeringly valuable from some rich or powerful penitent; and they came in bullion and precious stones, in currency or in kind, but were always the most that the donor could afford. A William Palfreyman in 1387 had presented a mare worth 10s, and the smith William Prentis in 1401 donated a leaf-shaped arrowhead of flint or agate, while a Hartlepool fisherman in 1415 gave a dogdrave (a sub-species of cod, usually caught on the North Sea's Dogger Bank) which must have been sizeable because it was sold for fourteen pence. Silks made their appearance so frequently that Durham became one of the

---

[8] The pectoral cross itself, of gold with arms of almost equal length, inlaid enamel, and a central garnet set in a white shell which came from the shores of the Mediterranean, and much intricate decoration, was buried with Cuthbert and is now kept in the Treasury of Durham Cathedral.

greatest repositories of the fabric in the land; but ostrich eggs were not uncommon, and the horn of an ibex was once deposited at the shrine. Until the fourteenth century the Lords Neville of Raby regularly brought a stag for the September feast of the Translation of St Cuthbert, which usually finished up in the Prior's household.

Nothing, however, was comparable in value to the emerald which was the centrepiece of an elaborate arrangement of rings and silver chains which hung in the western gable of the shrine; and which, in 1401, was valued by Henry IV's lapidaries at the scarcely credible £3,336 12s 4d, a sum that could have easily ransomed a prince and much else, anywhere in the known world; though who was so extravagantly generous in offering it is something no scholar has ever been able to trace.[9] Such was the profusion of gifts from the wealthy that in the sixteenth century it was observed that Durham was 'accounted to be the richest church in all this land ... so great was the rich Jewells and ornaments, Copes, Vestments, and plate presented to holy St Cuthbert by Kings, Queens, Princes and Noblemen as in these days is almost beyond belief'. Among these offerings were the banners of the Nevilles, the local magnates and patrons of the Cathedral and monastery, and that of the Scottish King David, who was taken after the great victory of 1346.

Queens and other women, however, were required to keep their distance from the corpse itself, whatever liberality they offered the saint. Across the floor towards the west end of the church was a line of blue marble set into the pavement with a cross at its centre, and no female was ever allowed to step beyond it towards the east end and the shrine. According to Symeon, when Cuthbert was a Bishop he had been so shocked by the lax behaviour of a mixed community of monks and nuns at Coldingham, whose monastery (clearly by divine intervention) had been destroyed by fire in punishment, that on Lindisfarne he decreed that women 'who wished to hear masses and the word of God ... should never approach the church frequented by

---

[9] Relative money values across six hundred years are notoriously difficult to assess, but in 1401 a highly skilled craftsman earned 6d a day. It would have taken him more than 365 years of uninterrupted labour to buy the Durham emerald at that price.

himself and his monks' but should gather on the green outside: a custom so diligently observed ever since 'that it is unlawful for women to set foot even within the cemeteries of those churches in which his body obtained a temporary resting-place, unless, indeed, compelled to do so by the approach of an enemy or the dread of fire'. Symeon then went on to recall the separate cases of two women who had defied the instruction by walking through the cemetery at Durham, thereby suddenly losing their reason and subsequently taking their own lives.

Other legends had grown through the ages to account for Cuthbert's supposed misogyny, which led to a ban in Durham which did not exist in other English cathedrals and lesser churches containing important shrines.[10] Some were more plausible than others but, these apart, there were two other factors that may have accounted for the proscription. One was that William of St Calais was well known for his aversion to women, refusing to countenance them at his abbey in Le Mans before he came to England, and he may have been responsible for a dictum that in the course of time became more associated with the saint. The other was the tradition among Benedictines – nowhere mentioned by St Benedict himself because it was probably thought too obvious to need raising – that women should not be admitted to their enclosure.[11] It has been suggested that in building the Galilee in the twelfth century, Bishop Hugh du Puiset created it as a lady chapel in order to accommodate women, who were then able to see through the open west doorway of the Cathedral, the shrine at the far end of the church.

A great deal of the monastic regime was dominated by the presence of Durham's patron saint, with much time and energy spent in attendance on the shrine in the Feretory behind the high altar, where the coffin was set upon a raised platform of marble surrounded by an iron railing, with enough space recessed under the shrine's canopy for four

---

[10] Canterbury and Norwich cathedrals allowed women full access, as did the Benedictine abbeys of Bury St Edmunds, Evesham and Malmesbury.
[11] It has also been suggested that the descendants of the Lindisfarne monks who set out with Cuthbert's body in 875 eventually became a married clergy who thereby appeared scandalous in the wider Church; and that resentment of these men was rationalised by attributing misogyny to Cuthbert in order to strengthen the position of the celibates (see AA Vol. XII (1954), pp. 157–67).

people to kneel and say their prayers; and a little altar 'adjoined it for mass to be said only upon the great and holy feast of St Cuthbert's day in Lent', which commemorated the moment when he died. The office of Sacrist, indeed, which never entered St Benedict's calculations, had become important enough in Durham to be occupied by a senior member of the hierarchy because of the need to supervise the wealth generated by Cuthbert's presence; and in time he was assisted by another obedientiary, the Feretrar, who was the official shrine-keeper, responsible for maintaining everything in the Feretory, including the complicated apparatus of ropes and a pulley with which to haul up and down the shrine's canopy.

These ropes were hung with six silver bells, 'so that when the cover of the same was drawing up, the belles did make such a good sound that it did stir all the people's hearts that was within the Church, to repair unto it and to make their prayers to God and holy St Cuthbert'. The canopy was gilded and decorated with 'four lively Images curious to the beholders', including a picture of Christ sitting on a rainbow in judgement ('very lively to the beholders') and another of the Virgin with the Child on her knee, its upper surface being covered from end to end with 'most fine carved work cut out with Dragons and other beasts most artificially wrought, and the inside was Varnished with a fine sanguine colour that it might be more perspicuous to the beholders'. The canopy had a lock at each corner, so that it could be kept firmly closed 'but at such times as was fit to show it'. So seriously was this security taken, that four different monks had one of the keys apiece for safekeeping. The relics and the most precious gifts associated with the saint were kept in a cupboard within the Feretory, and this was panelled in oak, which was varnished, and finely painted and gilded 'with little images very seemly and beautiful to behold'.

At the two great liturgies associated with Cuthbert, the entire community of monks were vested in copes for the High Mass, which was otherwise the case only on the most important feast days of the Church as a whole, celebrating Christmas and Easter, Pentecost, the Assumption and the Nativity of Our Lady: on these two Cuthbert days, a unique Mass had been sung in four or five parts ever since John Stele, Cantor in 1447, had been charged with this responsibility on assuming office, as had his successors Thomas Foderley (1496), John Tildesley (1502) and Thomas Ashewell (1513). And in that already richly decorated place, with incense drifting up to the stone vaulting high above, and with music playing on the Cathedral church's three organs, with the six singing boys of the choir adding their voices to those of the monks, the heavy and vivid garments in this most solemn act of worship, this intricately constructed drama, must have made many of the great congregations which gathered there for the principal occasions of the community believe that indeed they had been vouchsafed a foretaste of the kingdom of heaven.

Bede, too, was celebrated with great fidelity in Durham, especially at his festival on 27 May, when his coffin was carried by four monks round the church, pausing in the Feretory for special prayers because the Venerable (and eventually blind) historian's remains had originally lain there beside Cuthbert's until Hugh du Puiset transferred them to the special shrine in the Galilee. There can be little doubt that the separation was made at least partly in recognition of Bede's own great reputation, which by the twelfth century, four hundred years after his death, extended far beyond the English North. For he was not only the first but one of the greatest monastic historians, a man of exceptional critical judgement as well as of conspicuous sanctity and moral courage, who once wrote a letter to Bishop Ecgbert warning him of the dangers that beset monastic independence, which could be usurped by kings, powerful nobility – and even bishops: a dangerous thing to announce without anonymity during the Middle Ages. His writings were so esteemed in the English South and even further afield that the legend of Cuthbert was kept alive in such places almost wholly because of them. He influenced every monastic writer who followed him, and was 'the only teacher of the first rank the West knew between Gregory the Great and the eleventh century. Wherever in England Latin was read, Bede's *Ecclesiastical History* was read, and it would be hard to exaggerate the strength of its influence'. So highly was Bede regarded in Durham itself that, every holy day and Sunday, a monk climbed into the iron pulpit with a brass rail, which stood at the west end of the Galilee, and preached at one o'clock in the afternoon. Bede's shrine attracted so much attention in its own right that the Italian Aeneas

Sylvius, thinking it was Cuthbert's, knelt beside it in 1455 and said his prayers there by mistake.

There were other liturgical processions, apart from those held in memory of Durham's two most exalted figures, and none was more impressive than the one attached to the feast of Corpus Christi on the Thursday after Trinity Sunday, when the days were among the longest in the year and the weather (in theory at least) was at its most clement. The Corpus Christi shrine, 'all finely gilded, a goodly thing to behold', reposed in the Church of St Nicholas, in the market place at the narrowest neck of the peninsula. On top of the shrine was a crystal box, which enclosed the Sacrament and which, on this one day of the year, was taken out by four priests and carried through the street leading to the green outside the Cathedral, preceded by the congregations of all the churches in Durham, with their parish banners lining one side of the street at intervals, with flaming torches likewise held on the other side. Before the green was reached the procession stopped until St Cuthbert's banner was brought out of the Cathedral by the Prior and his brethren, who knelt and said prayers at the sedilia, which Hugh Whitehead then censed before leading it and the procession and the banner-holders and the torchbearers into the monastic church. The crystal casket was first placed reverently in the middle of the quire, whereupon *Te Deum* was sung and the organs played and a service began, while the casket and the whole congregation, with their banners and their torches, processed into the Feretory where St Cuthbert lay, and out again, into the open air and back the way everyone had come, to the Church of St Nicholas, where further prayers were said and the Corpus Christi casket was restored to its own shrine.

On this day, too, liturgical plays were traditionally enacted, 'elaborate cycles, which dramatised the whole of the Bible, from the Fall of the Angels to the Day of Judgment, besides introducing many apocryphal legends': it was because these mystery plays went on for hours that, since the festival of Corpus Christi was established by Clement V in 1311, they were staged in the long daylight of midsummer instead of at Christmastide and Easter when the days were much shorter, as had been the custom originally. Once they had been performed in church by clergy, but for over three hundred years they had been in the hands of layfolk who belonged to the dozen or so trade guilds in the city and acted out their parts *al fresco*, usually in Durham's market place.

In Holy Week now, a great paschal candle in a seven-branched candlestick (which a Jew would have recognised as a *menorah*, such as was used in the temple at Jerusalem) was set up on Maundy Thursday in the quire, where it was lit two days later on Easter Eve with new fire struck from a flint, a beryl or a piece of crystal, its flame then wavering continuously until Ascension Day. There was no other candle like this one in all England, for it rose as high as the triforium, the lower of the two galleries running the length of the church under the roof.[12] In Holy Week, too, the Passion was sung by three voices (one reciting the narrative, another the words of Christ, the third those of Pontius Pilate and of a chorus demanding the divine life); on Palm Sunday St Matthew's Passion was heard, on Tuesday St Mark's, on Wednesday St Luke's and on Good Friday St John's. Good Friday's was a 'marvellous solemn service', when two of the senior monks took a large gold crucifix to the lowest steps beneath the altar, the cross lying on a velvet cushion upon which St Cuthbert's arms were embroidered in gold.[13] Each monk in the community, led by Prior Whitehead, then came out of his stall, removed his shoes and crept to the crucifix on his knees to venerate it, while everyone sang the hymn *Pange Lingua* ('Sing, my tongue, the glorious battle').

And when the veneration was done, when every monk had made his most humble obeisance, the two seniors carried the crucifix with great reverence to the Easter sepulchre, which had been set up that morning on the north side of the high altar, and there they laid it down with another picture of Christ; and lit two tapers which burned on into Easter Day. This candleglow illuminated the sepulchre as the Easter service began before Sunday's dawn, when the two seniors returned to find it transformed from the bleak place it had been into an arbour that was vivid with red velvet and gold embroidery, and removed from it the picture of the Resurrected Lord and the Blessed

---

[12] It has been estimated that the Durham candlestick was about 38 feet high, the candle itself rearing another 30 feet on top of that.
[13] Cuthbert's arms were *Azure*: a cross patonce *Or* between four lions rampant *Argent*.

Sacrament, which had been placed there, too, taking these to the high altar where they were censed before being carried to the south door leading into the quire. Four old men from the Prior's own household awaited them there with a canopy of purple velvet decorated with red silk and a gold fringe, which was held over the monks as they processed round the church, while everyone else sang of glory and wondrous things, the place now ablaze with light from a hundred candles and more; until the high altar was regained and the image was reverently placed upon it, together with the Blessed Sacrament. And there these sacred things remained until Ascension Day.

The great feast days with their processions, their special music, their rich garments and their other dramatic stage props may have represented a sublime zenith in the monastic calendar, but the habitual round of offices and other liturgies were the spiritual lifeblood of the community. In the Priory church of Our Lady and St Cuthbert, Masses were sung every day of the year at more than twenty different altars, mostly situated in the transepts or in the chapel behind the Neville screen (where there were nine) for the repose of recently dead souls, in memory of some benefactor or event, at the behest of anyone who might feel in need of consecrated prayer and had the wherewithal to pay for the wax candles and other appurtenances of public worship; and these were sometimes intoned by secular chantry priests, but more frequently by monks in rotation, charged with the duty as part of their vocation. There was also a Mass of Our Lady sung in the Galilee, which was significant enough to require the attendance of the Cantor and his six choristers.

The High Masses, of which there were two each day, were sung before the high altar, the focal point of all the most exalted liturgies throughout the year. Above it hung a canopy which sheltered the Blessed Sacrament in its pyx of pure gold, which was girt about with very fine lawn embroidered with gold and red silk, and was crowned with a silver pelican in her piety, offering her blood to her young in token of Christ's blood shed for the sins of the whole world. When the Mass began, three monks stepped up to the altar in line ahead, one after the other, preceded by a verger bearing a wand, all bowing reverently to the Sacrament as they came. There were two chalices on the altar, one gold and one silver, their feet inlaid with precious stones; and two gilt cruets, two silver censers for everyday use, and two silver vessels to carry the incense; also two candlesticks. There were two silver basins for the priests to cleanse their hands in so as not to pollute the Host, in accordance with the Psalmist's injunction 'I will wash my hands in innocency, O Lord: and so will I go to thine altar'; and there was holy water for the cleansing, itself purified with a small quantity of salt, which was conveyed in a silver scallop shell.

All these services, these gorgeous festal occasions and the drabber offices when the monks were clad simply in their Benedictine black and the only decoration in the church was that written into its stones – all this prayerful activity was central to the *Opus Dei*, to the Work of God, which St Benedict had adamantly made the very first priority for any monk, that which must come before all else. This was so in the Priory church and Cathedral towering above the River Wear, just as it was in every monastery in the land and across Christendom as a whole. But in Durham there was an intriguingly different element, which was not to be found anywhere else, a singular thing in which the monks of Durham rejoiced. For they saw themselves above all other things as guardians of St Cuthbert's shrine, as the ministers and servants of 'a saint to be feared as well as loved. Above all he was a saint to whom they owed their gratitude.' The truth was that, in December 1539, Durham's patron saint and the *raison d'être* of its monastery still ran the Almighty pretty close when it came to adoration and awe.

A PRINCE AMONG BISHOPS

✠

'An abbot who is worthy to rule a monastery should always remember what he is called and realise in his actions the name of a superior. For he is believed to be the representative of Christ in the monastery, and for that reason is called by a name of his ... Abba, Father. Therefore the abbot ought not to teach, or ordain, or command anything which is against the law of the Lord; on the contrary, his commands and teaching should be infused into the minds of his disciples like the leaven of divine justice.'

RULE OF ST BENEDICT, CHAPTER 2

Durham differed in many respects from the customs and ambience of other English religious houses, but in nothing was it more singular than in its embodiment of power. When Sir Walter Scott composed his memorable verse in the nineteenth century, he was referring to the adjacent shapes of both Cathedral and Castle. By the sixteenth century, these had long since ceased to be separate entities, the one catering for spiritual needs and the other a purely temporal bastion; for the Castle was by then nothing less than the home of the Prince Bishops of Durham, who moved effortlessly from one building to the other in response to the complementary demands of both Church and the King's Majesty. 'Half church of God, half castle 'gainst the Scot' could therefore be read as a description of ecclesiastical power alone, which resided here by force of circumstance: especially, once again, the always dangerous confluence of northern geography and Border politics.

It was because of the simmering animosity between the English and the Scots, the occasional invasions and the perpetual raids across the

Border, and because the area of real and potential conflict was a great distance from London (involving several days of hard riding and the exorbitant cost of moving a royal army from the capital and its hinterland to the country's remotest extremity) that the Bishops of Durham became the monarch's viceroys in the North. It was they who were expected to pacify the Borderlands in time of trouble, they who were obliged to raise military forces within their region, they who administered justice everywhere within their bishopric, which was also a palatinate, one of just three in the realm, and the only one that was effectively autonomous.[1] Geographically, it extended from the River Tyne to the Tees and inland as far as the source of the Wear, with occasional enclaves elsewhere, such as the Bishop's estate at Crayke, a dozen miles north of York, and the great landholding which stretched from Norham beside the River Tweed to the coast just below Lindisfarne.[2] Within this territory the Prince Bishop's rule was absolute in secular as well as in religious terms so long as he did not offend his sovereign. There was very real substance in the boast of Bishop Antony Bek's steward in 1302 that 'There are two kings in England, namely the lord king of England wearing a crown as a sign of his regality, and the lord bishop of Durham wearing a mitre in place of a crown as a symbol of his regality in the Bishopric of Durham.' The Prince Bishops ruled in much the same way as their monarchs, with a council of close advisers – consisting of the great officers of their household and of the Palatinate – which exactly imitated the role of the King's Council in London.

So close were these prelates to the kings of England that they had a central role in every coronation, traditionally walking at the left hand of the newcomer to the throne as he moved up the nave at Westminster to the chancel steps, where Durham assisted in his anointing and his

---

[1] The other two were Lancashire and Cheshire, but these had been assimilated by the Crown in 1399 and 1246 respectively, the ruling Duke of Lancaster and his neighbour the Earl of Chester being thereafter the sovereign himself. The loyal toast in Lancashire to Queen Elizabeth II is therefore to 'The Queen, the Duke of Lancaster'.
[2] The Durham Palatinate was not synonymous with the Durham diocese, which extended over what are now the counties of Durham and Northumberland, together with the parishes of Alston and Upper Denton in Cumberland.

crowning there. This exalted position – in which the Prince Bishops were ecclesiastically inferior only to the Archbishops of Canterbury and York – was underlined in 1333, when Richard of Bury's own episcopal enthronement in Durham was attended by Edward III and his Queen, as well as Scotland's David II, both Archbishops and a large proportion of the English nobility. Hugh du Puiset was even closer to his sovereign than that, being the cousin of the Anglo-Norman Henry II in the twelfth century, a relationship which enabled him to extract charters confirming numerous privileges in the Palatinate. One of these was freedom (in theory at least) from royal taxation, it being held that the Prince Bishop's responsibilities as guardian of the northern Marches,[3] which were discharged out of his own income, resulted in a sizeable reduction of the monarch's expenditure.

The military forces that could be deployed from Wearside depended largely on the ancient feudal obligation of tenants taking up arms in whatever cause a lordling chose to support, which effectively meant every able-bodied man between the ages of sixteen and sixty and was the basis of all recruitment throughout the kingdom. Such episcopal musters were not necessarily made for purely defensive operations, as Bishop Bek demonstrated in 1300 when he twice took an army into Scotland on punitive expeditions which the Bishop himself led on horseback, though his successor John Fordham more cautiously deputed his fighting command in the Palatinate to Sir William Bowes of Barnard Castle and three other knights, who were all paid retainers to attend to military matters in peace and in war. On one occasion in 1388, they mustered 2,000 mounted men and 5,000 of foot at the Bishop's behest in order to protect the English Border against the Scots. So important was this responsibility in the career of any man elevated to the see of Durham, that one of his principal dwellings was the Castle which overlooked the Tweed from high ground on its south bank at Norham, where the river ran shallow enough to be fordable, thus providing the easiest access between the two countries inland of Berwick, where there was a bridge; and even now, in the fourth decade

---

[3] The Marches were tracts of land running along the borders with Wales and Scotland. The word was derived from the Old English *mearc* = boundary.

of the sixteenth century, its staff included half a dozen gunners who cost Bishop Cuthbert Tunstall £6 in wages every month.[4]

Two hundred years earlier, Edward II had been in no doubt at all which had the greater priority as far as the Crown was concerned in the dual role vested in every incumbent of Durham Castle. Berating the fourteenth-century Bishop Louis de Beaumont for his perceived failings as a warlord, which had turned out to be as great as those of the man he followed, Richard Kellaw, the King wrote that 'it was through the negligence and lukewarmness of your said predecessor that portions of your Bishopric had so often been wasted by the Scots … But behold! We now positively know that, through your default, negligence and lukewarmness, greater damage has happened and still daily happens in parts of your bishopric and the other neighbouring places than in the time of your aforesaid predecessor, notwithstanding the promises of advice and assistance offered by you, your kinsmen and friends.' Thomas Ruthall was exactly the sort of Prince Bishop the English kings relished, for he personally raised the northern troops who marched with the Duke of Norfolk to wipe out the Scots army at Flodden in 1513; and it was he who, in leaving us with one of the most graphic descriptions of the carnage there, rejoiced in a victory which 'has been wrought by the intercession of St Cuthbert, who has never suffered injury to be done to his Church unrequited'.

Second only to his military mandate in matters temporal was the Prince Bishop's function as a dispenser of justice. His authority was exercised in his halmote (manorial) courts, which heard actions for breach of contract, trespass, libel, slander, assault and other minor infractions; it extended to his borough courts in Durham, Stockton and Darlington, which made by-laws to regulate local trade and could

---

[4] The Prince Bishops had one other major dwelling in the North besides Durham and Norham Castles: it was at Auckland, ten miles or so upstream of their Cathedral, which Antony Bek had built in order to put some distance between him and the Priory's Benedictines, with whom he had a difficult relationship. They also had Durham House, between the Strand and the Thames in London, which they occupied during their frequent attendances at court and in the House of Lords; and manor houses at Darlington and Stockton.

punish anyone infringing them; it was the supremely last word at the Quarter Sessions, whose executive officers were the Bishop's own attorney-general and his solicitor-general, and which sat in judgment on criminal matters, from murder and riot to horse- and sheep-stealing, and to theft; and it was the ultimate reference point in the operations of the Durham Chancery, which issued charters, commissions of the peace, assizes, gaol delivery and array, pardons for outlawry, appointments of the Bishop's chancellor, escheator (the official who supervised dealings in property) and sheriff. There were four coroners in the Bishop's service, their payment made in part with corn from the Bishop's manors, their duties including the scrutiny of offences against the public order within the Palatinate.

The pardoning of felons, which was within only the Bishop's power, was very closely linked with the Durham tradition of sanctuary, which involved his Cathedral and its monks and exemplified the delicate nature of the relationship between the lord Bishop on the one hand, the Prior of Durham and his monastery on the other.[5] Sanctuary was intended to provide a refuge for those who were oppressed in any way, which included possibly criminal offenders in flight from a hue and cry, who could thereby be protected by the Church (even though in Durham they might simultaneously be pursued by the Bishop's own officers acting with his authority) and given a respite until an impartial hearing of their alleged offence could be arranged. The tradition had been maintained in England since the seventh century at least, and St Cuthbert's dying injunction to his brethren on Lindisfarne certainly reflected his anxiety that culprits might make for his shrine in the hope of his posthumous protection, and thereby be a nuisance to the holy island's monks.

In Durham, anyone seeking sanctuary made for a door on the north side of the Priory church and shouted for help while hanging onto an ornate bronze attachment in the shape of a lion's head with a flowing

---

[5] The origin of the sanctuary concept was Biblical, in the injunction received by Moses to create three cities of refuge 'that the slayer might flee thither, which should kill his neighbour unawares, and hated him not in times past; and that fleeing to one of these cities, he might live'.

mane, and a large ring held securely between its teeth.[6] Above that doorway were two chambers for watchmen who slept there throughout every night, for the express purpose of admitting anyone who sought sanctuary at any hour of the twenty-four; and as soon as someone was allowed in, the Galilee bell was tolled to signify the fact. The supplicant then had to declare the nature of his supposed offence, toll the bell himself, and was afterwards clad in a distinctive black gown with a yellow cross (St Cuthbert's) on the left shoulder. Bedding was provided on a grate near the Galilee's south door, and for the next thirty-seven days the man was fed and watered at no charge to himself. During that time he could move freely not only within the Cathedral church but also in the churchyard outside, and no one could harm or try to take him, without being drastically penalised: Symeon in the twelfth century had recorded fines of £96 for this offence, but in more recent times, imprisonment, torture and even the death penalty had been imposed. And when the thirty-seven days were over, the fugitive was surrendered to the Bishop's law officers, for due process and trial, which the man could only avoid by going into voluntary exile. But until that moment came, not even someone in fear of hideous execution for supposed treason could be touched, because Edward IV half a century ago had endorsed Durham's offer of sanctuary to cover even that.

Examples of conflict between the Bishop's writ and the Priory's tradition did occasionally occur. William Lynsdoe, a horse thief, got out of prison and took refuge with the monks, who continued to give him their normal sanctuary in spite of the Bishop's attorney-general arguing that he was in the Priory not as a fugitive but as a blacksmith. Giles Whitfield, accused of robbery in 1500, had pleaded that his offence was committed in York, and fled to the Bishop's liberty of Crayke to gain immunity, but His Grace's attorney-general this time argued that the episcopal location was not covered by the custom of sanctuary; nevertheless, the judges of his case postponed his trial until

---

[6] The original knocker is now in the Durham Treasury, a perfect reproduction having been affixed to the north door many years ago, as a precaution against unprincipled souvenir hunters or the corrosive effects of the local weather.

they reached the conclusion that he had a point, and therefore they allowed his appeal. Some wretches, however, did not survive the idiosyncratic dispensation of justice in Durham. William Brisco, a labourer, was charged with putting arsenic in a drink for his wife, sought and was given sanctuary, but 'Being found unable to read he was hanged'. Another labourer, John Grenewell, was accused of murder in 1504 and asked for the Priory's immunity, after which 'being found literate [he] was branded on the left hand with "M" before being delivered to the Bishop's ecclesiastical court'.[7]

The Prince Bishop's emoluments were considerable. The most influential clerics in the land, men who generally had some administrative background in government and were well favoured at court, habitually jostled for preferment to Durham, to which they were attracted by two things above all else: its power and its wealth. By 1539, the net annual value of the bishopric of Durham to its Prince was reckoned at £2,821 in the *Valor Ecclesiasticus*, the great assessment of the Church's wealth which had been completed only four years earlier; and only two men in the ecclesiastical hierarchy were worth more than that. This was largely an income derived from tenant rents and other sources in the extensive episcopal landholdings, as well as in commercial transactions, which were sometimes vastly complicated in their ramifications. For several centuries now, the Bishops of Durham had been in what was effectively a trade war with Newcastle-upon-Tyne, centred on control of the river's south bank opposite that town, which was partly their own demesne land and was entirely along the edge of their Palatinate (it would be settled within another sixteen years, when the Bishops were obliged to concede a rare defeat before the King's Council).

In claiming all lands which had been forfeited by those who had

---

[7] Between June 1464 and September 1524, the following indictments were made of people seeking sanctuary in Durham: murder and homicide 195; debt 16; horse-stealing 4; cattle-stealing 9; escaping from prison 4; housebreaking 4; rape 1; theft 7; backward in his accounts 1; for harbouring a thief 1; for failing to prosecute 1. Husbandmen (8) were the most frequent offenders, though there were also 3 ecclesiastics. Staves were the favourite offensive weapons (14) but some poor soul was 'Trodden to death'.

committed treason (traditionally reserved to the sovereign), the incumbent of Durham Castle added significantly to his prosperity. One other source of income was the Bishop's own mint beside the green which separated the Cathedral from the Castle, an invaluable concession which had been secured by Geoffrey Rufus's support for King Stephen during the twelfth-century civil war in which the Church was seriously divided, and which was at one time managed by a Florentine, though by the end of the fifteenth century the mintmaster was a local merchant, William Richardson. Not a great deal of all this wealth filtered into the local community, though the Bishop's Borough (one of five local boroughs by the sixteenth century), which included Durham's only market area and was where most of its butchers functioned, was easily the most prosperous. His Grace pocketed most of the profit, however, in tenantries and market tolls.

The Bishops were rarely seen in their Cathedral except on the great feast days or 'such times as they were to consecrate priests, or to give any holy orders', but on those occasions their rank and relationship with the monastic community was signified by the fact that on the south side of the quire there were two places where they might sit. One, and nearer to the high altar than any of the monastic stalls, was the episcopal throne, which was so elevated (up sixteen steps from the pavement of the quire) that the Bishop could survey, at almost the same eye level, the series of grotesques that embellished the springers of the roof vaulting along the length of the nave, whose faces sometimes pouted, often condescended, occasionally oozed piety or self-satisfaction, but were mostly benign or glaring stonily. There was nothing remotely as lofty as this throne in any other English cathedral. It was intended to convey its incumbent's secular as well as his spiritual dignity, and was better described as a gallery such as musicians might play from, with plenty of room for chaplains to sit on either side of the Bishop's own marble seat, which lay beneath a canopy elaborate with panels, niches, mullions and traceries. The whole edifice itself formed a canopy above the tomb of Thomas Hatfield, Bishop in the fourteenth century, who had thought up the entire structure as a fitting and lasting monument to his own eminence; and, as the man who financed the building of Durham College in Oxford (subsequently Trinity), to which the most promising young monks were sent to complete their education, he had more reason for vanity than most. But any man sitting up there in all his episcopal glory, surrounded by acolytes and chaplains, together with an assortment of other priests and religious and a deeply dutiful congregation of townsfolk, would find it very hard to hang on to any innate modesty as he contemplated his mortality. Some had been endowed with that particular virtue, but almost as many were supremely arrogant.

None more so than Antony Bek, sometime Patriarch of Jerusalem, who treated the monastic community as though every one of them, from the Prior downwards, were his tenants. At the same time, he was prepared to take on the even higher and mightier than himself, memorably refusing to answer the Archbishop of York's summons to a Convocation in 1291. He was eventually buried, on his own instructions, behind the high altar: 'the first bishop', as a reproving voice later pointed out, 'that ever attempted to lie so near the sacred shrine of St Cuthbert'. One Bishop of Durham, however, as arrogant as any of them, conspicuously never went anywhere near his Cathedral, and he was Thomas Wolsey, who occupied the see from 1523 until 1530, what time he prospered exceedingly from his secular dealings in the Palatinate, but concentrated most of his energies on becoming the most powerful man in Henry VIII's government, and in lobbying Rome assiduously for a Cardinal's hat, which in time he also secured. Absentee he may have been until he exchanged the see of Durham for that of more convenient Winchester, but he was to influence most profoundly the evolution of the community on Wearside.

The peculiar (and sometimes tricky) relationship between the Prince Bishops and the Durham Benedictines was indicated by the seat maintained for the prelate in the chapter house, where the most important and intimate business of the monastery was transacted; but where 'His position was that of an interested outsider admitted, by virtue of his personal dignity derived from the church, to honorary membership of the body which actually owned it, and, in all his relations with that body, the purely honorary character of that membership excluded him from the control of its internal affairs'. The peculiarity of this arrangement was underlined by his stall in the quire, which pointed up the fact that – as in every other monastic cathedral – the Bishop enjoyed a public status *in situ* normally belonging to the abbot of a monastic house. An abbot always sat in the first stall on the south side of his abbey after entering the quire, while the Prior, his subordinate, sat in the same stall on the other side; but it was the Prior, in this place, who was the *de facto* Abbot of Durham, with all the abbatial powers and prerogatives vested in him and not in the more illustrious figure who very occasionally sat on the opposite side of the quire.

Cuthbert Tunstall, Bishop of Durham in 1539, was in his tenth year on Wearside, after succeeding the absentee Wolsey whose own predecessor had been the bellicose Ruthall. Tunstall was as unlike either of these men as it was possible for a Prince Bishop to be. He was not particularly interested in wielding his considerable power and he was certainly less than enthusiastic about his military responsibilities, which may or may not have had something to do with the fact that his eldest brother had been killed at Flodden Field. Though he had been born in the North Riding of Yorkshire in 1474, he came from an old Lancashire family whose seat was Thurland Castle, some miles upstream of Lancaster on the River Lune. He was a deeply spiritual man with an instinct for scholarship, which had been nurtured at Oxford before an outbreak of plague there caused him to shift to the other place, and after emerging from Cambridge he furthered his education in Padua. He was a well-respected theologian, also skilled in Greek and Hebrew, mathematics and civil law: he was to publish, in *De Arte Supputandi*, a mathematical treatise which won golden opinions across the Continent. He made friends with many of Europe's leading intellectuals, including Erasmus and Sir Thomas More, and after returning to England from Italy, priested and at the age of thirty-two, he served in a number of parishes (including Stanhope in County Durham) before he came to the notice of William Warham, Archbishop of Canterbury, who made him his chancellor. From that moment, Tunstall's career in high places was assured, which meant that he was destined to prosper at Henry VIII's court, where presently he became Master of the Rolls.

He was entrusted with diplomacy on a mission to the Netherlands, where he lodged with Erasmus, and was subsequently appointed ambassador at the Emperor Charles V.'s court in Cologne, where he encountered Martin Luther's doctrines and urged Erasmus to write against them. Later still, he deputised for Wolsey – Lord Chancellor of England and Archbishop of York, lately the most powerful figure in the land apart from Henry VIII himself, but now on the verge of banishment by the King – on the diplomatic expedition that secured the Treaty of Cambrai and an uneasy balance in the perennial European power games. Throughout this period, Tunstall was also steadily rising in the English ecclesiastical pecking order, first as Archdeacon of Chester, then as Dean of Salisbury, finally as a very popular Bishop of London in 1522, the year before he was also promoted at court to Keeper of the Privy Seal; that same year, he made the King's speech at the opening of Parliament. And then, in February 1530, he was translated to Durham, commended there by a Bull of Pope Clement VII, the pontiff who was proving to be a massive stumbling block to the English King's domestic ambitions. Tunstall's attitude to the papacy was not uncritical. Though he was devoutly Catholic, and vehemently disapproved of the English Bible on the grounds that William Tyndale's translations of 1526 were sometimes faulty, he was equally scathing about papal nepotism, particularly the Pope's habit of bestowing benefices on ignorant dependants in Rome, 'such as cooks and grooms', instead of sustaining men of character and learning with them.

Tunstall climbed for the first time into his prominence above Bishop Hatfield's tomb just as the English Church was becoming convulsed as a result of Henry VIII's attempts to divorce Katherine of Aragon, and the inevitable consequences this had for the King's relations with Rome. Twelve months after Tunstall's translation, almost to the day, following a sustained period of bullying by the monarch, the English clergy were pardoned for their intransigence in not complying instantly with his wish that they support him in his struggle with the papacy, on payment of a collective £100,000 into the royal coffers (which the Province of York later augmented with another sweetener of £18,840 0s 10d, a whimsical figure arrived at by the jaw-cracking precision of Tudor accountancy), and on recognising Henry as 'their singular protector, only and Supreme Lord, and, as far as the Law of Christ allows, even Supreme Head' of the Church in England. Yet at the York Convocation which debated these matters in January 1531, Tunstall had dissented from the official document which recognised the King's position in those terms and chose to do so by selecting the phrase 'as far as the Law of Christ allows, even Supreme Head' for closer examination. He asked Convocation to think very carefully whether the words in question meant 'that the King is after Christ supreme head of his realm and of the clergy of England in worldly and temporal things' or whether they meant simply that 'the king in both spiritual and temporal matters is Supreme Head of the Church ... permitted by the law of Christ'. If the second interpretation was placed upon them, said Tunstall, 'I expressly dissent from this view, the words being understood to have this meaning, lest I seem to dissent from the Catholic church, outside which there is salvation for no Christian man'. This would not be the last time the Bishop of Durham was prepared to risk antagonising his sovereign in standing by some long-held principle. No one could have described Cuthbert Tunstall as one of the warrior Prince Bishops, but he was not lacking in courage when he recognised clearly whose side he was on.

He received from Henry in reply a letter that combined injured reproach and peevishness, a form in which the King specialised when he was offended but hadn't yet thought up his strategy for hitting back viciously. Tunstall's expressions of loyal devotion were acknowledged perfunctorily, but then Henry pointed out that the Canterbury Convocation had acceded to his demands without a single voice of dissent and asked 'why do not you, in this case, with yourself, as ye willed us in this great matter, conform your conscience to the conscience and opinion of the great number? Such was your advice to us in the same our great matter, which now we perceive ye take for no sure counsel; for ye search the ground, not regarding their sayings.'[8] By this time

---

[8] The 'great matter' was Henry's euphemism for his attempts to shed Katherine so that he could marry the coquettish Anne Boleyn, who had made it plain that she would not be his in any sense unless he made her his Queen.

Wolsey had been unseated in disgrace for his failure to engineer Henry's divorce, and his position as the power behind the throne of England would shortly be taken over by his protégé Thomas Cromwell, who was on his way to becoming Lord Privy Seal. And in May 1532, Cromwell, by then a Privy Counsellor, was responsible on Henry's authority for a raid by the Earls of Westmorland and Cumberland, accompanied by Sir Thomas Clifford and their men, on Tunstall's house at Auckland 'where his chief abode was, and most of his substance lay', while other officials were sent to the episcopal dwelling at Stockton to await further instructions. The strategy had been devised.

Auckland Palace was searched in his absence from top to bottom and two books – one by the Bishop of Hereford-designate, Edward Fox, on the difference between ecclesiastical and regal power, the other 'which he [Tunstall] himself had penned against them that would take possessions from the Church' – were appropriated, together with some other documents. The investigators reported to Cromwell that they were 'surprised at finding so little, he being so great a student, and so stiff in his opinions, as appeared by other of his writings...' From Auckland, they 'went to his place at Durham, hearing of money lying there. Found in a very secret place in Durham Abbey £300 11s 7d. Took an inventory of other goods there, and went to Stockton, where they did the same.' They thought 'he must have looked for this business long ago, and made all things clean beforehand. Have locked and sealed the doors where any of his books lie.' This, as many people across England were beginning to find out, was a very typical operation by Thomas Cromwell in the service of his King: stealthy, efficient, coldly calculated, and completely single-minded. One of the Lord Privy Seal's commissioners, John ap Rice, who examined all the documents a few days later, found them 'of no great importance' and agreed that if the Bishop had written anything incriminating, he must have 'done them away before'.

Tunstall was alarmed enough by this violation of his privacy, this blatant attempt to intimidate him, that two months after the raid he was writing to Cromwell as a supplicant rather than as the Lord Privy

Seal's social superior.[9] He protested that Henry's letter had 'sore grieved me: that ... if the King's highness knew my mind, as God doth, sure I am those words had not been put in. For I have been as sore against such usurpation of the bishop of Rome, as daily did grow, as any man of my degree in this realm. And ... I beseech Almighty Jesus, of his infinite mercy, that I may leave the King's highness in his most prosperous reign many years after my decease, to much increase of his honour, the wealth of his subjects and the propagation of his most royal patronage.' He signed this effusion 'your mastership's most humble bedeman Cuthbert Tunstall'. Effectively, in his own best interests, he was accepting the Royal Supremacy.

Yet that was not the end of it. The bishops in 1536 were required to hand over to the Crown all the papal bulls that had conferred their appointments and Tunstall had apparently been laggardly in this; now he was delivering up five sealed documents and asking Cromwell to intercede on his behalf with the monarch for pardon over the delay, his ultimate fear made very plain in the letter: 'Asks him to show the King that if he is to leave the bishopric he will not only lose his living, but many of his subjects also, who are his servants, will be left destitute of succour.' The Bishop's abasement went even further when he transferred to Cromwell a number of endowments in his gift which carried distinct pecuniary advantages. In July 1537 he granted 'the office of steward of the manor or lordship of Howden and Howdenshire, to be held and exercised by Thomas for the term of his life, in person or through his sufficient deputy'. This was a parish in the East Riding of Yorkshire and it carried an annuity of £20. During this period, Tunstall also transferred the advowson (patronage) of St James's Hospital in Northallerton, which might come in handy as a small bargaining counter should Cromwell find himself in need of such, together with a gift of £10 every New Year's Day, plus occasional fees from various other sources – all of which meant that the Bishop was giving the Lord Privy Seal, for his private use, up to £40 a year in protection money.

---

[9] Thomas Cromwell was the son of a London artisan and tavern-keeper and, in spite of (or because of) his high office of state, he was much despised by the nobility in particular as a jumped-up commoner, a snobbery that many bishops shared.

This was no more than the way of the world in sixteenth-century England. The significant thing is that the powerful Prince Bishop of Durham felt constrained to follow the unwritten rules more usually applied to much lesser folk.

At the same time, he did not abandon his most deeply held religious convictions. This placed him just off-centre in the spectrum of allegiance held by senior English clerics during the great debate between Catholicism and Protestantism that was now beginning to rage across Europe. Resolutely committed to Rome and all that went with it were John Fisher, Bishop of Rochester, and Reginald Pole, at this time a Cardinal in the Vatican but destined one day to become Archbishop of Canterbury; and they were supported strongly by the lawyer Sir Thomas More. Inclining the opposite way were Thomas Cranmer, the current Primate of All England, and Hugh Latimer, Bishop of Worcester. Between these two extremities stood moderates (temporisers, some would have said) such as Stephen Gardiner, Bishop of Winchester, John Stokesley, Bishop of London, Edmund Bonner, a canon lawyer who would eventually be elevated first to Hereford, later to London – and Cuthbert Tunstall. Whose essential stance was perfectly exemplified by the fact that on three separate occasions after the final break with Rome, he advised the King to be cautious in tampering with theology. Henry may have taken heed of this, because whenever he was disposed to exercise his rudimentary grasp of theology, and there were alternatives to be considered, the sovereign invariably chose the more conservative option: he persuaded himself that he was a good Catholic to his dying day and never lost his belief in Transubstantiation.

But Tunstall's instinct for self-preservation was sharpened by the great turmoil which possessed the North of England at this time as a result of the King's increasingly truculent attitude to the Church. An inflammatory sermon in Louth, Lincolnshire, protesting against the new policies in October 1536, had led to the popular rebellion known as the Pilgrimage of Grace, which quickly spread across the Humber until people were taking up arms against the Crown in all the northern counties, though rather less conspicuously in the Palatinate than in Yorkshire, Lancashire, Cumberland and Westmorland. Nevertheless, rebels had despoiled Tunstall's home at Auckland and invested his alternative residence in Durham Castle because they associated him with all that was anathema to them by his having finally accepted the King's Ten Articles, which ratified Henry's position as Supreme Head of the Church in England; at which the Bishop fled in alarm to his Border fortress at Norham. He would later denounce to Cromwell a man named Gervaise Cawood who, he believed, had 'spoiled the bishop of 50 fat oxen' at the same time as the episcopal domiciles were being mauled. 'Such a weed', wrote Tunstall, 'is meet to be put out of a garden where good fruit in peace should grow.'

The Pilgrims took St Cuthbert's banner from the Cathedral Feretory and thenceforth it was brandished at the head of a contingent which marched down from the North-east to join comrades from elsewhere in a confrontation with the forces of the King at Doncaster. There, for a brief moment on 26 October, it looked as if the royalists would be swept away before a tide of rebels who would then have marched on to London, to tackle Henry in person and force him to yield up Cromwell, whom they detested above all and much more than their King, who they thought had simply been ill-advised in his new policies. The Pilgrims had mustered 30,000 armed men and these outnumbered the King's men by almost five to one, which would have meant a walkover if the expected battle had taken place. But Henry and his chief commander, the Duke of Norfolk, offered concessions (which they had no intention of making good) and the Pilgrims were persuaded to lay down their arms and go home. St Cuthbert's banner was never seen again.

There was more trouble in Durham at the end of the year when Thomas Miller, Lancaster Herald, was sent on a progress through Yorkshire and on up to Berwick, charged with announcing the King's peace, which included a conditional pardon for all offenders. Unfortunately for him, the version of his proclamation in Newcastle-upon-Tyne differed from the text he had promulgated on Wearside, the two communities had compared notes while he was still on the hoof, and on his return through Durham he found a mob of angry citizens awaiting him. He was 'ungodly handled and did not escape without danger', getting away only by setting his horse into a gallop which outdistanced any pursuers on foot. This episode was to cost some citizens dearly when 1537 arrived. In the New Year some hotheads tried to reignite the Pilgrimage, which gave Henry the perfect excuse to repudiate all the promises he had made at Doncaster, ratified in the proclamation; also to let loose Norfolk in savage reprisals across the northern counties. Perhaps 700 people were slaughtered in a rout outside Carlisle, and there were 200 judicial executions to follow that. Many of the ringleaders were sent down to London for trial before being put to death hideously, but there were other venues across northern England where the same thing happened, and one of them was Durham. Henry Coke, a local shoemaker, had been on a list of the most wanted men since November, so he never had a prayer of surviving. Sixteen of his neighbours in all were taken for their part in the sacking of Durham Castle or the roughing-up of Thomas Miller.

In April 1538, the King was further informed that five people had just been found guilty of treason at Durham and executed there. They had been brought to justice before the King's Council in the North, the arm of Henry's government which had been revived after the Pilgrimage to do his bidding in the most unruly part of his kingdom, and was presided over initially by a reluctant Cuthbert Tunstall, whose appetite for the job was not whetted by the £800 per annum that went with it. He gave eight distinct reasons why he should be passed over, which ranged from the fact that he owned no house outside the county of Durham, and what property he had there was still in need of repair after being damaged by the Pilgrims, to the fact that he was hated by people in the North; but the clincher for him was probably contained in one sentence, which expressed his intention henceforth 'only to preach and teach in his diocese, and to discharge as well as God will give him grace the cure there committed unto him, and to meddle with no further worldly business'. Accept the job he did, however; but he relinquished it again after less than nine months, from October 1537 to June 1538. Tunstall was not a robust Prince Bishop and he had little stomach for condemning men to death. Nevertheless, the first signature on the document telling the King that justice had been done in the North was his. But he took care to be in London when the Durham executions were carried out.

THE THIRTIETH PRIOR

✠

'Therefore must we establish a school of the Lord's service; in founding which
we hope to ordain nothing that is harsh or burdensome ... so that, never
abandoning his rule but persevering in his teaching in the monastery until
death, we shall share by patience in the sufferings of Christ, that we may
deserve to be partakers also of his kingdom. Amen'

RULE OF ST BENEDICT, PROLOGUE

Tunstall's coeval in Durham, Hugh Whitehead, enjoyed a prestige
and an influence scarcely less than that of his Prince Bishop. As
Prior of the monastery of Our Lady and St Cuthbert, Whitehead
was not only the superior of the community, a position normally
held by an abbot, but he was in a succession whose occupants had
always been regarded as 'the most considerable ecclesiastic north of
the Humber', after the Archbishop of York and their own diocesan.[1]
Not even the Priors of Canterbury enjoyed as much power within
their region as did their counterparts beside the River Wear. Priors
of Durham, moreover, were garbed distinctively in order to convey
their eminence. On all ceremonial occasions they had a mitre on
their heads and moved with a crozier to assist their steps, which

---

[1] The relationship between the Priory and the Archbishop of York had been a tricky
one since the thirteenth century, when the latter disputed Durham's rights of spiritual
jurisdiction, visitation and other matters relating to the Priory's Yorkshire possessions.
The issue was a recurring vexation in Whitehead's time and it never would be
resolved, the paperwork still awaiting a conclusion in some probably forgotten corner
of the York archives.

were otherwise the tokens of only abbatial or episcopal rank, as were the special ring and the sandals they also wore. This was a distinction first granted by Pope Urban VI in 1379 to Robert Walworth (1344–91), who was notable for simultaneously presiding over the General Chapter of the Black Monks, the generally triennial gathering of English Benedictine superiors to discuss matters of concern to them all.[2] It was not won without some difficulty from Archbishop Neville of York, who did not take kindly to inferiors being indistinguishable from himself and challenged Walworth's right to wear these things; but unsuccessfully. One other dignity indicated the eminence of men who occupied the same position after Walworth: each was known as 'the Lord Prior', and generally conducted himself accordingly.

The evolution of such monks to the precedence now held by Hugh Whitehead followed from the phenomenon of the monastic cathedral, which was almost peculiar to England. Here, there were eight other examples besides Durham: at Winchester (founded in 964), Worcester (*c.* 974–7), Canterbury (*c.* 997), Rochester (founded in 1083, the same year as Durham), Bath (1088), Norwich (*c.* 1100), Coventry (1102) and Ely (1109). There was in addition the rather different position of Carlisle, which had been a priory of Augustinian canons since *c.* 1122 and became a cathedral eleven years later: different because in the technical distinctions of the religious life, a monastery strictly speaking was inhabited by monks, not by canons, friars or any other form of religious, and monks were only professed as Benedictines or Cistercians; the difference meant that Carlisle's rule and constitution were significantly unlike any of the others. Nevertheless, scarcely anywhere else in Europe did a monastery also function as the site of the local bishop's *cathedra*. It did not happen in France, or Austria, or on the Iberian peninsula; and in Italy there was the solitary example of the Benedictine cathedral at Monreale on Sicily, which was built – including some of the most stunning mosaics ever to embellish a church –

---

[2] The General Chapters were held for centuries in Northampton, though Coventry had been the venue from 1495 to 1519, and the last one, in 1532, took place at Westminster.

with that purpose in 1176.[3] That apart, the only case was at Downpatrick in Ireland, where St Patrick was buried and where monks from Chester had been sent over to found a monastery attendant upon the residing bishop's throne in *c.*1185.

In England, for some years after the Conquest, bishops who were also monks still supervised these foundations: in Durham, an era which had begun with Elfsige (963–990) and had seen seven monastic bishops, ended with William of St Calais in 1095. There was an inherent problem as long as this dual role was fulfilled by one individual, and it was that his monastic vocation – which, strictly applied, meant scarcely ever going outside the enclosure – and his duties around his diocese were incompatible. At first the monk-bishops thought they had solved the problem by appointing the Prior, their immediate subordinate, to act in their stead whenever they were absent. But gradually the monks became restive at being ruled by someone who, though one of their own, was increasingly missing from the community. And in 1215, by King John, they were given licence to elect their *de facto* superior themselves, the bishop thenceforth having no more than a nominal say in the matter.

The powers of the Lord Prior of Durham were, by the sixteenth century, only marginally less than those of the Prince Bishop, one measurement being the fact that whereas the Prior had only one chancellor to attend to and stand guard over his numerous juridical privileges and his liberties, the Bishop had both a spiritual chancellor to act for him *qua* bishop and a temporal chancellor to safeguard his more mundane interests in the Palatinate. The biggest differences between the two clerics were military and in the realm of attendance upon the monarch and his administration. The Prior had no armed forces at his disposal, though on several occasions in the fourteenth century he was required to provide support for military ventures. In

---

[3] Dom David Knowles was of the opinion that Monreale's founder, the Norman King William II ('the Good'), might have been influenced by English models. He noted that three Englishmen were Sicilian bishops at that time, in the dioceses of Compsa, Syracuse and Palermo. *(The Monastic Order,* p. 619). Although that was the one Continental example of a truly monastic cathedral, it excludes the Chapter of Premonstratensian canons at Ratzeburg, Schleswig-Holstein, who also supported a bishop.

1313, Edward II demanded a loan of 300 marks from William of Tanfield and his monastery to help him and his army on the way to Scotland, an expedition that ended ingloriously the following year with a heavy defeat at Bannockburn.[4] That was doubtless the reason why, when the Scots invaded in the wake of their great triumph, St Cuthbert's banner was taken out of the Feretory so that its magically victorious properties could be waved in the face of the enemy; and a monk, with grooms and three horses, receiving 12d a day in expenses, was sent with it to make sure it came back undamaged.[5] Later still, with Edward III on the throne, Prior William Cowton was told to provide a wagon and ten oxen which were needed to carry tents for the English troops who were then besieging Berwick; and this, together with similar demands at that time, so drained the monastery's resources that the King wrote off a debt of theirs for £100 later that year.

As for the Prior's involvement with the King's government, it was almost non-existent except to comply with periodic demands for funds: in particular, the collection of all the clerical subsidies in the Durham diocese granted by the Convocation of York as its contribution to the royal revenues. This was, in fact, a duty which ought to have devolved upon the Bishop but one from which he had gradually distanced himself at the expense of the Prior. Apart from the laborious business of the collection itself – which meant the absence from the house of one or more of the obedientiaries, who did the parish rounds to acquire the money – this involved periodic visits by the Prior to the capital, in order to be interrogated by the King's Treasurer and other luminaries of his exchequer. The duty had become particularly irksome since the Tudors came to the throne, for they were obsessive accountants down to the cuffs of their costly gowns and the gaudiest flourish of all their other extravagances.

---

[4] A mark was a unit of accountancy, not a coin, representing the weight of metal originally valued at 128 silver pennies, but thereafter variable. In 1539 it was reckoned at 13s 4d.
[5] The banner was, of course, also taken out to assist the English victory at Flodden in 1513: whether it was gladly lent to the rebels during the Pilgrimage of Grace or was simply seized by them (perhaps the more likely scenario) is something we shall never know.

The Priors had unusual powers of punishment and regulation outside their monastery as well as within, which had at times led to testy relations with the Prince Bishop, whose jurisdictions covered the same territory. The most turbulent period was when Antony Bek and Prior Richard de Hoton were locked in combat at the turn of the thirteenth and fourteenth centuries, when the Bishop attempted to overrule every decision the Prior made and excommunicated ninety-four monks who defied his authority. Yet an earlier conflict ought to have resolved such problems. A long dispute between Bishop Richard Marsh and Prior Ralph Kerneth dragged on through the third decade of the thirteenth century and was largely to do with judicial prerogatives and the income arising from them. Unlike a number of southern monasteries – Ramsey, Battle and Bury St Edmunds were the models – the convent at Durham had no clearly defined area of jurisdiction in its surrounding district;[6] and it was in a determined effort to obtain this that the Prior attested before the King's law lords, with a multitude of learned witnesses supporting his case, 'the comprehensive and far-reaching powers of the priory in matters as diverse as the return of writs, jurisdiction over forest and waste lands, fines, amercements [discretionary penalties], rents and farms'. The case also raised the issue of the Prior's authority over suspected felons, and one of Kerneth's witnesses testified that during the time of Bishop Hugh du Puiset, or a little earlier, 'he saw the monks erect a gallows and dig an ordeal pit in priory lands outside the borough of Elvet'. Kerneth mustered no fewer than one hundred and eight witnesses in support of the Priory's case. And in spite of the fact that part of the case rested on the reliability of certain documents issued in the time of Henry II, which were almost certainly forgeries concocted by the monks themselves in order to strengthen their position, the Bishop conceded 'the court that King William of glorious memory granted to them, as freely and honorifically as [we hold] our own court, with all the liberties and customs pertaining to it within the town [of Durham] and beyond,

---

[6] 'Convent' was used throughout the Middle Ages and for some time after to signify religious communities of either men or women; it did not, as it does in England now, refer exclusively to female houses.

with sake and sole, toll, team and infangentheof, and wreck of the sea'.[7]

As a result of this concession, the document known as *Le Convenit* was drawn up 1229 in the time of Marsh's successor Richard le Poore, which in part dealt with the standardisation of weights and measures throughout the monastic and episcopal boroughs of the Palatinate. It agreed that the Bishop's men should take the lead in all breaches of the peace, but that the Prior's bailiffs must be notified if the suspects were monastic tenants; and, if such people were found guilty, half the revenues extracted from them in fines should go into the Priory's exchequer. The Bishop alone could try and punish felons accused of homicide, but it was allowed that 'if a robber shall be taken in the land of the Prior and shall be tried in his [the Prior's] court, the execution of the judgement shall be done by the bailiffs of the Prior at the gallows of the Bishop, freely and without hindrance. Likewise, when a duel shall be adjudged in the court of the Prior, or when anyone in the same court shall be condemned to the pillory or tumbrel, the execution of the judgement shall be done by the bailiffs of the Prior, and without impediment, at the place and pillory and tumbril of the Bishop.'

Le Convenit did not bring to an end the traditional frictions which had long existed between Bishop and Prior, as Antony Bek's high-handedness exemplified (and there would be other examples after him), but at least it was a reference point for anyone adjudicating the settlement of all such disputes in future. The most persistent of these involved the money that accrued from penalties imposed by one or other of the Durham courts, and what profits the Bishop and the Prior could expect from the exercise of their jurisdictions. There were ten such courts operating in the city and its hinterland – quite apart from the common law courts which functioned in parallel with the national judicial system – and in some of them (the three prerogative courts, for example, dispensing forest, admiralty and marshalsea justice) the

---

[7] Grants of sake and soke diverted to the owner of an estate the fines and other profits that would otherwise have gone to the Crown; toll was a lord's right to take a commission on all cattle sales on his estate; team was his right to fine anyone accused of cattle-stealing; infangentheof was the right of a lord to pursue and hang a thief caught red-handed.

Bishop's officials and the Prior's men were liable to appear either in tandem or as adversaries.[8]

But revenue was not the only source of tension between the Castle and the Priory. Prior John Fossor 'took the sheriff to task in 1342 for refusing to hand over his share of the incomes arising from pleas in the bishop's court' and Bishop Bury conceded his point; whereas Bishop Hatfield forty years later was frustrated by the appearance of Prior Robert Walworth's bailiff at an episcopal court up in Norham, where he successfully prevented three men entering any plea at all to the charges they were facing. The Lord Priors of Durham and their monks were very jealous indeed of their privileges, at every stage of their history. It has been well noted that frictions most commonly occurred during the period immediately following a new Bishop's installation, before he had properly understood how much episcopal arrogance was likely to meet monastic resistance on Wearside. And, on at least one occasion, the monks received regal backing for their intransigence, when Henry VI in the fifteenth century wrote to Bishop Robert Neville and warned him not to forget that Prior William of Ebchester's own privileges must on no account be infringed.

The boundaries of ecclesiastical jurisdiction were further complicated by the presence and the claims of two archdeacons in the Palatinate. These subsidiary figures in the hierarchy had existed since the twelfth century, the Archdeacon of Northumberland's pedigree being fractionally shorter than that of the Archdeacon of Durham, and names with a ring to them had occupied both positions in the past: Antony Bek had been Archdeacon of Durham from 1275 to 1283, immediately before becoming Prince Bishop, while the Archdeacon of Northumberland between 1174 and 1195 was William, son of the Hugh du Puiset who had given the role of Bishop its first unmistakably princely lustre and had inspired the building of the Galilee. Essentially, the archdeacons were the Bishop's principal ecclesiastical assistants within their respective territories, and there they also had their distinct prerogatives and privileges

---

[8] The admiralty court heard marine matters (e.g. shipwreck and fishing disputes along the Palatinate's coastline and estuaries), the marshalsea adjudicated on anything involving the King's servants.

which were as susceptible to encroachment as anybody else's. In particular, there was an historical residue of rivalry between the Priory and the archidiaconate, which contributed to the forging of monastic charters as both a defensive and an aggressive measure in the twelfth century, and which included the right to enthrone Bishops, an arcane ritual embodying many fine nuances of precedence: in 1143 and 1153 'the election appears to have been made by the archdeacons and some of the higher clergy in the diocese under the presidency of the Prior of Durham'; but in 1333 'Richard Bury had been installed by Prior William Cowton in the presence of the king of England, his wife and mother, two archbishops, five bishops and seven earls'. Even a fifteenth-century Archdeacon of York had attempted to usurp this function, by following the habit of Canterbury, whose Archdeacon had a mandate to enthrone diocesans in the southern Province under the authority of his metropolitan. In spite of persistent pressure from York (which included an attempt to intimidate Prior John Wessington in his own chapel), Archdeacon Thomas Kemp was seen off by the monastic superior and sent packing back to the Ouse, but only after the monk had made a direct appeal to Rome in 1439. Thenceforth, all Prince Bishops were enthroned by the current incumbent of the Durham Priory.

Whose greatest source of power lay in the very considerable amount of patronage at his disposal, particularly in the advowsons of northern churches which lay in his gift. Only the Bishop himself could muster a better tally, with thirty-four benefices in his diocese, the Prior having twenty nominations there, the next most influential patron controlling no more than five. At one stage, no fewer than seventeen rectories and twenty-eight vicarages, together with the numerous prebends and vicarages attached to the collegiate church of Howden in the East Riding of Yorkshire, lay in the presentation of the Prior and Chapter of Durham, with seven rectories and six vicarages in the York diocese also theirs to bestow, plus five vicarages down in the diocese of Lincoln.[9]

---

[9] A rector was the incumbent of a parish, who received all its tithes as income. When a monastery acquired a parish by bequest or other means it became its absentee rector, and received the full emoluments, appointing a vicar to fulfil the incumbent duties, for which he received in return only a proportion of the income. A prebend was the stipend derived from a manor or other holding on the monastic estates. A collegiate

The monastic holdings had even extended into Scotland, where nine vicarages were at one time available for suitable candidates. The huge church at Howden (almost the size of a cathedral, and with its own chapter house) and the nearby collegiate Hemingborough were regarded as the most desirable benefices that the Prior of Durham and his Chapter could bestow, and it has been reckoned that no other monastery in England had anything as rich as these two livings with which to acquire income, to satisfy influential supplicants, to be used as a negotiating item in the everlasting ploys and counter-ploys of local (and even national) politics, both spiritual and temporal. Even now, in the sixteenth century, there were parishes in the region (like Edmundbyers) that yielded no more than a few marks a year in income – perhaps £5 – and others, regarded as moderately gainworthy (like Aycliffe, Billingham or St Oswald's, Durham), which would provide its incumbent with up to £16 per annum. But Howden, even at the beginning of the thirteenth century, had been worth at least £200 to its incumbent and had more than held its place since in the scale of enviable benefices.

Nor was ecclesiastical patronage the limit of the Prior's bounty, for he also had many secular rewards to disburse. There were any number of jobs he could offer, ranging from the servile to the artisan and the extremely responsible, which provided security as well as a reliable income, available in his private household, in the Priory's wider needs (nightwatchmen to invigilate the north door of the church, should anyone demand sanctuary during the hours of darkness; and there were many other such tasks to be disbursed) and on the Priory's lands. Then there were the four hospitals maintained by the monks for the more fortunate indigents in the local community and for pilgrims visiting St Cuthbert's shrine: one of these, at Witton Gilbert, some miles into the countryside, had been founded originally to take care of lepers; another, dedicated to St Mary Magdalene, was in the borough of St Giles and was used as a guesthouse for the pilgrims; a third was just

---

establishment was a superior parish church, endowed to support a college (a community) of secular priests instead of a solitary incumbent and (if he was absentee) his vicar.

outside the Priory gatehouse and not only accommodated four old ladies in separate rooms, but housed a school for 'certain poor children ... being altogether maintained by the whole Convent with meat, drink and learning'; and the fourth, tending elderly dependents of the monks, was close by it. Lay workers were needed to clean and victual and run all these premises, and such jobs were much sought after by respectable townsfolk and their sponsors. Yet another avenue of patronage existed far from the North, in Oxford, where, since 1381, there had been a number of vacancies for secular pupils at Durham College, which had originally been founded for novice monks, and where education for any layman was a guarantee of great prosperity in whatever life he was likely to follow.

One last benefit that the Prior and his brethren could offer the merely prosperous and the exceedingly rich was the security of premises that were less likely to be broken into by thieves or pillaged by more ominous adventurers than almost anywhere in the region. The monastery, quite simply, was a place of stability and safety in an otherwise uncertain and frequently disordered world. It therefore became the depository for other people's wealth in the shape of cash, plate and jewels, and many of the northern nobility took advantage of it as such; also as a place in which to leave their most precious documents, the deeds and titles that legalised their prosperity, however they had come by it. This habit was occasionally followed by monarchs, too, Henry V being one who entrusted the Durham treasury with some of his valuables. The Prior often acted as treasurer of the King's money required to fight the Border wars against the Scots, a duty which Hugh Whitehead certainly discharged in 1535, when he was required to pay the garrison at Norham (even though the castle there belonged to the Bishop), which was guarding the ford across the Tweed as a responsibility to the realm.

All gratuities were in great demand by the high-born as well as by the merely ambitious and covetous. The Lord Prior of Durham was constantly beset by supplicants from amongst the most powerful men in the North of England (and even royalty was not exempt from such craving). Great magnates asked the Prior to present a favoured chaplain of theirs to a living within his gift, as both the Earl of Westmorland

and the Earl of Northumberland did in the fifteenth century after they had spotted vacancies in the vicarages of Bywell St Peter and Bedlington respectively. Between 1419 and 1446, Aycliffe was provided with incumbents who had in the first instance formerly been an executor of Sir Ralph Eure, in the second an Oxford graduate who had been clerk to Cardinal Beaufort, and in the third a suffragan bishop who had served under two different Prince Bishops (Langley and Neville, whose time spanned 1406 to 1457), and whose position had obviously been secured as a sympathetic gesture to an old man who had earned favour from his superiors. The prebendaries attached to Howden in the same period were occupied by four future bishops, two barons of the royal exchequer and a motley collection of lesser functionaries who had served the Crown or the Prince Bishop in some capacity or other.

Such gifts were not only an assurance of prosperity; they opened up the way to much wider prospects as well, for the ambitious retainer who could rely on a sponsor to bring him to the Prior's attention. In exchange, the monastery could be tolerably sure of help from that direction, should the need arise for a patron or a protector in difficult and unforeseeable circumstances: there was always a quid quo pro in these transactions. And then there were the smaller, token presents (but they all added up in a recipient's pocket) that could be disbursed to contacts who might be in a position to assist the Prior at some future date in some way or other. Hugh Whitehead and his brethren of the Durham Chapter in November 1537 had granted an annuity 'or annual rent of £5, to be taken and issuing from and in all and sundry their lands and tenements in the township and manor of Wingate, to be held by Thomas Wrythesley for the term of his life, to be paid to him at Michaelmas'. Wrythesley (or Wriothesley) was a coming man in Henry VIII's firmament, who would finish up as Earl of Southampton and Lord Chancellor of England.

At the same time, such dalliance with the powerful and the influential was not without its problems for the Lord Prior, both actual and potential, for if he offended any one of them he would probably suffer for it in at least some sidelong way on a day of reckoning yet to come. Prior Wessington seriously affronted the Earl of Salisbury in 1438 after declining to make the Earl's man William Cowhird the forester out at Bearpark, where the Priory had an estate which the monks used for recreation, and where they bred horses; and, though he appears not to have suffered for this lapse, some form of retribution must have been a lurking possibility afterwards. So much were the Priors accustomed to accommodating those with even more power than they had, that they often found themselves giving away benefices they would otherwise have bestowed nearer home. Wessington's successor-but-two, Richard Bell, doubtless spoke for many when he lamented in 1476 that 'I and my brethren are so oft times called upon in such things by diverse lords of right high estate that we may not have our liberty to dispose such small benefices as are in our gift to our friends, like as our will and intent were for to do, as God knoweth and me repenteth'. One of the more delicate skills required of men in his position was the art of writing letters to powerful people (they were known as *littera excusatoria*) regretting their inability to place a retainer in some vacancy or other, as requested. They quaked when they opened correspondence beginning with 'Reverend father in God and my right trusty friend', or 'Right worshipful and reverend and my full good and worthy master' or some other fulsome salutation, for it was invariably followed by something more pressing than a modest petition and was often enough written in anticipation of a future vacancy. It was in this fashion that Lord Montague, Lieutenant of Carlisle, sought to place a servant of his in 'the office of Keeper of your park called Beaupark whensoever the same office by the decease of John Rakette may ... happen to be void'. The Nevilles, too, were persistently on the lookout for jobs for their retainers and even for friends of their acquaintances.

So the Priors of Durham distributed largesse like princes when they were able to, and they themselves lived like the lords they more than nominally were. They had their own lodging adjacent to the Cathedral's south transept, and it was not much less palatial than the various dwellings of the Prince Bishop. It is likely that only at Westminster was a monastic superior accommodated in more luxurious surroundings than these, particularly after John Wessington's residence, for he was responsible for an unprecedented schedule of improvements which absorbed almost half of what was spent in his time on the monastery buildings as a whole (and was specifically financed by the profits from the monastic coal mines). Between 1429 and 1432 some twenty workmen, including three masons, were permanently employed on extensions to the fabric of the Prior's Lodging. At the end of Wessington's tenure, there were eight very large chambers and numerous smaller ones: one of the principal being the private chapel dedicated to St Nicholas, where the Prior said Mass with his domestic chaplain every day and received officials (including the sovereign's) whose business required the swearing of an oath. It was equipped with a font for the baptism of highly favoured infants – such as the Earl of Westmorland's son, who also received a christening present worth £7 6s 8d from Prior Wessington's successor, William of Ebchester.

Next to the chapel was a hall in which important visitors – and the other monks periodically – were entertained by the Prior, for the traditions of his office included generous hospitality, and having some of his brethren round in rotation was a kindly gesture and a compensation for the fact that he generally dined with them in the Fraterhouse (as the refectory was known in Durham, where it ran along the southern side of the cloisters) only on the great feast days and other special moments in the calendar, such as Maundy Thursday. If royalty or nobility or someone in high office was staying at the monastery, then the best silver plate was brought up from the buttery, and with it also the guests could enjoy furniture which often reflected each individual superior's taste (sometimes very expensive indeed) and frequently accompanied him on his various progresses round the monastic lands in a long cart, which awaited his pleasure in the stable beside the gatehouse. Between the hall and the chapel were bedchambers for important guests, both of them hung with expensive fabrics, which has led one authority to speculate that Wessington enjoyed 'a style of living not easily matched anywhere else in fifteenth-century England'. But there were many other visitors who were given more modest quarters in the monastery during every incumbency and they included heralds, envoys in transit from here to there, visiting players for the Corpus Christi mystery cycle and mummers to provide entertainment on other days of high feasting.

The scale of hospitality is indicated by the fact that in the twelve months which started in May 1430 the Bishop of Durham was given dinner twice in the Prior's Lodging, while the Bishop of Carlisle, the Prior of Tynemouth, the Abbot of Whitby, Sir Robert Umfraville (Sheriff of Northumberland and Vice-admiral of the North) and a number of lesser dignitaries and officials each supped there once, the Prince Bishop's suffragan in Durham many times. On one occasion, twenty-six guests sat round the Prior's table, including two abbots, the Sheriff of Durham, the Prince Bishop's receiver-general, the rectors of the richest local benefices, and eight university graduates who were the senior priests of the collegiate churches in the diocese; a proportion of the Durham monks was also present. Between the spring of 1437 and that of 1438, the Duke of Norfolk, then the King's Warden of the East March, visited the monastery on no fewer than five occasions, on one of which he stayed for five days with a retinue of 300.

The Prior's private household, generally staffed by something over (but not much more than) a dozen people, was dominated by his domestic chaplain, who said Masses with him and was his aide at all the other services, accompanied him whenever he left the monastery to attend to the community's business outside, and generally acted as his personal assistant-cum-secretary. Not far behind this monk in influence and authority was a second chaplain (often referred to as steward and occupying an office above the stairs leading into the Prior's hall) who ensured the smooth running of the Lodging, controlled its staff and handled financial matters requiring the Prior's attention. Under him in a clearly stratified and rigid hierarchy came the members of the household who were not professed, who were led by one of their own as lay steward, and who corresponded to the esquires, yeomen and grooms found in every nobleman's household. Their rank was signified by their dress, which was of better quality at the top of the scale than at the bottom and with more vivid livery; the lay steward was often garbed in a mixture of red and green, the esquires *(generosi)* in just one colour which was usually fixed at the whim of the York

66

merchants who supplied the cloth.[10] There were also some boys on the staff to run around on errands, and women who attended to the Prior's laundry. Some of his domestics stayed in his employ, and that of his successor, for the whole of their working lives and could look forward to a pension and/or a place in one of the hospitals at the end of it. Many of them were related to the monks, who in this way exercised their own particle of patronage.

The nature of the relationship between the superior and his brethren was to some extent dependent on the character of the individual himself. Prior Bell (1464–78) couldn't have endeared himself to his monks by forbidding them to wear linen shirts and thick woollen slippers like lay people, insisting on coarse wool for their bodies and leather on their bare feet instead. But he never antagonised his brethren as much as did John Fossor (1341–74), who was reprimanded by his Bishop for sending monks to the monastery's prison (situated in an outer wall above the river, which could only be reached in a prehensile stoop down exceedingly steep steps and was provided with a window too high for the wretched occupant to see out of)[11] simply for questioning him in Chapter or for no good cause at all: an imperious attitude which so inflamed them on one occasion that they actually attacked him after he had dismissed a generally held position of theirs out of hand.

But even in the most harmonious times, the Prior was set apart from the rest of the community, both by virtue of his wider responsibilities and his manner of living. He dressed more opulently than they did, for a start, his black Benedictine habit expensively lined and trimmed

---

[10] The 'steward' of a monastery might also be someone much more exalted, however. During Henry's reign the Earl of Shrewsbury was steward of eleven abbeys, the Earl of Derby seven, the Earl of Rutland six, Anne Boleyn's father (the Earl of Wiltshire) six, the Duke of Norfolk four, and Thomas Cromwell himself five. Such stewards as these represented an abbey's interests if these were ever contested in a court of law, or if they simply needed an impressive figurehead in civic affairs.

[11] There were, in fact, two prisons for erring monks at Durham. The one high above the river was reserved for those guilty of serious offences (felony, immorality, etc.) for which they might spend a full year in chains. Smaller offences (habitual slothfulness, say, or repeated failure to turn up for the office on time) were punished by a much shorter stay in a cell between the chapter house and the Prior's Lodging.

with fur. He ate better, too, even when he ate alone and even though his food was prepared in the same kitchen that produced everyone else's victuals. Malmsey and other wines regularly appeared at his table, as did oysters and salmon, dates and raisins, currants and figs, and a tremendous assortment of spices and condiments, while the rest of the community were refuelling each day on loaves of bread, two pots of ale apiece, pulses and beans, and generally coarser fish, with an emphasis on dogdraves and other kinds of cod, which had usually been salted down so that they remained edible (just) more or less indefinitely; it is very likely that every other Benedictine in Durham counted the days before his turn came round again to share the Lord Prior's more satisfying mealtime. And although it is true that at Durham the relationship between the superior and his community at large was a great deal closer than was the case in some other English Benedictine convents (Christ Church, Canterbury and Worcester being cases in point), the fact is that the Lord Prior of Durham was only *primus inter pares* at the saying of the offices and the other rituals in the Cathedral church. Otherwise, he represented absolute authority, with a loftiness that clearly separated him from his brethren, just as St Benedict had intended when he composed his Rule: it was the Prior who had the major say in appointing the obedientiaries, the only elected office being the one he occupied himself.

Hugh Whitehead had risen to this eminence along a path well trodden before him. Priors of Durham tended to be notable as men 'of learning and good conversation' and this one showed signs of scholarship early in his life as a Benedictine monk. Having been professed at the end of the fifteenth century, and priested on 18 December 1501, he was simultaneously despatched to Oxford, where Durham College had been endowed specifically for young religious such as himself to be refined intellectually and thus prepared for senior status in the monastery on Wearside.[12] After studying beside the Isis for seven

---

[12] Durham monks had, in fact, been despatched to Oxford since the time of Hugh of Darlington, who was Prior from 1286 to 1292 and bought five acres of arable land from the Abbess of Godstow on which the new establishment could be built. The College was re-endowed by Bishop Thomas Hatfield in 1387.

years, with another two of serious application in the library at home, Whitehead emerged with a degree in theology in 1509, his doctorate following in 1513, by which time he had already proceeded upwards to serve as Prior Thomas Castell's domestic chaplain. From there he returned to Oxford, this time as the College's Warden, and if anyone had still doubted where he might be heading in due season, that appointment should have turned doubts into likelihood: no fewer than six Wardens of Durham College had eventually become Priors of the mother house. First, though, he was brought home as an obedientiary, serving as Terrar and Hostillar between 1515 and 1520, two functions which gave him experience in handling the miscellaneous expenses of the house and its estates (for mending roads, for maintaining a sheep farm and suchlike) and in tending to the needs of guests. By his time, the Terrar was seen as the senior obedientiary, with more overall authority even than that enjoyed by the Bursar.

And then, on 27 November 1519, Thomas Castell died, the last of the great Durham builders (the east gatehouse into the monastery garth was his outstanding legacy) and sometime Warden of Durham College, 'leaving us destitute and desolate of a head and ruler to order and govern this your said regular and cathedral church and monastery', as the sub-Prior Robert Werdell pointed out when beseeching his Bishop, Thomas Ruthall, for the licence to elect a successor. Ruthall's response was couched in appropriately florid language ('I not only understand how it hath pleased Almighty God to call from this transitory life to his infinite mercy your religious governor and devout father, the late Prior of that my church, but also have well considered your petition and desire…') in the middle of which 'I have not only granted to you liberty and licence for your free election … but also have given ample commission and full authority unto them in mine absence to perfect all things appertaining to my pastoral cure and foundatory power, for the entire accomplishment of the said election …'. The permission was written at Ruthall's London residence 'beside Charingcross, the ix day of December'.

Hugh Whitehead was one of the two monks who took the petition south for Ruthall's approval, the other being the bibliophile Thomas Swalwell (another graduate and former Warden of Durham College) who had lately assumed for the second time the obedientiary role of Almoner, whose principal task was to oversee the four hospitals and the almonry school.[13] He was fifteen years older than Whitehead and it would not have been improper for him to entertain some hope that he might be the next Prior of Durham. The procedure for election was ritualised, like everything else of significance in the monastery, and the entire community gathered for a preliminary meeting in the chapter house on 18 December, which must have been almost as soon as Whitehead and Swalwell dismounted with the precious licence after their long winter journey up from London. The first thing to be done was to summon the superiors of all Durham's dependent cells, to join their brethren of the mother house in the elective process itself, and these were spread across an improbably long swathe of the country, down as far as Lincolnshire and across into Lancashire.

The nearest was at Finchale, three miles downstream of Durham, where the Wear ran over great slabs of rock and teemed round a bend foaming with rapids, and where the nine dependent monks dwelt in a priory of their own which was as impressive as many a mother house in the land, and was the richest of all Durham's outposts. The Northeast was where the greatest concentration of dependencies lay, with much smaller cells and a couple of monks in each case at Jarrow and Monkwearmouth, the oldest priory of all on Lindisfarne with three monks, and an anchorhold on Farne which barely sustained two religious at best and was occasionally left without even a solitary hermit. Then there was the most distant priory at Stamford, again with only two residents, though these were frequently joined by one or more monks from Wearside, for whom it made a very convenient stopping-place on journeys between the North and London. Lytham, beside the Irish Sea, owed its existence to the fact that a local magnate with a devotion to St Cuthbert had built and endowed it to Durham late in the twelfth century. No monk from the mother house was ever overjoyed at the prospect of serving in any of the dependencies, but secondment to Lytham was particularly unpopular because its residents had over a

---

[13] The children of the almonry were taught and maintained as an act of monastic charity in the loft which extended north from the Priory's gatehouse.

long period of time been regarded with hostility by the locals, for no apparent reason other than their Durham connection, that had been so extreme on one occasion in 1425 that it had resulted in the excommunication of xenophobic Lancastrians.

The Prior of Stamford, Henry Thew, the Prior of Lytham, Richard Caley, the Master of Wearmouth, Richard Evynwood, and the Warden of Durham College, Edward Hindmarsh, assigned proctors to cast their votes in the election of Thomas Castell's successor, and there were one or two other absentees; but on 3 January 1520, sixty-three monks celebrated Mass at the high altar of the Cathedral and heard a sermon preached by Richard Herrington, the Communar; and, after 'certain monitions and protestations had been publicly set out by Christopher Wylie, proctor of the sub-Prior and Chapter, at the doors of the chapter house and at a certain place in the cloister, against those having no voice in the election, the sub-Prior and chapter sang the hymn *Veni creator spiritus* on bended knee for the grace of the Holy Ghost . . .'. A versicle and a collect followed, the Bishop's licence was read out, 'those who ought not to be present at the election were expelled by word and, whilst certain jurists, notaries and witnesses remained, the chapter house and cloister doors were firmly closed and placed under guard, the constitution *Quia propter* of the council-general was read out, and everything else required by right and custom was observed'.

And Hugh Whitehead became the thirtieth Prior of Durham 'without debate in or out of Chapter, but rather by the inspiration of the Holy Ghost, unanimously (excepting only Mr Hugh himself) and suddenly'. The sub-Prior declared the result and Whitehead was at once led to the high altar, where the canticle *Te Deum laudamus* was sung and the Cathedral bells were rung. The singing finished and the customary oration extolling Whitehead's virtues having been made, the election was expounded 'to the clergy and people gathered before the high altar in the presence of the Chapter . . . in the common tongue' and there followed a strange little ritual of mock reluctance by the new Prior. Thomas Swalwell and two other monks 'in the presence of the elect residing in a chamber within the infirmary of the monastery, exhorted him to give his assent to his election, and although he put off giving his agreement many times, at length, not daring to resist the divine will and to the honour of the Holy Trinity and the glory of SS Mary and Cuthbert, "with a fearful spirit, a heavy heart and tearful eyes", he clearly and publicly offered a written statement whereby he, Hugh Whitehead ... gives his consent to his election'. There was also an interlude after the election when Whitehead was obliged to appear at eight o'clock on a Saturday morning in the nave of the Cathedral before Robert Davell, Archdeacon of Northumberland, who was wearing his alternative hat as the Bishop's Vicar-General that day. There, the new Prior 'in monk's habit and wearing a doctor's cap, sitting on a stool in the midst of his fellow monks seated about him as the Chapter' underwent 'examination and other incumbent things concerning confirmation of his election'. Next day, on Sunday 8 January, he was escorted from the Cathedral door to 'the stall on the north side of the quire of old used and wont to the Prior of Durham' and duly installed while *Te Deum* was sung yet again 'with the choir continuing and the organs harmonising with the singing until the end of the psalm, and the bells having been rung'.

The electoral process was over at last. A new chapter was beginning in the monastic epic of the English North. But the thirtieth Prior could scarcely have guessed, on his inaugural day in 1520, what the future held for him and for the other Benedictine monks of Durham, to whom he was now divinely appointed as a father in God.[14] His sovereign, Henry VIII, was yet to be declared Defender of the Faith by Pope Leo X for writing a scathing tract against Martin Luther's philosophy.

---

[14] There were, in fact, thirty-one occasions when a new Prior was installed in Durham; but Richard of Darlington served two terms, 1258–72 and 1285–9.

V

SUBSTANTIAL POVERTY

✠

'Let no one presume to give or receive anything without the abbot's leave, or to have anything as his own, anything whatever, whether book or tablets or pen or whatever it may be; for monks should not even have their own bodies and wills at their own disposal.'

RULE OF ST BENEDICT, CHAPTER 33

In composing his Rule, St Benedict clearly intended that his monks should live, according to the norms of sixth-century Europe, in holy poverty. Not only were they to be deprived of all personal possessions, but their dwelling place also was to be stripped bare of everything but the minimal necessities for life at a very frugal level; and they were most certainly not to have any form of intercourse with the world outside, for their purpose within the enclosure was the worship of Almighty God, the salvation of their souls and nothing else. In pursuit of these objects, their way was therefore to be one of ascesis, but in a moderate form that had no precedent in the religious life: they were not expected to mortify themselves to the point of maceration in order to imitate the Desert Fathers of the Church, as did the coenobites of early Irish monasticism, who were of the tradition by which St Cuthbert had been formed. Benedictines were required only to live within precisely defined limits which excluded even the mildest forms of self-indulgence. They were to form utterly self-sufficient communities, which had nothing at all to do with the commerce and other arrangements of the society around them.

And yet, less than a century after Benedict's death in *c.* 547, the

73

Italian abbey of Bobbio (which had actually been founded by the Irish missionary Columbanus before accepting the Benedictine obedience) and its 150 monks owned twenty-eight farms and in AD 643 produced 2,100 bushels of corn, 1,600 cartloads of hay, 2,700 litres of oil, 5,000 pigs and cattle, and 800 amphoras of wine for sale in the markets of provincial Piacenza. Benedict's monks, in other words, had discovered that although individual ascesis was quite possible provided a strict discipline was maintained, total isolation from the rest of mankind was certainly not feasible. Thenceforth, Benedictine monasteries developed as rather vigorous corporations, some of which were to become very substantial indeed.

Durham Priory was just such a community, its substance based very largely upon its possession of lands, the fruits of those lands, and the income coming from them in various forms including, most importantly, tenantries and tithes which replenished the Durham treasury from the numerous benefices in its gift; other than this there was a certain amount of sustenance from the fisheries of both rivers and coasts. Its wealth was also increased by whatever pilgrims might offer in devotion to Cuthbert, and by various forms of gratuity from other benefactors; but land was the bedrock on which the monastic economy was based, and there was a great deal of it. The Priory's territorial possessions were spread widely across north-east England and down from the Borders into Lincolnshire and the East Midlands; and until repeated Scottish encroachments forced it to close its dependent cell at Coldingham in 1478, Durham had also controlled lands in Roxburghshire, especially along the valley of the Tweed. As it was, in 1539 its stake extended into Nottinghamshire, with holdings at Gotham, Kingston-on-Soar, Sutton Bonington and elsewhere, as well as in the city of Nottingham itself. In Lincolnshire it had land (and a house) in Lincoln city, in Blyborough, in Bescathorpe and in Boston; and although the income from these properties was largely diverted to the upkeep of the dependent St Leonard's Priory in Stamford, a proportion generally found its way into the coffers of the mother house as well.

The complexity of Durham's acquisition of and dealings in land is typified by the transactions which occurred over a long period at Wolviston, on the lower reaches of the Tees and some fifteen miles south-east of the monastery. It's not clear when the monks first acquired land there, though it most probably came to their predecessors in Cuthbert's time, but in 1128 Bishop Flambard 'restored' a carucate he had evidently seized from them sometime in the previous twenty years, to which his successor Geoffrey Rufus added half a carucate between 1133 and 1141.[1] In the thirteenth century there were two demesnes, 'one dispersed in the three fields and the other at Bewley, where some tenants owed works'. There was, at the same time, a perpetual traffic in freeholdings, in which the convent secured in 1180 or thereabouts 'in return for land at Pittington and £10 6s 8d, Richard the Engineer's holding', with further transactions in the thirteenth century, as follows:

a toft and 30 acres with 1 acre of meadow, granted out by 1213 at 12d a year, a toft and 24 acres with 2 roods of meadow, granted out between 1218 and 1234 at 2s a year, also apparently the toft and 40 acres with 2 acres of meadow granted out at 2 marks a year and a toft and 24 acres with 1 acre of meadow granted out between 1234 and 1244 at 2s a year; a holding of at least one messuage and 34 acres with 2 acres 1 rood of meadow, and probably also the rent of 3s 8d due from it by 1280; eight tofts and 300 acres with 20 acres of meadow by 1296 in return for a substantial corrody. Between 1298 and 1346 one messuage, four tofts and 152 acres with 7 acres of meadow were recovered; in 1367 30 acres, perhaps with one toft, by the priory's representatives; in 1377 one messuage and 65 acres with 3.5 acres of meadow . . .

and so on, right up to 1430, by which time the monks had seventy-two distinct holdings in the area, amounting to 689 acres.[2]

---

[1] A carucate was the amount of land that could be tilled in one year by a single plough with a team of eight oxen. It might be anything between 60 and 180 acres, depending on the nature of the soil.

[2] A toft was a plot of land on which a building stood; a rood was a quarter of an acre (i.e. *c.* 1,200 square yards); a messuage was a house and the ground around it; a corrody was an annual allowance granted for an advance of money or services rendered; a bovate was approximately one eighth of a carucate and therefore a variable measurement, sometimes known as an oxgang; a vill was a division of a parish, synonymous with a township, a manor or a tithing.

There was a similar history of intricate land dealings at Burdon, a few miles north of Darlington, which in the thirteenth century

> was held by them as four carucates for 10s a year by Roger son of Acaris; apart from two bovates that he had previously granted to the monastic almoner, he sold the whole vill in three stages, starting in 1218, to William Brito, who became the direct tenant of the monks at 2 marks a year after Roger's son Roger had sold them his intermediate lordship. By 1234 William Brito had conveyed the estate to the monks; they undertook in return to maintain a chaplain at Darlington and another at Dinsdale at 4 marks a year each and to pay William's daughter Agnes 1 mark a year. This gave the monks the manor-house with the demesne and the mill, and the services of a number of free tenants, among them the almoner whose interest had more than doubled following a grant by Stephen of Canterbury ...

Typical again was the way in which income was raised from the monastic lands, in a group of townships situated in the eastern half of the Palatinate and which coexisted alongside other estates belonging to the Prince Bishops. In the fourteenth century there had been about 825 holdings in the hands of some 740 tenants, and of these only about one hundred were freeholds, clustered thickly around Wolviston and Burdon, as well as in Billingham, Ferryhill, Aycliffe and Hebburn, where some freeholders had become substantial tenants (like William Mayr who, in 1349, had 260 acres in Hebburn, which was two-thirds of that township) though most holdings were between 30 and 60 acres. The majority of tenants at that time, however, paid no rent in money (as did William Mayr) but were obliged to serve the monks with their labour instead; like a Monkwearmouth tenant who was required to work at Fulwell Manor for eight days with two men; and a freeholder in Kirk Merrington, who was recruited for manorial service there for two days with one man, and had to harrow a rood of land as well. Other tenants had to turn out for the monastic benefit on several days a week between June and September, when agriculture was at its busiest, and how long they were thus employed, and in what tasks, often depended on their exact status in the confusing pattern of medi-

St Cuthbert (*c.* 635-87) was the ascetic Prior and sometime Bishop of Lindisfarne (Holy Island), whose reputation for working miracles made him the supreme cult figure for centuries in the English North. He was eventually buried behind the high altar of the Durham Priory church in 995, and has remained there ever since. Fenwick Lawson's sculpture *The Journey* (which stands in St Mary's church on Holy Island) depicts Cuthbert's brethren carrying his coffin in a perambulation which lasted well over a century, after Danish raiders advanced on the island and the monks fled, taking their saint with them.

Cuthbert's pectoral cross, of garnets set in gold, the central one lying within a white shell from some Mediterranean shore. It was buried with him and was overlooked by the royal commissioners when they ransacked his tomb at the Dissolution of Durham Priory in 1539. It is now kept in the Treasury of Durham Cathedral.

ABOVE: From sometime in the fourteenth century until the period of the Commonwealth (1649–1660) Durham's Priory church (and cathedral) flourished lead spires on its two west towers: this is what it looked like at the Dissolution in 1539. The oil painting by Samuel Buck, however, was not produced until early in the eighteenth century. It hangs in the Dean and Chapter Library.

LEFT: In the Middle Ages and for some time after, criminals (and others) fleeing from the law, or simply from a mob, were protected by the Durham monks for 37 days, provided they could lay hands on the knocker attached to the north-west door of the church. Made of bronze *c.* 1140 in the image of a lion's head, it acquired a hole above the left eye which appears to have been caused by a bullet or an arrow, though no one knows how or when. The original Sanctuary Knocker is kept in the Durham Cathedral Treasury, having been removed some years ago and replaced *in situ* by an exact (but synthetic) copy.

The tradition of scholarship and bibliophilia, including the copying and illumination of manuscripts, was established very early in the history of Durham Priory. The monk shown here in a twelfth-century manuscript is working in the scriptorium of the monastery, steadying a page with one hand while he inscribes with the other. The knife in his left hand would have been used to sharpen his quill and to erase mistakes quickly before the ink dried. The monk is thought to be Lawrence, who was Prior of Durham from 1149 to 1154.

Cuthbert Tunstall was Bishop of Durham from 1530 to 1552 after eight years as Bishop of London, which was regarded as the inferior position. He was tried for high treason during the monarchy of Edward VI but reinstated when Mary reached the throne in 1554. A man of principle who deftly avoided trouble if at all possible, he enjoyed an ambiguous relationship with Henry VIII, and served the King as President of the Council of the North, after the Pilgrimage of Grace failed in 1537. Lacking belligerence, however, he was untypical of the Prince Bishops of Durham, who were traditionally the most powerful and sometimes the most aggressive figures in the English North.

Hugh Whitehead was the very last Prior of Durham from 1524 until the Dissolution of his monastery in 1539. He then became the first Dean of the Anglican cathedral until his death in 1551. Like Cuthbert Tunstall he was a survivor, and he steered his priory and his brethren to safety during a hazardous time, which saw many die because they would not submit to the King's will, and many great monasteries destroyed. This is a page from Hugh Whitehead's breviary …

… and this was his signature.

John Brimley was Durham's Cantor and Master of the Choristers from 1535 until 1573, when he died at the age of 74 and was buried in the Galilee. He therefore began by working for the Benedictine monks of Durham and finished in the service of an Anglican Dean and Chapter. Together with three former monks, he took part in the last (and illicit) Catholic mass ever sung in Durham Cathedral, in November 1569. He composed music as well as directing singers, and this fragment of a manuscript is part of Brimley's setting of the *Te Deum*.

Ricardus Richardson vxor   Robertus Richeman

Margaret et Ysabella   et Thomas keth pat'

Margaret mat'

Wyll'm xpofer   Iohn keth p vicar

Ric Whelden moch'   pat' et illius

Ioges ffelan

Ioges peyrson   Robt heryngton moch'

Elizabeth peyrson vxor ei'   Ioges Coode moch'

Robt Thomson   Robt ffost moch'

Robt peyrson

Margareta Browett   henric Skypton

Robt Browett   dns Richard' whley

Margaret Browett vxor ei'   Richard' whley

Agnes ffelton   thomas whley

dns' Richard' Smyth

Ioseph worley et   dns' thomas hawkhs

Agnes vxor ei'

Alicia morley

dns' thomas whley   dns' Ioges Georghs stot

dns' Stephanus whley   whley alian vxor ei'

dns' Robt whley   Robt' haspett   Dompny thomsta

Isabella whley   wyll'm duchit

agnes whley

Iohna morley   Robes stot

dns' Nicholas whley

Robin Erdys   Iohn mychell

Ianet mychell   arget   Lyan swaynston

Alian hodgys   Iohn duch'ht   Thes worley

Katerin stot   Robt stot   hugh mychell

Gregory swaynston   Iohn mychell

Iohn swaynston

Henry VIII (after Holbein) in 1536, the year the Pilgrimage of Grace erupted across northern England in protest against a number of things, which included Henry's dismissal of his wife so that he could marry Anne Boleyn. Essentially the rebellion, which at one stage threatened Henry's throne, was against his repudiation of the papacy and his establishment of an English Church, of which he was head. Durham Priory survived as a Benedictine foundation for two more years after the Pilgrimage was savagely put down.

OPPOSITE PAGE: The Durham *Liber Vitae*, the Book of Life, was first compiled in the ninth century, with the names of over three thousand people associated with the early Church in Northumbria; and from *c.* 1100 the names of Durham monks were added, year by year. It lay on the high altar of the Priory church where, at the high mass, the celebrating priest laid his hands on it during his intercessions for the living and the dead. It is now kept in the British Library, the oldest volume of its kind to have survived from Anglo-Saxon England. This page consists of some names from 1529.

LEFT: Sir Richard Rich was a lawyer knighted in 1533, the year he also became Henry VIII's Solicitor-General. Three years later he was appointed first Chancellor of the Court of Augmentations, a position he held until 1544. As such, he supervised the dispersal of assets seized by the Crown at the suppression of one religious house after another. He was one of the most powerful officials in Henry's government, generally loathed in the country at large.

BELOW: Thomas Cromwell, Lord Privy Seal, was the great bogey figure to most people during the crucial years of Henry's separation from Rome and creation of the Church of England. He masterminded the King's religious policies and the Dissolution of the Monasteries was his brainchild, as a means of increasing the royal wealth as well as of distancing England from the Vatican.

eval English social structures (were they bondmen or husbandmen, cotmen or bovaters, or did they fall into some other category separated by very fine distinctions from the rest?).[3]

By the end of the fifteenth century many changes had taken place in this part of the Palatinate and the 825 holdings had been reduced to 375, the number of tenants falling from 740 to 330, with a commensurate increase in the size of almost all the holdings. A new pattern had emerged, with syndicates of individuals obtaining the leases to entire townships in which they had equal shares and equal responsibilities in the payment of rent to the Priory. At the same time, labour services had been almost wholly abandoned and cash rents had taken their place as a policy, though in practice tenants sometimes paid their dues in the produce of the land.

The monastic way of organising and profiting from its lands was similarly complex. Central figures in this were the Terrar (Roger Watson in 1539) and the Bursar (Robert Bennett) who controlled approximately two-thirds of the entire operation, but the rest of Durham's estate – apart from those segments which, as in the case of St Leonard's, were allotted to the dependent cells – was apportioned between the five other obedientiaries, each of whom had responsibility for particular endowments and received the monies that came in from them for the discharge of their various functions within the community. Each of these seniors had his own office, known as a checker, which were scattered about the monastery, handily positioned for the efficient discharge of their occupants' duties. The Bursar's checker was therefore strategically placed just off the entrance to the cloisters from the Priory garth, right opposite the hall of the Prior's Lodging, which everyone having transactions with the outside world was bound to pass on his way in and out of the Priory. The Cellarer's checker consisted of two ample chambers alongside the great kitchen, the Terrar's office 'was as ye go into the Guest Hall, on the left hand as ye go in', where Roger

---

[3] Bondmen were unfree peasants (comparable to the villeins and serfs of an earlier period), husbandmen were tenant farmers; and whereas the first owed labour services to the landowner, the second paid money rent only. Cotmen and bovaters were tenants in medium-sized holdings (12 acres was typical) and paid the lord in both cash and in labour; the terms were synonymous, varying from place to place.

Watson was perfectly situated to make sure that all the guest chambers were kept clean, with all their linen 'sweet and clean', and with two hogsheads of wine always at the ready against the arrival of unexpected guests. The Sacrist's checker could only be reached from the Cathedral itself, through a door in the wall of the north aisle of the quire but, given that John Porter's business was the proper conduct of services in the church, there would have been no point in placing him and his assistants anywhere else.

These and the other senior monks were the convent's principal connections to the world outside, in their dealings with the tenantries, the farms and the other holdings which produced the income enabling them to discharge their internal duties. The farm which Roger Watson had to keep an eye on at Elvethall Manor, therefore, was only exceptional in that it was just across the river from and well within sight of the monastery, on the east bank of the Wear; otherwise, its relationship with the monks and its working differed little from any of the monastery's more prosperous holdings across the North.[4] It covered 434 acres of mostly south-facing land of which 150 acres consisted of woodland, with 50 acres of meadow and the rest under the plough. The farm buildings, surrounded by a stone wall, were dominated by a huge barn, but there was also a granary and three subsidiary barns for the storage of wheat, barley and oats. There was a byre for the plough-oxen, a stable for horses, a storehouse for tools and other tackle. There were houses occupied by the reeve, who was foreman of the workforce, and other members of the farm's permanent staff: the forester, the carter, the smith, the stockman, the pinder (who impounded other people's animals which had strayed onto the monastic land, evidently a problem locally) and their assistants. This was, in short, a substantial holding whose primary purpose was the production of corn, with wheat and rye growing through the winter, oats and barley following them in the spring. There were no other crops and the only animals

---

[4] Elvethall Manor had traditionally been one of the Hostillar's responsibilities, but there are grounds for believing that the Hostillar's function may have merged with the Terrar's sometime shortly after 1529, in which case the farm would have come within Dan Watson's scope.

apart from some fowl were the oxen (usually thirty-three of them) and the horses, which were used for working the land and nothing else until they dropped dead, whereupon their hides had some commercial value.

Barley was the most prolific grain grown at Elvethall, some of it required for the monastery's own purposes, otherwise largely sold to the many Durham brewhouses. After that, oats were the principal crop, most of it destined for use as fodder for the horses on the farm and elsewhere in the convent's service. Wheat was both a cash crop and necessary for the internal economy of the monks; some, obviously, was sent to monastic mills on the riverbank (one of which was for the Prior's sole use) and thence to the bakehouse, but a great deal of it was given as a dole and part of their wages to the reeve and the other monastic employees, with any surpluses finding their way onto the open market. Rye was grown almost entirely for paying the farmworkers' wages. The other product of the cereal crop was, of course, straw; and while some of this was used as bedding and fodder for the monastery's animals, and for roofing material, a great deal of it was sold to an always waiting queue of civilian purchasers, who were also interested in obtaining the oxen and the horses when these were available, draught animals being in great demand by a wide range of civilian buyers. And though it was not the purpose of Elvethall to breed stock specifically for sale outside (that went on at Muggleswick in the hill country to the north-west and at Le Holme, a grange the monks ran just outside Billingham), Roger Watson often judiciously balanced his books by replacing an animal while it still had enough working life left in it to attract the more needy customers.

The animals had a manifestly crucial role in working the farmland, but this depended most of all on human labour, which was provided by the seven permanent staff at Elvethall, by the obligation of customary tenants, and by the seasonal work of local people. Shincliffe men were hired every year for up to forty-two days to cart manure to Elvethall, to supplement what the farm animals themselves produced for fertilising the fields, in an example of economic efficiency that produced richer dividends at Durham than in most English monasteries. Most of the other hirings, as well as the obligatory labour, were made in the same satellite township, for weeding the corn, for catching moles, for bringing in the harvest, for threshing and winnowing during the winter months. Sometimes the villagers were required to help out with the ploughing, normally done by the reeve's men. Outsiders were also hired to scour ditches and repair hedges, to mend buildings and walls, and this was the supervising monk's direct responsibility, while his reeve took care of the routine care and upkeep of farm equipment, hiring carpenters to fettle carts, and buying the iron (which usually came from Spain via the dock at Newcastle) for his smiths to make ploughshares, horseshoes and other items. The reeve also purchased harnesses in Durham city, and various tools, and quantities of sack-cloth; but he acquired from the Cellarer the tallow, as much as 16 stones of it annually, he needed to dose sick animals with (mixed with tar it also made an efficacious ointment to cure sheep on other monastic granges of the pernicious orf and rotting mange), and to lubricate wheels and axles. Then there were the six cartloads of coal he bought every year to provide the farmworkers with their house fuel. The economy of Elvethall itself was much the same as for any civilian community, in microcosm.

Roger Watson had also inherited from the Hostillar the farms at Muggleswick and Le Holme; there was another such manor farm at Houghall, which fell under the Bursar's direct supervision, and two that came within the Sacrist's province, remotely at Ayhope Shield up in Weardale and also at Sacriston Heugh, five miles from Durham itself. Most of the Priory's sheep-farming was conducted in the hill country to the west (though the grange at Le Holme near the mouth of the Tees was, in fact, the biggest holding, where sheep were fattened as well as cattle), the stock-raising largely being in the northern farms, the grain being chiefly grown on the rich arable land which lay to the south of Durham. But sheep-farming was never as important economically to the Priory as it was to the monks of Yorkshire, where the Cistercians of Fountains, Kirkstall, Jervaulx and Rievaulx in particular had huge flocks running into thousands, as did several monasteries in East Anglia. At Le Holme, the resident shepherds and the monk who supervised them tended no more than a few hundred animals. The Priory's kitchens had first call on the slaughtered carcasses, any surplus meat being sold on the open market, as was the whole of the wool clip.

Similar arrangements existed at the monastery's salt flats adjacent to Le Holme in the Tees estuary; and from its fisheries along the Tyne, which were a recurring source of trouble between the Priory and the burgesses of Newcastle, who disputed its right to catch salmon there. But after farming in its various forms, the monks principally looked to coal for a certain amount of income as well as for fuel – it had replaced wood wherever the monastery needed fires, to bake or cook with, as well as in the warming-house and the Prior's Lodging, although some wood was still used as kindling – and several pits were worked on behalf of the convent, all of them (exploiting seams at Ferryhill, West Rainton, Bearpark and elsewhere) situated within ten miles of the Priory. These working mines were invariably small-scale affairs, requiring only a handful of hewers, but some of them had shafts deep enough underground to require the use of candles by the workers.

Coal deposits existed on other properties as well but, as these were rarely situated beside a river or near the coast, the difficulty of shifting the fuel over even moderate distances economically was a crucial factor, and they were not often exploited. Even at the operational mines, the coal was generally sold to the local lordlings and to monastic tenants, who collected the fuel from the pithead at their own expense, or by using their own muscle power. The income the coal seams produced was scarcely substantial enough to keep the Bursar happy in his budgeting, but it was at least reliable and didn't depend upon the weather for prosperity, as the monastic farmers did. Finchale did as well out of mining as either Durham or any of its dependencies, with about £30 coming in annually. The largest amount that appears to have accrued from this industry in the sixteenth century came when Thomas Wolsey was absentee Bishop, and let out the pit at Raily Fell on behalf of the monks, for £180 per annum.

There was nothing at all tidy about the arrangement of the monastic economy except in the way each part of it was run and in the meticulous tracking of every operation, every item, every transaction, every margin of profit or loss in the accounts kept by each of the obedientiaries, to be scrutinised in Chapter by their brethren if there was any cause for concern, or by the Prior (who had himself already been an obedientiary in his turn and therefore well knew how things should be run) in an example of careful accountancy that had been operating fluently for centuries before the notoriously calculating Tudors came to the throne.[5] There had, in fact, been one infamous lapse from this highly efficient norm, and the Priors of Durham had been extremely careful ever since to make sure that it would never happen again. In 1432, faced with the need to appoint some twenty-five of his brethren as obedientiaries and their assistants, Prior Wessington had given the Bursar's pivotal role to Thomas Lawson, evidently because no one better qualified was willing to accept what had always been recognised as a particularly onerous appointment: previous Bursars had often offered their resignation because, they said, 'the labour of the said office was unbearable for one man'.

Lawson was relatively junior in the community and his only preparation for the most taxing role of all except for that of the Prior himself, had been four years working as the Cellarer's assistant. On being asked, after his first year in the higher office, to present his accounts for inspection, he said he hadn't had time to draw them up properly and offered instead an inventory of thoroughly muddled figures, which had doubtless been cobbled together hurriedly as the deadline approached. Wessington's own failure was to realise that something had gone seriously amiss and to resolve the matter without further delay, and so Lawson's incoherence was allowed to continue for five full accounting years, by which time he was so distressed that some of his brethren feared he might be contemplating suicide. By 1438 it was at last abundantly clear that he had been fiddling the accounts in order to conceal his incompetence and, in particular, he had suppressed any evidence of the enormous debts he had been incurring on behalf of the monastery, to the tune eventually of £1,210, which was a crippling sum in the fifteenth century even for a prosperous

---

[5] The various Durham accounts survived to the present day and have been extensively published in book form at intervals since the nineteenth century by the Surtees Society, to form a body of historical evidence without parallel in the annals of English monasticism. See Bibliography.

Benedictine corporation. It was only after investigation by the Terrar, Henry Helay, that the discrepancies were finally revealed in the absence from the Priory of Lawson himself, who was then fulfilling another part of the Bursar's duties by touring the conventual estates. Hearing of his exposure, Lawson fled and went into hiding, so that his subordinates in the progress round Durham's properties were unable to report whether he was alive or dead. 'In which situation', Wessington informed his Bishop, Robert Neville, staying uncommonly cool at this unexpected turn of events, 'the Prior took the advice of his brethren, who thought it best to appoint someone else to the Bursar's office; he accordingly offered it to various monks, as insistently as he could. But they all refused absolutely, believing that the labour would be too much for them ... In which perplexity, the Prior ... talked to his brethren about the possibility of dividing the bursary, to which division they all agreed and no-one objected.' We have no clear idea of what happened to Lawson, except that he died in 1442 or in the following year.

For the next seven years, from the summer of 1438, the Bursar's income was divided equally between himself, the Cellarer and the Granator, the three monks accounting for their portions separately to their Prior and to the Whitsun Chapter. They were thus equally responsible for the monastery's solvency and under this arrangement the Granator now bought his own wheat and barley, instead of acquiring it through the Bursar, the Cellarer continued to purchase meat and other provisions, the Bursar himself being relieved of everything except his responsibility to provide the community with cloth and wine, and the Prior with enough money to take care of his private expenses, which included the wages of his servants. For a number of reasons, including external factors like wildly fluctuating market prices and poor harvests, the experiment was abandoned after Wessington admitted to his Bishop that 'certain members of the convent argued that this division cost more in horses and servants, as well as causing the absence of more persons from divine services'; and it must, indeed, have been quite difficult sometimes for a monk who found himself smothered in accountancy, to remember the principal reason for his having become a religious. From November 1445, therefore, the old system was restored and the Bursar again became the economic lynchpin of the community.

Without fail, in bounteous times as well as in the leaner years, the Durham obedientiaries totted up their figures annually, every Whitsun, for presentation to their superiors and to their brethren in full Chapter. They and other monks with important roles in the Priory's scheme of things also had to keep detailed account of even the smallest item that passed through their hands, as the Bursar's Book for 1531–2 makes clear. 'Distribution of napery: And, 18 December, to the clerk of the Infirmary a good yard for 6 napkins. And to Nicholas Browne 8 yards for the convent's table, and 9½ yards for 2 towels. And to Gilbert Walker, 26 February, 16 yards for 4 towels. And to the same man 21½ yards for 3 tablecloths, and 6 yards for another tablecloth on the same day. And to the same man, 1 March, 8¼d yards for the convent's table. And to the same man for the novices' table 6 yards. 107½ yards.' Among the Bursar's other purchases were 'Buying of soap: And in half a barrel of soap brought from Ralph Whytwode 10s. Paid to his wife in Jarrow in an old noble, and he is quit. And from Master Swynburne 2 barrels of soap at 22s – 44s. In the account. There remains half a barrel for the account in the year 1532. Buying of tar. And from Master Swynburne 3 barrels of tar at 5s – 15s; quit in the account between us. And from Thomas Jonson 1 barrel 5s. Paid in wool.'

Thomas Holborne, meanwhile, Master of the Infirmary in 1534–5, noted that he had received 'From the Hostillar £3 2s 10d; from the Bursar 26s 8d; from five officers 10s; from various tenements 6s 6d'. He also kept tally of his expenses for that accounting year.

First to the King 20s; to the Feretrar 16s; to the Cantor 6s 8d; to the clerk of the infirmary 12d; to his servant 5s; to the laundress 2s 6d; for parchment and paper and to the clerk who writes the account 12d; for thread, soap, and sewing of tablecloths 6d; for 12 wagon-loads of coal at 7d, 7s; for carriage at 9d, 9s; for 12 wagon-loads 5s 6d; for carriage of coal 6s 10d; for the carriage of one wagon-load of fuel 10d; in wicks/rushes 8d; on a pittance that was made 3s 4d; on a pittance made for the Lord Prior and the convent on the Vigil of St Andrew and on St Andrew's day 25s 1d; for the ironwork of one shool [shovel?] 2d; for mending one lock and two keys for the postern 7d; on white candles

13d; for 4lb of wax 2s 4d; for making of candles 4d. Expenses £5 16s 4d.
Excess of expense 10s 4d [should be 9s 10d]

It was by taking such great pains as this, almost as much as by the extent of its territorial acquisitions and the various forms of income that grew from them, that the Priory had become so prosperous over the centuries. Its income had, in fact, declined rather severely since the thirteenth century, largely because what came into the treasury from its 'spiritualities' had dropped from £1,466 16s 4d in 1293 to £359 1s 10d in 1537, though the last figure represented a small recovery from the glum year of 1464, which brought in only £316 10s ¹/₂d.[6] This alarming state of affairs had very largely been caused by a series of famines early in the fourteenth century, followed by the Black Death which repeatedly swept England from top to bottom between 1348 and 1379 and recurred periodically throughout the later Middle Ages. The plague wiped out approximately one third of the population, including 45 per cent of all the clergy, which meant that tenantries and benefices were simply abandoned through lack of souls to take them up, or enough people who could afford to pay the tithes and other monies to the landowners and patrons.[7] It also cost Durham fifty-two of its monks. But even in any financial gloom that might have pervaded the first half of the fifteenth century, Durham had been in a position to lend Henry VI £100; and it was in looking back on those years from the end of the sixteenth century, that the chronicler George Bates would wistfully remember how the Cathedral was 'accounted to be the richest church in all this land ...'.[8] He might have noted also that Durham's wealth was regarded enviously by some: in 1410 a number of

---

[6] Monastic income was derived from *bona temporalia*, which came in from manors, vills, pastures, tenements and mills, and included the sale of wool, hides, tallow, straw, timber and surplus livestock etc; and from *bona spiritualia*, which consisted of tithing and other monies coming in from benefices. The *bona temporalia* were consistently the most important source of revenue.

[7] The civilian mortality rate has always been a matter of debate; the clergy figure is more precise (see Chapter 14 of *The Black Death* by Philip Ziegler (London, 1970), especially p. 236)

[8] Bates was almost certainly the author of *Rites of Durham*, and may have been the monastery's last registrar before the Dissolution.

Lollard knights, followers of the reformer John Wycliffe but even more persistent critics of the Church of Rome than he, had campaigned for the secularisation of all Durham's wealth, as well as that of the Prince Bishop.[9]

Fifty years before Bates composed his threnody, the Church in England was given the most penetrating fiscal examination in its history, when commissioners appointed by Henry VIII's very new Vicar-General, Thomas Cromwell, toured the land with instructions to assess every religious institution and record its financial position, in a document that was presented to the government within twelve months (though Cromwell had ambitiously expected it to be done in five), which was remarkably expeditious in the circumstances: there were, after all, at that time some 650 monasteries and monastic dependencies alone in England and Wales, not to mention the hundreds of parish churches that also had to be accounted for. The resulting inventory was called the *Valor Ecclesiasticus*, which was as comprehensive in its more restricted field, and just as revealing, as the Domesday Survey of 1086.[10] What the commissioners came up with was imperfect – these were men working under intense pressure, not always with the co-operation of the people they were investigating, and they had no particular training for the job in hand, so that errors and inconsistencies were bound to crop up – but it was more illuminating than any assessment that had ever been made before.

It showed, for example, that in 1535 just under 10 per cent of the religious houses had gross incomes (including both spiritual and temporal monies) of less than £20 a year, that 35 per cent averaged something between £20 and £100, with the same percentage recorded at £100–£300, that 16 per cent could rely on £300–£1,000 coming in, and that 4 per cent exceeded all those figures. Twenty-eight convents were in the last category, and between them they enjoyed one quarter of all

---

[9] The etymology of Lollardy is interesting. Deriving from the Middle Dutch *lollen* or *lullen*, meaning to sing, it came to signify in English 'a mumbler of prayers', clearly in retaliation for the trenchant criticism by Lollards of the Catholic Church. See *Oxford Dictionary of the Christian Church* (ed F.L. Cross and E.A. Livingstone, 1997), p. 994.

[10] *Valor Ecclesiasticus* can be translated as 'What the Church is Worth'.

the income generated by the religious houses in the country. Richest of all the Benedictine foundations was Westminster, with an income of £3,912 4s 3/4d, followed by Glastonbury (£3,642 3s 3/8d), Christ Church, Canterbury (£2,909 17s 4 3/8d), Bury St Edmunds (£2,336 3s 10 1/4d), St Albans (£2,102 7s 1 3/4d), St Mary's, York (£2,091 4s 7 1/8d), Peterborough (£1,979 7s 7 5/8d), Reading (£1,938 14s 3 3/4d), Abingdon (£1,876 10s 9d), Ramsey (£1,849 8s 4 1/4d), Winchester (£1,762 19s 2d), Gloucester (£1,744 11s 1/2d), St Augustine's, Canterbury (£1,733 9s 11 3/4d), Durham (£1,522 14s 1/2d), Tewkesbury ((£1,478 7s 11d), Worcester (£1,444 14s 3 1/4d), Evesham (£1,313 5s 3 1/2d), St Werburgh's, Chester (£1,104 14s 2 1/2d), Ely (£1,084 6s), Crowland £1,050 17s 9 3/4d), and Norwich (£1,061 14s 3 1/2d).[11] Two non-Benedictine religious houses were wealthier than Durham – St John of Jerusalem in London (the Knights Hospitallers' Priory, worth £2,286 13s 10 1/8d) and the house of Bridgettine nuns at Syon in Middlesex (£1,943 11s 85/8d). Five such communities in the top 4 per cent were rather poorer: Fountains (Cistercian, £1,178 19s 3 1/2d), Cirencester (Augustinian, £1,325 12s 8d), Lewes (Cluniac, £1,091 9s 6 1/8d), St Mary's Leicester (Augustinian, £1.0561 8s 2 3/4d) and Merton (Augustinian, £1,036 1s 3 1/2d).

There may have been thirteen Benedictine communities better-off than the Priory, but only a couple of monastic cathedral establishments (at Canterbury and Winchester) were more prosperous when Thomas Cromwell's men came to look at the books. The figures these revealed may have been a source of some anxiety to Hugh Whitehead, his Terrar and his Bursar as they tried to keep their monastery solvent, when such a thing could no longer be taken for granted, as it doubtless was three centuries earlier. To anyone casting covetous eyes on Wearside, however, Durham was a very appetising prospect indeed.

---

[11] Dom David Knowles was of the opinion that the *Valor* underestimated Durham's resources, which he reckoned to be £1,600 or thereabouts in 1531–2 (see *The Religious Orders* Vol. III, p. 263).

Part II

✠

VI

THE GREAT MATTER

✠

'These are the devices of Cromwell, who boasts he will make his master more
wealthy than all the other princes of Christendom...'

EUGENE CHAPUYS TO THE EMPEROR CHARLES V,
19 DECEMBER 1534

The Dissolution of the Monasteries might never have happened had
Henry VIII not lusted after the coquettish younger daughter of one
of his counsellors, Sir Thomas Boleyn. He had already had a relationship with her elder sister Mary (by whom he may have had a son)
and both were among the highly privileged ladies who waited upon
Henry's wife, Katherine of Aragon, at court. The marriage of Henry
and Katherine had been unusual because she was then the widow of
his brother Arthur who, before his death from consumption at the age
of fifteen, had been expected to succeed their father on the throne; by
which time Henry VII would probably have installed his notoriously
pious second son in Lambeth Palace as Archbishop of Canterbury. As
it was, he decided that Prince Henry should inherit the widow before
he succeeded to the Crown, a decision that had nothing at all to do
with sentiment but was entirely a matter of securing international
alliances for the safety of the realm and the continuity of the Tudor
line upon the throne of England. For Katherine was the daughter of
Isabella, the doughty warrior Queen of Castile (who carried on a
campaign against the Moors when she was pregnant with the princess)
and of the equally formidable Ferdinand of Aragon, who united two
quarrelsome Iberian neighbours at their betrothal and sent Christopher

Columbus on the voyage that secured rich pickings in the New World for their people; they also unleashed the Inquisition on the peninsula and were acknowledged thenceforth by the Aragonese Pope Alexander VI (who was a Borgia) as The Catholic Kings of Spain.

Not only could Katherine claim such a politically desirable pedigree, but she was also the aunt of the Hapsburg Prince who would within a few years have become the Holy Roman Emperor Charles V. No alliance could possibly have been more attractive to an English sovereign. In making a treaty which obliged his younger son and his daughter-in-law to marry, therefore, Henry VII of England was simply following the instincts of every ruler throughout Christendom, even though Prince Henry at the time was not yet twelve and his future wife barely seventeen. There was also the even more cynical matter of the dowry that would tumble into the royal purse, in spite of the fact that Katherine's parents had already been milked of one at her ill-fated betrothal to Arthur.

Henry VIII had only just succeeded his father when, in June 1509, he and Katherine were married in the Franciscan church in Greenwich, he then being seventeen, she twenty-three. It had been intended that the wedding should take place much earlier, when Henry was fourteen, but Katherine's first union had been an impediment to this. Canon law forbade the marriage of a woman to her dead husband's brother, and it was therefore necessary to obtain a special dispensation from the Vatican, which was duly supplied, but only after a lengthy period of deliberation which was doubtless engendered at least partly by a need not to seem too compliant to such a controversial request.

The couple were happy enough to start with, but within a few years they were struggling, although Katherine gave birth to the Princess Mary (who would one day be Queen) in 1516. She then had three miscarriages, but bore another girl and a boy, who each died a few weeks into infancy. It became very clear to Henry that his wife would never fulfil her principal obligation to him, which was to provide him with the legitimate son and heir he craved above all things and, from that moment, Katherine's days as his consort were probably numbered. His roving eye, which had settled on another of her ladies-in-waiting, Elizabeth Blount, as well as on Mary Boleyn, would doubtless have been accommodated by his wife, and the marriage might well have survived his compulsive need for infidelity had she satisfied his urge to perpetuate a Tudor dynasty. But then Anne Boleyn attracted his attention, too, he fell hopelessly in love with her, and any such possibility disappeared when Anne made it plain that she would not share his bed unless he made her his Queen. This was a very high-risk strategy with a volatile man who had a streak of viciousness waiting for anyone who thwarted his plans or otherwise incurred his displeasure. And before very long she would pay for it with her life.

By 1527, everyone at court was ready and waiting for Henry to seek a divorce, for which he first petitioned Pope Clement VII in April of that year.[1] He based his case on the proposition that his marriage to Katherine was invalid because she had earlier been his brother's wife, and he adduced two passages from Leviticus in support of this.[2] But there was a passage in Deuteronomy which flatly contradicted these,[3] and it was not until Henry's theologians and canon lawyers had argued themselves to a standstill that the matter was resolved – to their satisfaction at least – by pretending that the problem didn't really exist; and on that basis the petition was forwarded to Rome. This time, the Vatican took much longer to respond than it had in granting Henry's earlier dispensation, and three years later the King was still awaiting a formal reply, after ambassadors had regularly been trundled out to Rome, while papal legates shuttled back and forth between Italy and England. Impatiently, Henry drew up another letter, after bullying Parliament (which hadn't met since 1523) and the two Convocations of Canterbury and York to support him, as well as a clutch of divines from Oxford, Cambridge and a handful of Continental universities;

---

[1] But John Longland, Bishop of Lincoln, in 1532 claimed to have heard rumours of divorce 'nine or ten years ago'.

[2] Chapter 18, verse 16: 'Thou shalt not uncover the nakedness of thy brother's wife: it is thy brother's nakedness'. And Chapter 20, verse 21: 'If a man take his brother's wife, it is an impurity: he hath uncovered his brother's nakedness; they shall be childless.'

[3] Chapter 25, verse 5: 'If brethren dwell together and one of them die, and have no child, the wife of the dead shall not marry without unto a stranger: her husband's brother shall go in unto her and take her to him as wife, and perform the duty of a husband's brother unto her.'

and now he dropped heavy hints that his patience was almost at an end, that if the pontiff did not accede to his request without further delay, he would seek other ways of achieving his aims. At the same time, he respectfully suggested that Clement ought to 'declare by your authority, what so many learned men proclaim ... as you not only can but, out of fatherly devotion, ought to do'. Henry was adept at applying pressure with a cosmetic touch of conciliation in order to persuade himself that he was a reasonable man.

This document was sent Romewards garnished with the seals and signatures of the two archbishops, four bishops, twenty-five abbots, forty-odd members of the nobility and a dozen or so courtiers below that level of society, but those of Cuthbert Tunstall and Hugh White-head were not among them. The Prior of Durham may not have been canvassed for his support, but his Bishop most certainly was, at least indirectly through Convocation. Tunstall, in fact, was to change his mind about Katherine's position during the protracted negotiations that went on between Henry and the Vatican, and even afterwards, when the King had dispensed with his Queen and installed Anne Boleyn in her place at the beginning of June, 1533. Within a month Henry was threatened with excommunication by Clement and given until September to renounce Anne and resume his marriage with Katherine, but backtracking was not in this monarch's nature, and in this instance it was certainly impossible.[4]

Katherine never gave up fighting her corner, insisting to all who would listen that she had been grievously wronged. She maintained this position when Edward Lee, the Archbishop of York, and Tunstall went to see her twelve months after Henry's second marriage, by which time she had been officially downgraded to the rank of 'Princess Dowager'. The two prelates had been charged with persuading her to

---

[4] The Vatican's patience with Henry was extraordinary. Having threatened him with excommunication in July 1533, it did so again in 1535 after John Fisher, Bishop of Rochester, had been executed, but did not actually carry out the threat until 17 December 1538, when Paul III at last enforced the ultimate Catholic sanction, and placed England under an interdict, by which all Sacraments were withheld from the population by every priest in communion with Rome; except the final one, *unctio extrema*, which was administered to the dying.

abandon her claims to still being Queen, which were embarrassing and infuriating Henry in equal measure. At their meeting, Tunstall 'in reply to an observation she made, that he and the rest of her counsel had always told her her matter was just, said the point on which they had been consulted when the Legates were here was only upon the validity of the bull and brief; but divers other questions had arisen and been debated by the chief universities of Christendom ... And it was concluded that ... no dispensation would enable the brother living to marry her ... Tunstall had accordingly altered his opinion, and advised her to do the same ...'.

The legalised annulment of the marriage to Katherine of Aragon (which was pronounced on the authority of Archbishop Thomas Cranmer, who had suggested lobbying the European universities and now dared to do what the Pope had ultimately refused to grant) and the enthronement of Anne Boleyn changed the course of English ecclesiastical history. It was the fundamental cause of Henry's conclusive break with Rome, and it consequently led to the monarch setting himself up as the Supreme Head of the Church in England. It also produced the circumstances that culminated in the Dissolution of the Monasteries. For the young King who had won golden opinions from everyone in his youth, who was a devout Catholic and who had, indeed, been proclaimed Defender of the Faith, had incurred the enmity of almost all Europe, which was still dutifully in alliance with the Vatican, by snubbing the papacy as no one had ever attempted to before. Only those north German states and a growing but still relatively small number of enclaves elsewhere which subscribed to Martin Luther's teaching and had regarded themselves since 1528 as Protestant, were not positively hostile to Henry, and even they did not look upon him with much warmth because of his early attack on Luther.

The possibility of having to fight off aggression on several fronts – from the Scots and the French in particular, and from the armies that the Holy Roman Emperor (Katherine's nephew) could muster from Spain to Mitteleuropa – would have been disconcerting enough in any circumstances: it became a matter of dismay when Henry took stock of his resources. Wars were expensive follies (occasionally necessities) to conduct, and the English King had been a belligerent fellow from the moment he reached the throne, when one of his first acts had been to build the warship *Mary Rose*, to begin a programme of naval expansion that would continue throughout his reign. Only four years after his coronation he had simultaneously taken on the Scots and crushed them at Flodden, while personally conducting an invasion of France which gained a little territory and enabled Henry to flex his muscles on the battlefield at the so-called Battle of the Spurs (which was, in fact, no more than a brief skirmish that may have cost fewer than half a hundred casualties, whereas the bloodbath at Flodden left 10,000 Scottish dead on the field). The French were to be a perpetual incitement to battle, both on land and at sea, which had something to do with the fact that Francis I, who succeeded his father, Louis XII, in 1515, was as truculent as his English rival, with exactly the same ambition – to be the King of Kings whose name and deeds would ring incomparably across Europe. They would fight it out for the title, on and off, till the pair of them died within days of each other at the beginning of 1547.

Henry was also a King who lived extravagantly, never happier than when he was ostentatiously on public display in all his regal finery, with a huge retinue similarly tricked out, or when bestowing expensive gifts lavishly on favoured recipients. The day would come when a French admiral, lately at war with the English, paid a courtesy visit to London, where Henry presented him with a cupboard full of plate worth £1,200 as well as horses and greyhounds. But nothing taxed his exchequer disproportionately so much as the extravaganza which became known as the Field of the Cloth of Gold, which signalled a rare moment of amity between him and Francis (it lasted only a few months, and hostilities broke out again within two years) and was hailed as a great stroke of diplomacy but in reality was no more than eighteen days of lavish entertainment, with interludes of jousting and other manly events in which the two monarchs could display their virility.

Henry had built a royal yacht, the *Katherine Pleasance*, especially to convey himself and his Queen (who was still Katherine of Aragon) across the Channel for the meeting near Ardres in Picardy, and he took more than five thousand people with him, together with 2,865 horses, hundreds of tents and pavilions, tons of plate and staggering quantities of food and drink, much of it still on the hoof or wing when it left England.[5] Two thousand craftsmen had preceded this multitude three months earlier in order to construct the accommodation for the royal party, and it was not Spartan. The entire event was arrayed in gold cloth (hence the name attached to it), which provided clothing, horse blankets, tents, tapestries and sundry other trappings, offset by baubles, platters and pieces of cutlery also made from gold. Henry's wardrobe, including gold cloth tunics galore, and many, many jewels, cost him a fortune and the whole episode set him back £15,000 – approximately £4.5 million in today's currency. It took him a decade to clear off his debt for the rendezvous in the Val d'Or, yet this didn't persuade him to curb his spending. Eventually he would have to go to the moneylenders of Antwerp, who charged interest of 14 per cent, and two years later he owed them £100,000. It has been calculated that over a period of eight years after the Field of the Cloth of Gold, Henry's outlay on war and preparations for war amounted to the breathtaking sum of £2,135,000, of which £265,000 had gone into funding his navy.

Long before that, however, he had been struggling financially. At the time of his marriage to Anne Boleyn he was close to bankruptcy, having spent all the money his father had left him, amounting to £1,800,000. Ten years before the wedding he had already become so strapped for funds that he introduced two new taxes, one of them euphemistically called the Amicable Grant, which took one sixth of everyone's income apart from that of the clergy, who had to yield one third of theirs. This produced so much rioting throughout the land that Henry had to repeal the taxes, a humiliation he was unaccustomed to; and so his difficulties continued, not to be abated until, faced with the prospect of huge additional expenditure in national defence measures and in fighting off the alliances forming against him in the wake of his breach with the papacy, he saw a solution in the great wealth of the Church.

---

[5] This included 2,200 sheep, 1,300 chickens, 800 calves, 340 beefstock, twenty-six dozen heron, thirteen swans, seventeen bucks, 9,000 plaice, 7,000 whiting, 700 conger eels, four bushels of mustard and vast quantities of other spices, wine and beer victuals worth £8,839 in all.

Or, rather, Thomas Cromwell did. The man who by 1536 was the power behind the throne in all things as Lord Privy Seal had led an unusually varied life before entering Henry's service under the patronage of Thomas Wolsey. Like Wolsey, he had emerged from the trading classes, his father being a blacksmith, brewer and fuller in Putney and/or Wimbledon. As a young man he had acquired some legal training before quarrelling with Walter Cromwell and leaving home to become a mercenary in Italy, where he had fought for the French against the victorious Spanish at the Battle of the Garigliano in 1503. Remaining there, and being befriended by the banker Francesco Frescobaldi, he set himself up as a merchant in Florence and then as an accountant in Venice, before moving to Antwerp to engage in trade as an agent for English dealers in the Flemish marts. He returned to Italy in about 1510 in the company of one Geoffrey Chambers, who was bound for Rome as a representative of the Gild of Our Lady in St Botolph's Church, Boston, charged with obtaining indulgences from Pope Julius II that would ease the hardship of Lincolnshire parishioners during the annual severities of Lent.[6]

Though these years are still clouded in some uncertainty about the dates of his various movements, it is very probable that Cromwell returned to England in 1512, and he may have married in the following year Elizabeth Wykes, daughter of an usher of the chamber to Henry VII, with whom he had a son, who was still an adolescent when she died in 1527. For a while Cromwell was in the service of the Marquis of Dorset and at the same time he maintained his many commercial connections with the Continent, as a cloth merchant (and wool-dyer), also becoming notorious as a moneylender whose interest rates were higher than the English average. He had acquired a great deal of expertise during his years abroad, as well as a number of Continental attitudes: he had become a great admirer of Machiavelli and Caesar Borgia while in Italy. He was, however, a flawed man: his biographer

---

[6] A contemporary account, which may not be apocryphal, reckoned that Cromwell craftily induced the Pope to grant the Gild the indulgences they sought by procuring some delicacies, which awaited the pontiff when he returned from a day's hunting and so delighted him that he authorised the necessary permission on the spot.

would one day say that 'when not perfectly certain of his ground, and in the presence of those whom he wished to conciliate, none could be a more adroit flatterer than he; it was only when he was completely master of the situation (and he had a peculiar gift of discovering just what his position was in relations to other people) that he became contemptuous, overbearing and cruel'. He was also celebrated as a fluent conversationalist, with a sharp and agreeable wit in three or four languages.

After being admitted to Gray's Inn in 1524, Cromwell attracted Thomas Wolsey's attention enough to be employed by him in drafting legal correspondence. This impressed his patron so much that within a year he was made the instrument of an ambition that obsessed the Cardinal, who wanted to leave his mark on the intellectual life of the kingdom by building colleges associated with his name in Oxford and in his home town of Ipswich.[7] In order to produce the funds for these projects, he obtained permission from both the Pope and his King to suppress a number of the smaller English monasteries and use their revenues for his building programme. Starting with the Augustinian abbey of St Frideswide in Oxford, a total of twenty-one houses had been suppressed by the end of 1525, which yielded some £1,800 and displaced about eighty monks, nuns and canons; and in 1528 seven more convents were dissolved, though these produced no more than £200 in revenue between them, which had enabled a total of twenty-five religious to live modestly. The men and women concerned were allowed to choose whether they would transfer themselves to a larger house of the same congregation to which each belonged, or return to the secular world with a small pension.

Dr John Allen (who would one day be Archbishop of Dublin) was Wolsey's principal agent in this business, but Cromwell had a vital role in the suppressions because he had the necessary knowledge of the law relating to lands and property and was therefore in charge of the

---

[7] Cardinal's College, Oxford, which was not finished by the time Wolsey fell from power in 1529, eventually became Christ Church. The Suffolk college was even less advanced and came to nothing, the only evidence of it today being a brick gateway on a one-way street leading to the Ipswich docks.

complicated paperwork, which involved the transfer of fabric, the settlements with tenants, and the adjustment of claims. He also appears to have supervised the surveying and valuation of buildings, and the drawing-up of inventories of everything that was portable and could be sold to the highest bidders – altars, furnishings, bells, tapestries. It was the perfect training for what he would himself instigate a few years later on a much bigger scale.

Many protested against these suppressions, usually people living in the vicinity of the houses, as at Tonbridge, where the townsfolk petitioned for the Augustinian priory and its eight canons to be left alone. Their dissent was ignored and it never became more than a very local resistance, because the convents concerned had no great importance or national reputation: none was associated with any major saint and, though five of them had an income of more than £100 per annum, the average for the whole was under £50. But there were two other very good reasons for submission. One was that Cardinal Wolsey was the most powerful man in the land after his sovereign, with any number of sanctions available to him that he wouldn't hesitate to apply to offenders. The other was that he had the backing of his King, when the mystique of royalty was the most powerful phenomenon in the lives of every English man and woman after the mystique of divinity. It was something that no one would even dream of defying.[8] And so the demolitions continued and might have gone even further had Wolsey not been deposed and disgraced for his failure to persuade the Vatican that Henry's dearest wish should be granted in his pressing 'great matter'. Thomas Cromwell now attracted his sovereign's attention and was made a member of Council very shortly after Wolsey's death at the end of November 1530, though Henry chose not to make the appointment public for another four months. He had already obtained a seat in Parliament as the Member for Taunton the year before, at the instigation of the Duke of Norfolk, who was Henry's

---

[8] It was very striking, for example, that during the Pilgrimage of Grace none of the rebels held Henry responsible for the state of affairs they were protesting against, and blamed it all on his closest advisers. They remained ludicrously dutiful to their mendaciously treacherous sovereign even when they were on their way to the scaffold.

principal military adviser. He was, very palpably, the coming man.

His ascent to power thereafter was remarkable. In 1531–2 he became not only a Privy Counsellor, but Master of the Jewels, Clerk of the Hanaper and Master of the King's Wards.[9] By 1533 he was Chancellor of the Exchequer, by 1534 Principal Secretary to the King and Master of the Rolls; Vicar-General in January 1535, Lord Privy Seal and Vicegerent of the King in Spirituals by July 1536 as well as Baron Cromwell of Okeham, and Knight of the Garter within another thirteen months. His position by then 'was almost that of a despot. He was supreme in Convocation, Privy Council and Parliament; he enjoyed paramount authority in the direction of internal affairs, and next to the King was by far the most important man in the realm'.

If Eustace Chapuys is to be believed, from his vantage point as Charles V's ambassador in London, the speed with which Cromwell rose to power may well have had something to do with his boast about making Henry the wealthiest prince in Christendom. Certainly all scholars agree that shortly after Wolsey's death Cromwell obtained an interview with the King that transformed his own fortunes, and it is difficult to see what might have been a more galvanising topic of conversation between them than a solution to the divorce problem and a promise that the sovereign's growing financial difficulties would also be resolved if advantage was taken of the situation to repeat on a much greater scale the strategy that Wolsey had employed when he needed funds. The idea would have appealed to Henry even if he had not been facing ruin, for he had inherited the avarice that characterised his father along with the fortune that he had so swiftly dissipated. The Abbot of Colchester was not the only subject who would recognise before long that 'the King and his Council were driven into such inordinate covetousness that if all the water in the Thames were flowing gold and silver, it were not able to slake their covetousness'. The gathering rumours of Henry's intentions said that he proposed 'to usurp

---

[9] The Clerk of the Hanaper controlled the fees which had to be paid into Chancery for the sealing and authorising of charters and other documents. Hanaper is derived from an Old French word meaning a place or container in which plate or treasure was kept.

part of the Church goods and distribute the remainder to noblemen. Benefices will be given to laymen ...'. And the already well-to-do would indeed profit hugely from what was afoot; but only after they had bid successfully at an auction conducted by Cromwell for the financial benefit of the King's majesty. There were some exceptions to this rule, where old debts were paid off by an ostentatiously grateful sovereign; but for the most part the entire business would be conducted like any other form of hard-nosed commerce.

The possibility existed that the nation might rebel against any or all of Cromwell's projected measures (as, but only in the North of England and Lincolnshire, it did), though it is doubtful whether Henry himself ever seriously entertained the idea, believing as he did in the Divine Right of Kings even more fervently than any of his subjects. But his new henchman knew very well that dissidence could be obliterated as efficiently as a monastery, and he had no scruples about using widespread force or invoking the awful penalties for treason. He also calculated that popular resistance would be minimised if a plausible rationale for suppression could be introduced. The handiest one was the well-known laxity of certain religious in their observances, which ranged from gluttony to concupiscence. Monastic zeal had been on the slide for a hundred years and more, and instances had been revealed every time a Bishop's visitation took place. It was not at all uncommon for the episcopal officials to note that the Rule of an Order was not being kept, that the divine offices were being neglected, alms were being wasted, and hospitality was no longer what had been intended at the foundation.

In the huge diocese of Lincoln during one moment in the fifteenth century it had been observed that 'There is nothing here but drunkenness and surfeit, disobedience and contempt, private aggrandisement and apostasy, drowsiness – we do not say incontinence – but sloth and every other thing which is on the downward path to evil and drags man to hell.' At the Benedictine Ramsey Abbey near Peterborough in 1439, the Bishop's men had uncovered 'defaults, transgressions and offences, concerning the which we here keep silence, that we may spare your fame and honesty'. Among the Benedictine nuns of Godstow 'certain things forbidden and contrary to holy religion' were 'shamelessly committed therein', evidently with the help of 'the scholars of Oxford'. At Elstow 'no nun convicted, publicly defamed, or manifestly suspect of the crime of incontinency [should] be deputed to any office within the monastery, and especially that of gatekeeper'. At Dorchester (Oxfordshire) in 1441, the Augustinian canons were the most notorious reprobates of all, for after Compline each evening 'they repaired to Thomas Tewkesbury's room, to which women resorted, where they called for good ale and settled down to chess, that universal solace of the reprobate. Several were incontinent, while the abbot was accused of keeping at least five mistresses at the common expense.'

Things were no better when the sixteenth century arrived. Even though the Abbot of Wymondham had been dismissed a few years earlier, the Bishop's visitation of 1514 found the condition of his house disgraceful, with the eleven remaining monks fighting in the cloister as well as committing several other misdemeanours: the Prior had tried to kill two of his brethren with a sword, had thrown a stone at another, and had not been to confession for a year. At Walsingham Priory, which was dedicated to Our Lady and sheltered the most famous shrine in England apart from that of Thomas à Becket in Canterbury, the Augustinian Prior in 1514 was a dissolute man who dressed as a layman and kept a jester, had appropriated money and jewels and was suspected of immorality, while the canons generally were dissipated, frequented taverns, hawked and hunted. At Peterborough Abbey, which Bishop Alnwick of Lincoln visited in June 1518, the Abbot was found seriously lacking in responsibility, selling wood without the consent of his brethren, repairing his own tenements but allowing everything else steadily to decay, and slandering Brothers John Bernwell and Christopher Barnewell. Worse, 'Within the monastery there is a certain tavern in which the brethren drink in bad weather, sometimes too early, sometimes too late' and 'There is much too frequent traffic by the brethren into Peterborough without licence. Let this be reformed.'

Ramsey Abbey had not improved much in eight decades. The gates were not shut after the last office of the day, so that 'the monks ... can get out of the monastery at will in the night' and some individuals were found seriously wanting, too. The Prior was too rigorous and not impartial, correcting his brethren 'at the simple complaint of laymen and of people of low estate', whereas Dom John Stow was a blasphemer and great swearer, 'he reproves his fellows and does not wish to be reproved by them', and Dom John Burwell didn't pay the stipends of the monks at the proper time, and William Calyner, 'serving the brethren in the refectory, is not of honest conversation, nor does he show deference to the brethren of the monastery, but abuses them with censures'. All human life was to be found in such monasteries, and monks were much as other men are.

Yet not every religious community was riddled with vice, great and small, and Durham Priory was probably as rigorous as any, as it always had been: the profoundly disciplined example of Cuthbert had left its mark on Wearside in this as in so many other ways. In the middle of the fourteenth century, indeed, Bishop Hatfield had thought the discipline of these Benedictines rather too severe, urging the monks to have a decent period of recreation each week, and to provide more careful attention, with more delicate food, for those who fell sick. They appear to have still been model religious nearly two hundred years later, when they were inspected in 1513 by the Abbot of Winchcombe in his role as official Visitor of the Order, who thought Durham a 'monastery ... which in regular observance surpasses all others in the realm'. From a man in his position, who was a southron as well, that would not have been a judgement lightly made.

By 1539, the only detectable laxity on Wearside was a tendency for most monks to dine apart from the novices, in the loft, at the west end of the frater house, leaving the youngsters alone in the refectory, where the dietary regulations were strictly observed, and where meals were accompanied by readings, which were abruptly terminated when the novice Master struck a bell hanging over his head. Meanwhile, the professed monks of Durham enjoyed tablecloths and each brother had his own mazer (drinking-bowl) edged with silver gilt. They ate rather better than the Benedictines of Westminster, consuming nearly four times as much meat and 50 per cent more fish (especially herring and dogdraves), almost all of it landed from the North Sea at South Shields, though much salmon was bought from further up the Tyne. They also averaged twenty eggs apiece every week in the year, to go with the bread and the pulses or beans that were their daily fare, washed down with beer or, on feast days, with wine.

A general awareness of the most lamentable failings had been fuelled since 1528 by a tract entitled *A Supplication for the Beggars* by the pamphleteer Simon Fish. Nothing is known about his origins but, after Oxford, Fish had been admitted to Gray's Inn, and he belonged to a group of young men who became notorious for their public hostility to Thomas Wolsey and to the papacy, making such a nuisance of themselves that they were obliged to flee to the Low Countries in order to escape the Cardinal's wrath; and there their attachment to Protestantism was increased by contact with the exile William Tyndale, who had lately (in 1525) produced his New Testament in English, which was attacked by Thomas More and Cuthbert Tunstall among others. On Wolsey's fall from power, Fish dared to return home, where his pamphlet had already been circulating for months. There has always been a suspicion that Anne Boleyn made sure Henry saw it, though he never admitted this; but it certainly appeared on the streets of London in great quantity during the royal progress through the capital at Candlemas (14 February) 1529.

Addressed to the King himself, the *Supplication* began luridly with an appeal by

> your poor daily bedemen, the wretched hideous monsters (on whom scarcely for horror any eye dare look), the foul, unhappy sort of lepers, and other sore people, needy, impotent, blind, lame and sick, that live only by alms, how their number is daily sore increased ... by the reason that there is, in the times of your noble predecessors passed, craftily crept into this your realm another sort (not of impotent, but) of strong, puissant, and counterfeit holy, and idle beggars and vagabonds ... These are (not the herds, but the ravenous wolves going in herds clothing, devouring the flock) the bishops, abbots, priors, deacons, archdeacons, suffragans, priests, monks, canons, friars, pardoners and summoners.

Fish asserted (what was, in a manner of speaking, approximately true) 'that they have gotten into their hands more than a third part of all your realm'. He added that 'The goodliest lordships, manors, lands and territories are theirs. Besides this, they have the tenth part of all the corn, meadow, pasture, grass, wool, colts, calves, lambs, pigs, geese, and chickens. Over and besides, the tenth part of every servant's wages, the tenth part of the wool, milk, honey, wax, cheese and butter.'

Fish liked to apply the sweeping broad brush to his subject. He reckoned that there were '52 thousand parish churches . . . five hundred thousand and twenty thousand households' which yielded to 'the five orders of friars' a total of £43,333 6s 8d. 'Oh, grievous and painful exactions thus yearly to be paid! . . . The Turk now, in your time, should never be able to get so much ground of Christendom if he had in his empire such a sort of locusts to devour his substance.' And so the tract went on, inveighing against 'these greedy sort of sturdy, idle, holy thieves . . . that have made an hundred thousand idle whores in your realm' and been guilty of many other misdemeanours, including the Church's refusal to 'let the New Testament go abroad in your mother tongue, lest men should espy that they, by their crooked hypocrisy, do translate thus fast your kingdom into their hands'. They were stronger in the King's own Parliament than he was himself.

And Fish had a very simple remedy for all these ills. He doubted very much whether his sovereign could possibly make any laws that would right these wrongs, and anyway he preferred a more muscular approach.

> Set these sturdy lobies[10] abroad in the world, to get wives of their own, to get their living with their labour in the sweat of their faces, according to the commandment of God, *Genesis III* . . . Tie these holy thieves to the carts, to be whipped naked about every market town till they will fall to labour, that day, by their importunate begging . . . Then shall as well the number of our aforesaid monstrous sort, as of the bawds, whores, thieves, and idle people, decrease . . . Then shall you have full obedience of your people. Then shall the idle people be set to work. Then shall matrimony be better kept . . . Then shall the gospel be preached . . .

---

[10] 'Lobies' are 'lubbers', which derived from an Old French word for a swindler or parasite. Monks and laymen who worked for them were sometimes sneered at as 'abbey lubbers'. The expression was to be perpetuated in Edward VI's Vagrancy Law.

With vivid denunciations like that doing Cromwell's work for him, there was scarcely any need for government anathemas against scandalous irregularity in the religious life. They would be made, however, in the reports of the Vicar-General's commissioners, as they repeatedly toured the religious houses from 1534 onwards. That was the year in which Parliament passed an Act abolishing the authority of the Pope in England, which anticipated the Act of Supremacy by which Henry VIII assumed the pontiff's historic role as head of the English Church. Both these measures were fundamental to the changes Henry had set his mind to after deciding to break with Rome, and they were not directed at the existing ecclesiastical establishment alone: the universities of Oxford and Cambridge were also specifically required to submit to the new dictat, in what has been seen as 'the first intrusion of the power of the state into the internal affairs of English universities'. The primary object of all the legislation going through Parliament at this time was to inculcate the habit of obedience to the English sovereign in matters spiritual as well as temporal, but there was a very worldly element in it as well. The Ecclesiastical Licences Act of 1534 was almost entirely aimed at stopping the flow of money from England to the Vatican, referring to 'intolerable exactions of great sums of money as have been claimed and taken ... by the Bishop of Rome' in the way of pensions, fruits, Peter's pence, dispensations, licences, faculties and many more forms of traditional papal taxation.

It was also in 1534 that a document was drafted under Cromwell's supervision, whose purpose was announced in its first paragraph. 'Things to be moved for the King's highness for an increase and augmentation to be had for maintenance of his most royal estate, and for the defence of the realm, and necessary to be provided for taking away the excess which is the great cause of the abuses in the Church.' This was the preliminary to compiling the *Valor Ecclesiasticus*. It was also the veiled official warning that religious life in England would shortly be changed for ever.

VII

THE APPARATUS OF PLUNDER

☩

'To remember all the jewels of all the monasteries in England, and specially the cross of emeralds at Paul's ...'

MEMORANDUM BY THOMAS CROMWELL, UNDATED IN 1535

There was a bloody prelude to the Dissolution of the Monasteries, and it anticipated or followed the legislation which Parliament enacted in 1534. Most importantly, an Act of Succession ensured that the throne would pass to any children the lately wed Henry and Anne Boleyn might conceive, and another such Act made criticism of their marriage treasonable, as would be any suggestion that the King was a heretic or in schism from the Church as a result of his rejection of the papacy. And then, in November, came the Act of Supremacy, which made 'the King our Sovereign Lord, his heirs and successors ... the only Supreme Head on earth of the Church of England, called *Anglicana Ecclesia ...*'. The opponents of these proceedings included Sir Thomas More, who had resigned as Lord Chancellor two years earlier because he felt unable to support his sovereign's rejection of the Queen and the growing confrontation with Rome; John Fisher, Bishop of Rochester, who had openly preached defiance on a number of occasions; and a handful of religious who rebelled against Henry's ecclesiastical policies when the majority of English monks and nuns were studiously trying to ignore the issues at stake. By the end of 1535, all but those few rebels had subscribed to the Royal Supremacy (and, in Durham, Cuthbert Tunstall had renounced papal jurisdiction as early as March the previous year).

One of the dissidents was Elizabeth Barton, the somewhat deranged and visionary serving-maid (the Holy Maid of Kent) who became a Benedictine nun, and who had prophesied that Henry would cease to be King within a month of his second marriage and would die the death of a scoundrel (and was actually interviewed by him as a matter, it seems, of astounded curiosity). The others were Franciscan Observants, who belonged to the most rigorous of all the preaching Orders, and members of the London Charterhouse, whose distinctive mixture of individual reclusiveness within a contemplative community had been a unique form of coenobitic profession since their Order's foundation in eleventh-century France.[1] Richard Reynolds was another objector, second only to Fisher as an English theologian, who functioned as a chaplain to and spiritual director of the Bridgettine nuns of Syon in Middlesex, where Elizabeth Barton was 'a familiar and honoured visitor'. All these people went to the scaffold, at Tyburn or in the Tower, after interrogation and in some instances torture, in every case after trial. Barton and the friars were the first to go, in the spring of 1534, the Carthusians and Reynolds following twelve months later; John Fisher on 22 June 1535, Thomas More on 6 July.

A climate of legalised violence and terrifying penalties therefore existed when the machinery of Dissolution was assembled, and it was frightening enough to subdue any other religious who might have been tempted to voice the opinions that had sent the Observants and the Carthusians to their deaths. It was in this atmosphere that Thomas Cromwell carefully began to make his preparations with the utmost clarity, covering not only the conventual houses but the rest of the Church's holdings as well. In the document that he produced just as the Act of Supremacy was being passed in 1534, which aimed to increase and augment his sovereign's finances, the most notable thing is the preciseness of the financial and other calculations he had made. The

---

[1] The Observants belonged to a reforming variant of the Friars Minor who had been founded by Francis of Assisi in 1209; they had arrived from the Continent at the invitation of Henry VII, and they had acted as confessors both to his son and Katherine of Aragon. They were characterised by, among other things, 'a forthright bluntness of speech that was in striking contrast to the conventional outlook of the majority of the other friars of England ...'.

Archbishop of Canterbury was to have 2,000 marks per annum 'and not above, and ... the residue of the possessions of the archbishopric may be made sure to the King and his heirs for the defence of the realm and maintenance of his royal estate'. The Archbishop of York was to be allotted £1,000 a year, the residue of his estates similarly going to the monarch, while bishops would be limited to 1,000 marks.

The King's cut from the possessions of the two Primates was only to be the start of the plunder, however. Henry would also enjoy the first fruits of every bishopric and benefice 'for one year after the vacation, of whose gift soever it be', the lands and possessions of any convent with fewer than thirteen incumbents, a third of the revenues of every archdeaconry, the franchises and liberties 'to any archbishoprics, bishoprics, cathedrals, priories & ... the moiety ... of the dividend in every cathedral and college church' while 'The lord of St John's [was] to have 1,000 marks, and the rest of his possessions to go to the King, and at his death, the whole; and likewise the lands of every commandery at the death of the knights in possession, for the maintenance of the King's estate, defence against invasion and enterprises against Irishmen'.[2]

Cromwell had also considered what was to be done with some of the religious and secular clergy whose lives would be considerably, sometimes dramatically, changed by these swingeing subtractions from their incomes. Their arrangements, too, were sketched out with precision. In convents that were not to be closed down completely (that is, houses with more than thirteen monks or nuns in them), fixed sums were to be allotted for the maintenance of the religious, with £7 a year for the upkeep of each priest and £5 for the lay brethren, the abbot of every monastery having as much as the rest of his monks put together 'to keep hospitality and repair the house'. Nuns were to receive 5 marks (worth £3 6s 8d in 1534) if their house was allowed to continue, the

---

[2] First fruits, formerly known as annates, were the first year's revenues from an ecclesiastical benefice, which had traditionally been paid to the Pope; liberties were groups of manors or tracts of land outside boroughs; 'the moiety' was the half of an estate; the 'lord of St John's' was the head of the Order of St John of Jerusalem (the Knights Hospitaller) in England, and commanderies were subsidiary to the mother house, the extremely prosperous Grand Priory in London.

abbess or prioress to be treated in the same fashion as their male counterparts. The only thing the Vicar-General didn't take into account in his memo was the predicament of the poor souls who would suddenly find themselves without a home after many years of stability, sometimes the best part of a lifetime, and what settlement would be made in their cases. That would be worked out before long; but for the moment, it didn't enter Thomas Cromwell's calculations.

The first piece of apparatus set up for the ensuing operation was the Court of First Fruits and Tenths, to deal with all the paperwork involved in making the initial assessments for the *Valor Ecclesiasticus*.[3] This was ready for action early in 1535, after commissions had been set up on 30 January to deal with the survey in 'every diocese, shire and place in this realm and into Wales, Calais, Berwick and the Marches of the same'; and the clergy in each district were simultaneously ordered to appear before their local commissioners with the required information by the First Sunday after Trinity, which was 30 May. This was always likely to be a deadline too tight for many to meet, and there were other delays in supplying the necessary information to the Vicar-General. Only three auditors had been appointed to scrutinise the figures coming in from the whole of Yorkshire, Durham and Northumberland, a huge tract of land, much more extensive than anywhere else in the realm, and on 11 May Sir Thomas Tempest, one of the commissioners for the two northernmost counties, had to tell Cromwell that they were running late, largely because there was so much to do in Yorkshire that the work on its neighbours was much further behindhand than it should have been. Cromwell was not pleased when he received only the Yorkshire returns in the first delivery, and was in such a temper about this that on 21 July Cuthbert Tunstall had to write a mollifying letter, adding his own weight to Tempest's, which went in the same post as the delayed documents.

The men engaged for this investigation were mostly of the educated middling classes in English society, who had traditionally supplied the

---

[3] Tenths were originally a tax paid on any individual's movable possessions, but from 1 January 1535 a new 10 per cent tax was imposed on the net incomes of all spiritual benefices, which the new Court supervised in tandem with the first fruits.

government with its provincial managers and other agents: mayors, sheriffs, justices of the peace, official auditors and local gentry. Quite often the diocesan bishop acted as chairman when the *Valor* commissioners met to discuss their findings and to draw up the *comperta* they were required to submit to the government.[4] Sir Thomas (of Holmside, near Newcastle) was typical: a younger son with no inherited land but with legal training, who had served in the households of the Prince Bishop and the Duke of Richmond, as a result of which he had acquired estates in the Palatinate and the North Riding, and was both a JP and an MP. He and his colleagues could claim expenses for their labours but they received no salaries, and therefore the only rewards they could hope for in this operation were whatever favours Cromwell chose to bestow on those who impressed him most in the discharge of their duties; this was a powerful incentive to extreme application and to doing whatever seemed most likely to attract the Vicar-General's attention. They were rooted in their local communities, however, men who in many cases had a relationship with the religious houses in their districts, with ties of kinship or tenantry or simple familiarity. Most of them would have supped at the table of the abbot or the prior of the nearest monastery. For all these reasons it is unlikely that they bore the monks and nuns any ill-will, though they may well have been critical of religious excesses where these were known and gossiped about. But they were acting in the government service, and no one in that position was ever allowed to forget it. Thomas Cromwell was among the most vigilant of men, he took great pains over everything he did, and he perpetually checked up on how everyone discharged their duties.

The instructions to the commissioners were comprehensive in the extreme, and again bear all the marks of Cromwell's efficiency. The first thing they were to do was to summon 'such and so many of the bishops and archdeacons, scribes and ministers ... as they shall think most convenient for knowledge to be had of the numbers and names' of all the deaneries, dignities, cathedral churches, collegiate churches, colleges, hospitals, monasteries, priories, religious houses, parsonages,

---

[4] *Compertus-a* is 'that which has been ascertained/ is clearly known'.

vicarages, chantries, free chapels 'or other promotions spiritual' in the area. After carefully examining all relevant registers and other documents, the commissioners were to split up into threes or any other convenient number, and work their way through all these ecclesiastical properties; and there they were to interrogate the incumbents closely on every conceivable matter of interest to the authorities. They were 'to enquire, search and know the names of the dean or prior of the said cathedral church or monastery, of the names of the sub-deans and sub-prior, treasurer, residencer, chanter, sexton, almoner, hospitaller, bowser [bursar] and of every other person that hath any dignity, prebend, vicarship, petty canonry, or other office, chantry, cure or promotion spiritual in succession in the said cathedral, church, or monastery'. They were to discover 'the number, names and certainty of the manors, lands and tenements, demesnes, rents, farms, possessions, parsonages, portions, pensions, tithes, oblations and all other profits as well spiritual as temporal' attached to every place they registered.

The ultimate purpose of these investigations was to establish the gross annual income of each ecclesiastical establishment, whether conventual or otherwise. Nothing at all must be overlooked, no matter must escape investigation, and every individual must be interviewed exhaustively to this end. The Visitors were then to deduct various pensions, rents and fees due to lay administrators (such as bailiffs and stewards) as tax-free monies. And when they were done, 'the said commissioners . . . shall cause to be made a fair book after the auditor's fashion' containing every piece of information they had ferreted out of their shires and dioceses. Every book compiled by each group of commissioners was to be delivered 'unto the King's Exchequer under their seals, according as is limited by the tenor of the commissions as they will answer unto the King's highness at their uttermost peril, to the intent that the tenth of the premises may be taxed and set to be levied to the King's use according to the statute made and provided of the grant thereof'. It was as typical of Thomas Cromwell as it was of Henry himself, that a chilling reminder of power and the terrible consequences of giving offence should add a final twist to this relentless document. Which was also incongruously scrupulous in its allowance for monastic expenses.

Even more crucial to the master plan for stripping the Church of its wealth was the Court of Augmentations, which was not established until the *Valor Ecclesiasticus* had been compiled and presented to the government. On 14 April 1536, Parliament passed the Act which created this appliance for controlling and supervising the new wealth that would shortly be swelling Henry's treasury.[5] Such was the urgency informing the decision that the Solicitor-General, Richard Rich, was suddenly told to shed all his current responsibilities and concentrate on setting up and starting the new apparatus. Rich was a very typical Tudor careerist who had studied law, a Hampshire merchant's son of about forty years old at the time of his new appointment, an opportunist who trimmed his sails to make the most of any wind that blew, denounced by Thomas More at his trial as treacherous and unprincipled. Like Cromwell, he had attracted Thomas Wolsey's attention and took a great step forward in 1528 when he interested the Cardinal in a plan (which was never, in fact, carried out) to reform the common law. The following year he became Commissioner of Sewers in Middlesex and Member of Parliament for Colchester; by 1533 he had reached one of the three highest legal offices in the land and he had received a knighthood. It was as Solicitor-General that he had prosecuted all those who refused to accept Henry's Acts of Succession and Supremacy, in the course of which he personally examined More and Fisher before their trials. Now, he was in charge of a hitherto unheard-of instrument of government, with a staff of thirty-four to start with, though as its work (and its appetite for work) expanded, within a few years it had several hundred officials scattered across the shires of England, invigilating revenues for the Crown.

Rich conducted a great deal of his work from his home at Leighs in Essex, though the headquarters of Augmentations were within the Palace of Westminster, where Sir Thomas Pope, the first Treasurer of

---

[5] Ten days later, Henry authorised a secret commission to investigate all treasonable conduct, which was designed above all to rid him of Anne Boleyn – by then mother of the future Queen Elizabeth – who he suspected of the same conduct by which she had attracted him a few years earlier. She was executed on 19 May, and the next day Henry married Jane Seymour, who would give him his legitimate male heir and die in the act of doing so.

the Court and Rich's second-in-command, and the administrative staff worked. In chambers specially constructed for the new organism, no expense was spared to make an agreeable context in which people would administer the complexities which soon began to swamp them with detail. Workmen were employed for four months in plastering ceilings and wainscotting the walls with well-seasoned wood, in making the terraced grounds for the clerks to look out upon, in planting a garden with fragrant herbs. Because this was a Tudor operation, everything was noted carefully in the accounts, including the 13,200 nails which cost £6 1s 9d, the thousands of bricks at £8 per thousand, and the 400 loads of earth at 3d a time.

With the fabric and surroundings of the new building finished, the office equipment was installed: 'Green cloth for the accounting board, twelve presses reinforced with iron, strongboxes and bags in which to store the incoming money and valuables, scales, weights, locks and other essential paraphernalia were purchased as required. Quantities of ink, parchment and paper were consumed in the making of accounts or tripartite engrossing of official documents; also for Court sessions a book called a "jury book" was procured "with a silver crucifix fastened upon it". At the same time wax was bought for impressions of the Court's seals which were newly engraved for immediate use.' Everything was set down in the accounts, including the monies which would be disbursed as gratuities, the fuel required to keep the place warm, and the victuals to be consumed at Sir Thomas Pope's table. A pay scale was drawn up, and it was one that anyone outside the government's service might envy. Sir Richard Rich collected £300 per annum as Chancellor of the Court, Sir Thomas Pope £120 as Treasurer, with the attorneys and solicitors serving under them at headquarters earning between £40 and £20 a year at the beginning of the enterprise, significantly more later on. William Cowper, first Surveyor of Woods, started on £20, Richard Duke, Clerk of the Court, on £10, while the Keeper of Records (Walter Farr) earned 4d a day, the chief mason and the chief carpenter £6 1s 8d per annum.

The Augmentations officials were very busy men from the moment they moved in, which some of them soon found meant repeatedly moving in and out in order to confer with the King and members of his Privy Council. Thus, on 28 September 1536, were noted 'the costs of Thomas Pope riding with nine horse to the Court about the affairs of the Court of Augmentations, the King's Grace then lying at Dunstable, and for the same time, being 6s 8d per diem by the space of three days, that is to say, for myne expenses £3 7s 8d, and for my fee 20s; [*summa*] £4 7s 8d'. That was the second such journey in little more than a week by Sir Thomas and, on 3 October, off he went again, this time accompanied by Robert Southwell, one of the Augmentations attorneys, to see the monarch who by then had shifted to Windsor. There were others who must have found their new appointments even more exhausting, necessitating even longer absences from home. In the following summer, Richard Duke was obliged to travel from Colchester to Hampton Court, where he was busy for fifteen days before moving on to Windsor for another ten days, after which he was recalled to Westminster. But nobody labouring in the head office was nearly as mobile as the agents who did the real donkey work in the field when Cromwell's next strategy was implemented: a full visitation of the monasteries which, like the fiscal examination of the previous twelve months, had never been known on the same scale before.

Visitations of religious houses had been a regular feature of their lives for centuries and were enshrined in canon law. They were traditionally conducted by the diocesan bishop and they were supposed to occur annually, but in practice tended to be much less frequent than that: if the prelate got round to all the convents in his diocese every four years he was thought to be doing rather well. The procedure, however, was unvarying. The house was first given notice that His Grace would be arriving on a certain date, and those he expected to interview were instructed to prepare themselves for this.

Cuthbert Tunstall's citation to Hugh Whitehead and his brethren on 22 June 1532 was entirely typical of the form used. The Durham monks were first saluted elaborately with an explanation of what was afoot, 'Since nothing more becomes a shepherd than to keep care of the flock committed to him … for that reason it can be a very great help for the flock to be carefully visited, and if it is found to be infested with any kind of sickness, that remedies which can control a growing evil be looked for with all care …' It was therefore proposed that 'in the chapter house of the church of Durham' on Tuesday 16 July, 'and continuing and extending on the following days, as may be necessary, we shall in person visit you in head and members with the kind feelings of paternal love and in accordance with the pattern handed down in this respect . . .' Then the tone changed, from the fatherly to the lordly: 'Therefore . . . we peremptorily order you, the prior and chapter and each and every one of you, that you in all person be present before us in the place and at the time specified, in order to receive our visitation to be carried out in the canonical form handed down in this respect, and in order to undergo the visitation in person with due reverence.' Whitehead and his brothers were charged with 'seeking out meanwhile with intent minds every single thing which needs reform and correction . . . and then of informing us faithfully and with genuine feelings, so that with the help of our ministrations good men may be preserved from harm . . .' And they thereupon began to prepare themselves accordingly.

A bishop's arrival was always heavily coated with well-recognised ceremony, as the superior of the house presented his credentials 'together with evidence of the canonical foundation of the house' and a statement of its current finances. Everyone then went in procession to the chapter house, where a sermon was usually preached before the bishop interviewed every monk in the place, starting with the superior. Each had been supplied with a questionnaire beforehand, which sought their views on such things as fidelity to the Rule, the level of discipline and administration in the monastery, and gave every monk an opportunity to complain about anyone or anything he might be dissatisfied with. The bishop travelled with clerks on these occasions and so everything was carefully noted in writing before the visitation was concluded. But, if necessary, anyone found defective in any way might be interviewed again before the episcopal party left. And in due course, from the episcopal palace, there came an injunction setting out the changes (if any) that must be made, and the suggestions that ought at least to be considered by the religious.

Cromwell's visitation, therefore, was grounded in a long tradition, different from anything that had happened before chiefly in its intent, and in the composition of the Visitors. These were a different sort of animal from the commissioners charged with compiling the *Valor*, and they certainly did not resemble any bishop who had ever shepherded his flock, as they were sent about their business a few months before Augmentations was officially set up. A majority had been trained in the law and some of them were ordained as well, salaried professional employees with ambitions to satisfy and careers to advance. They were, when the Court began to function properly, the ten regional auditors and the seventeen particular receivers whose annual financial reward was '£20 plus profits' from whatever they could squeeze out of the religious houses and the ecclesiastical benefices. And although most of them seem to have been as reasonable as the commissioners who had supervised the initial *comperta* that resulted in the *Valor*, a number very quickly earned less savoury reputations as bullies with a rapacious gleam in their eyes at the sight of monastic wealth. Some, certainly, were not above blatant toadying in search of promotion. And sometimes they bickered and quarrelled among themselves.

Two who didn't get on at all well together were Thomas Leigh, an Old Etonian from Cheshire with a Cambridge doctorate in law, who had already been noted (by Eustace Chapuys) as a less than ideal ambassador to Denmark, and John ap Rice, an Oxford notary who had lately been Registrar of Salisbury Cathedral.[6] These two were sent off to trawl through thirteen religious houses between Somerset and Hertfordshire in August 1535, and rapidly discovered that they were not good travelling companions, now doomed to a month on the road together. From the outset they vigorously disagreed about appropriate courses of action, with ap Rice generally taking a lenient view of the religious, the self-important and truculent Leigh quite the opposite; and consequently they sent contradictory reports and advice to Cromwell. Eventually the Welshman blew the whistle on his unbearable colleague, and told their boss that Leigh was 'too insolent and pompous ... Wherever he comes he handles the fathers very roughly, many times for small causes, as for not meeting him at the door, where

---

[6] Leigh was to become much the more notorious of the two, but ap Rice was the more interesting man, who later in his life produced the first Welsh translations of the Lord's Prayer, the Creed and the Ten Commandments.

they had been warned of his coming ... He is also excessive in taking ...' What this exchange meant, of course, and frictions that sometimes occurred between other officials on similar errands, is simply that Cromwell's agents were human beings, just like the gluttonous and libidinous religious they occasionally came across.

Another tart view of Leigh was expressed by John Musard, monk of Worcester, who communicated with Cromwell at the end of September, and may have been in government pay himself as an informer, or was perhaps an exceedingly naïve and trusting man. 'Dr Leigh', he wrote, 'showed openly that he was comperted by many of our convent for his incontinency, and a sower of discord between us, when he was at Gloucester. Yet nothing is laid to his charge, which is greatly mused at amongst our convent.' Cromwell clearly took notice of this and ap Rice's comments, however, and must have reprimanded Leigh, for a month later the Doctor was writing defensively to his superior, telling the Vicar-General that 'though I was discomforted I was more surprised who should incense you against me. I pray I may not live to that day when I shall give any cause for deceiving your expectation of me. I shall always act as if you were present, and proceed for the glory of God and the King's honour ... sycophants would be glad to bring me out of your favour, though I have used no rigor at any time or place'. He followed this up with another letter five days later, refuting the monk's charges of incontinence – 'and though a man is given to sensual appetites I am not addicted to such notable sensualities and abuses as you are informed'. He had also been accused of taking his brother with him into the Midlands at the government's expense, and excused this on the grounds that 'As my brother buried his wife of late, and is not very expert in the world, I willed him to ride with me to see the countries and manners of men, and for no other cause; and as I did not dare to ask you to take him into your service, I have sent him for a time to my lord of Chester'.

Towering above most of his colleagues in stature and rectitude was John Tregonwell, a Cornishman and Oxford law graduate, who had been Principal of one of the Inns of Court (Peckwater), had acted as the King's proctor in his divorce suit, had been sent on diplomatic missions to Scotland and the Netherlands, had participated in the trials of the Carthusians, as well as those of Fisher and More, and would shortly be enlisted again for similar service at the indictment of Anne Boleyn. In 1535, before his recruitment for Cromwell's new enterprise, he was principal Judge in the Court of Admiralty. There were others, like John ap Rice, against whom no fault could be found except that they were charged with a scarifying duty and were prepared to carry it out to the letter; and they included William Cavendish, William Blitheman, Edward Gostwick, John Scudamore, John Heneage, Leonard Beckwith and a dozen more. There were one or two who came somewhere between the ideal and the repugnant: such as Thomas Bedyll, another Oxford man who had served as Archbishop William Warham's secretary at Lambeth, who worked as diligently at ingratiating himself with his superiors as he did in the tasks that they gave him.[7] He, too, had been busy at the Supremacy trials, at the exposure of malfeasance in the Charterhouse and at Syon.

Soon to be detested as much as Thomas Leigh was Dr Richard Layton, a Cumbrian who was distantly related to Cuthbert Tunstall (and also to the lawyer Robert Aske, who led the Pilgrimage of Grace) and who, on coming down from Cambridge with a law degree before taking holy orders, had started fashioning a career under Wolsey at the same time as Cromwell. With remarkable dexterity he managed to hold both his vocations in balance, enjoying several ecclesiastical livings up and down the country (Rector of Stepney, of Harrow-on-the-Hill, of Sedgefield respectively, Dean of the collegiate church at Chester-le-Street) until he became Archdeacon of Buckingham in October 1534. That same year he was also appointed a clerk in Chancery and Clerk to the Privy Council; and then he was unleashed on the monasteries. He quickly became noticed as one of the most energetic Visitors, and he wrote the most enthusiastic and fluent despatches that ever landed on Thomas Cromwell's desk. He was an official who obviously enjoyed his work, but there was something distinctly singular about his reporting that set him apart from others engaged in the same duties as himself.

---

[7] Dom David Knowles thought him 'one of the least attractive of Cromwell's minions ... in all of which his coarse texture of mind and snuffling accents show to peculiar disadvantage against the ... physical suffering accepted and endured by his victims'.

He was a man who entered every house of religion with his nose twitching for any scent of carnal activity, and when he found it he reported it in great detail, but switched from English into Latin to convey the most salacious bits. At the Augustinian house of Repton in Derbyshire Thomas Rede, the sub-Prior, and three of his brethren were identified as sodomites '*per voluntarias pollutiones*'; at Marham in Norfolk, the incontinent Cistercian nun Barbara Mason was '*peperit semel et fatetur se cognita a priore de Pentney*', three others were '*peperit semel ex conjugato*', and a fifth sister was '*peperit dual proles ex solutis*'. Not far away, in the same county, the Augustinian Prior William Wyngfelde confessed to masturbation and one of his canons '*cum duabus feminis et fatetur se passum esse sodomiticum*'. One is left wondering how the Archdeacon of Buckingham extracted such intimate information.

Tregonwell and his colleagues set off across England in the summer of 1535, as rain swept across the land for weeks on end. Their assignments cannot be isolated from the investigation of Church wealth then concluding, though it has been persuasively argued that this second bout of commissions had at least as much to do with Henry's need to subjugate the religious communities and leave them in no doubt who was now running the Church in England. Authority was clearly at issue in Cromwell's choice of the first houses to be visited: they were the Cistercians, the Observants, the Gilbertines, the Premonstratensians, the Cluniacs and one or two smaller Orders which had traditionally been exempt from the regular episcopal visitations to which Benedictines had long been accustomed, and which since the time of Edward the Confessor in the eleventh century had frequently been a source of tension between the monks, the bishops, the Crown and the papacy.[8] In picking on the exempt Orders first, therefore, Henry was throwing his weight about, demonstrating who was boss in the new order of things, telling the religious that drastic changes were afoot.

---

[8] The Premonstratensian canons (and canonesses) were founded in 1121 by St Norbert at Premontre, north of Paris, and lived according to the Rule of St Augustine. They reached England in 1143 and had thirty-four houses here in the 1530s.

The eighty-six questions which the visitors were instructed to put to the religious they were required to interview (seventy-four for the male communities, with another dozen for the nuns) reeked of a determination to convey authority and even to humiliate. Some, at the top of the list, simply repeated what Sir Thomas Tempest and his colleagues had been asking earlier in the year: how many monks or nuns were there in this place, what was its income, how had this been acquired, and so forth. A whiff of the intent behind the questionnaires came with enquiries about the rigour with which the religious were maintaining the traditions of the house, as set down in the original statutes conveying the founder's will. There were others designed to exploit any frictions between a superior and the rest of the community. How had the superior been chosen, how were the accounts presented, was the upkeep of fabric to everyone's satisfaction, were corrodies and other emoluments given by the superior to kinsfolk or secular friends, did he or she accept monies for favours bestowed (admitting a novice, offering tenantries), were the brothers or sisters treated equally in their dealings with the superior?[9] Then there were questions which asked what was usually taken for granted by outsiders, designed to test the sincerity of each individual's vocation: had these people entered the religious life with ambitions for advancement, or (in the case of nuns) had they been compelled to take up their profession reluctantly? How faithfully did they observe the vows they had taken, covering poverty, chastity and obedience? It was a form of interrogation that cynically presupposed jealousies and telltales in every community. But, then, so did the traditional form of visitation conducted by the diocesans. Only the tone was different in this case.

There was a lengthy sequence of queries covering the second of the great vows, and one imagines that Richard Layton might have enjoyed some small carnal sensation of his own as he pored over the answers. Was the abbot or prior in the habit of conversing with women? Did women enter the monastic enclosure? Young boys? What were the

[9] A corrody was a pension, more usually paid *to* a religious house when a family wanted to isolate (or protect) one of its members: e.g. the rebellious daughter placed in a nunnery so that she would be beyond the reach of unwelcome suitors.

sleeping arrangements in the community? Did anything resembling love letters or other amorous tokens ever cross the threshold? Whispered conversations through open windows or gratings? Nuns in particular were interrogated about any contact they or their sisters might have had with any male who was not very close family. Both they and the monks, the canons and the friars who were also being pressed hard on such matters, could scarcely have emerged from the experience without feeling that they had been very deliberately violated.

The zeal with which Leigh and Layton in particular threw themselves into this opportunity may be judged from a letter which the latter wrote to Cromwell on 4 June 1535, after the two men had worked in the West Country and clearly found themselves much more in sympathy than would Leigh and ap Rice a few weeks later. He asked the Vicar-General if he and Leigh could next do the North Country together, starting in the Lincoln diocese and working their way up to the Scottish Borders, 'down one side and up the other', and assured him that the King would not find anyone else who could do him such good service in that part of the country 'nor be so trusty to him'. Citing their own northern origins, Layton said that he and Leigh 'have familiar acquaintance within 10 or 12 miles of every religious house, so that no knavery can be hid from them, nor can they suffer any injury. They know the fashion of the country and the readiness of the people. Their friends and kinsfolk are dispersed in every place ready to assist them if any stubborn or sturdy carl proves rebellious'. The questionnaires, so Layton assured his employer, 'will detect all coloured sanctity, superstitious rules of pretended religion and other detectable abuses' by those 'who have found crafty means to be their own visitors, and do not intend any reformation nor increase of good religion, but only to keep secret all matters of mischief, selling their jewels and plate at half their value for ready money'. This communication revealed Richard Layton's own understanding of the work he was engaged in, and of its ultimate purpose. He and the other Visitors were to oversee both a religious conversion and a redistribution of wealth. This doubtless tallied with Henry's priorities. Thomas Cromwell, who had never been known to express great religious conviction, may have taken a narrower view.

Shortly afterwards, Layton pressed his suit again upon Cromwell, pointing out that the diocese of York had not been visited since Thomas Wolsey's time, that if he and Leigh could have the assistance of William Blitheman as Registrar, they might finish the whole northern Province by Michaelmas. Moreover, 'I should advise you to set forth the King's authority as Supreme Head by all possible means'; to which this North Country man added something that revealed another flaw in his nature, which knew no loyalty except to those who might assist his advancement and his prosperity. 'There can be no better way', he said, 'to beat the King's authority into the heads of the rude people of the North than to show them that the King intends reformation and correction of religion. They are more superstitious than virtuous, long accustomed to frantic fantasies and ceremonies, which they regard more than either God or their prince, right far alienate from true religion.' And Cromwell presently assented to the proposition, knowing full well the manner of men he was letting loose on the North.

Leigh and Layton were not only inordinately zealous, extremely efficient and rather unpleasant men: they had each at different times made it clear to the Vicar-General that their activities in the service of the Crown were not in the least disinterested. In October Layton had written again to the Vicar-General, this time about a benefice in the bishopric of Durham which he had heard was at the disposal of the dying Dean of Stoke-by-Clare in Suffolk, where there was a college of secular priests. According to Layton, Cuthbert Tunstall (a kinsman of his) had once promised him the living when it became available, and 'I beg you will write to him in my behalf ... for this benefice'. Layton's colleague had lobbied for preferment, too, and Tunstall was also involved in this transaction, for the Sherburn hospital was in his gift when the appointment of a new Master was eventually made and filled by Leigh; but it was Cromwell, not the Bishop, whom the Old Etonian thanked for landing this catch.

Months after Layton's request for the northern circuit, Cromwell at last decided in December to send him and Leigh on their way, and they joined forces in Lichfield at the turn of the year. They generally travelled together for the next couple of months, though occasionally they split up in order to cover the ground more quickly. Starting in the

East Midlands, they worked their way up through the Vale of York, branched off into the East Riding and west into the Dales, where there were Cistercians at Jervaulx and Benedictine nuns at Marrick, rode on up to Bamburgh on the North Sea coast, then came back across the inland moors by way of remote Blanchland and its Premonstratensian abbey, to Barnard Castle and Richmond, where there were Franciscans as well as Benedictine monks. They probably divided again there, one of them going west into Cumberland to visit the Augustinians of Lanercost, while the other traversed Westmorland to reach the Premonstratensians at Shap. They were certainly together again in Carlisle and then proceeded along the Irish Sea coast, with diversions to Whalley and Sawley, whose Cistercian monks would later in the year be deeply implicated in the Pilgrimage of Grace. Towards the end of February 1536, the two officials concluded their visitation in Chester, after inspecting more than 120 religious houses and covering well over a thousand miles of almost wholly difficult country in the depths of winter. These were robust men in every sense.

Wherever they went, they left a trail of mostly celibate men and women who wondered what on earth was coming next. All over England, as rumour of Cromwell's impending visitations spread, prudent superiors had begun to liquidise some of the assets of their houses against a much rainier day than even the dreary summer of 1535 had produced. They may have shrugged off the earlier examinations leading up to the *Valor*, as just another example of the scrutiny they had been under since Wolsey's time; and that critical point had passed without too much disturbance of the religious equilibrium. Now, however, there was a new and much more determined inquisitor abroad and everyone was well aware of it. So flocks of monastic sheep were put up for sale in the market place, lands were leased out on much longer terms than before, quantities of plate and other valuable items were sold or simply vanished one day. Even the civilian neighbours of some communities were helping themselves to monastic property, with or without the connivance of the monks, in order to make sure it didn't fall into the hands of Cromwell's men: so great was a general antipathy to the sovereign's new whims and fancies, which had begun with his lust for Anne Boleyn. And everyone waited, anxiously.

THE SMALL HOUSES FALL

✝

'The King and Council are busy setting officers for the provision and exaction of the revenues of the churches which are to be suppressed; which, it is said, will be in number above 300, and are expected to bring in a revenue of 120,000 ducats.'

EUSTACE CHAPUYS TO CHARLES V, I APRIL 1536

By the time Layton and Leigh had finished their visitation of the North, Cromwell was putting his finishing touches to the next shattering piece of legislation. By 3 March 1536 the rumours of something drastic were doing the rounds and 300 was the figure that recurred in most of them, though interpretations of it were inconsistent. Lord Lisle, sometime naval commander and ostentatious penitent, heard that it was 'bruited that abbeys and priories under 300 marks by year, not having twelve in convent, shall down', whereas Eustace Chapuys reported to the Emperor that 300 churches were involved.[1] 'The silver plate, chalices and reliquaries', he wrote, 'the church ornaments, bells, lead from the roofs, cattle and furniture belonging to them, which will come to the King, will be of inestimable amount.' There were people queuing up, he implied, to take advantage of the properties that might soon be on the market. Then he added an extra titbit of information. 'I am told that although Cromwell promoted in the first instance the

---

[1] Lord Lisle, when he was merely Arthur Plantagenet and the bastard son of Edward IV, had grounded and lost his ship in an action off Brest in 1512, and declared that he would eat neither flesh nor fowl until he had done penance at Our Lady's shrine of Walsingham.

demolition of the said churches, that nevertheless, seeing the dangers that might arise from it, he was anxious to prevent them, for which reason the King had been somewhat angry with him.'

The rumours were well founded, and the figure of 300 was as nearly accurate as makes no matter. What nobody knew (what scholars still haven't been able to fathom) is when the decision was taken to carry out the next phase of Cromwell's (and Henry's) master plan. But it certainly could not have been later than the back end of 1535; it may even have been before the local commissioners began to accumulate the material for the *Valor* at the beginning of that year. Or sometime during 1534, when the King finally broke with Rome, dismantling the Charterhouse at Smithfield and seven Observant friaries at the same time because some of their people had refused to submit to his will?

Nor are we clear whether Henry or his Vicar-General took the lead in deciding to emulate Thomas Wolsey by shutting down monasteries for gain. All we know for sure is that on 11 March 1536 a Bill was presented to the House of Commons for the confiscation of all property and the termination of the religious life in the smaller monasteries, nunneries and similar houses in England and Wales. It has always been understood that Henry was so intent upon this that he went to Parliament to argue the case for suppression personally before Members, and it would not have been foreign to his nature to have intimidated his politicians in this way. The evidence, though, is rather slender and depends largely on a letter from a Thomas Dorset, priest, to the Mayor of Plymouth (a Mr Horsewell), claiming that Henry went to the House on a Saturday when the Bill was before it 'and bade theym loke upon it and waye it in conscience, for he would not, he saide, have theym passe on it nor on any other thyng because his grace gevith in the bill, but they to see yf it be for a comyn wele to his subjectis . . . and on Wedynsdaye next he will be there agayne to here there myndes'.[2] Whether or not the sovereign was as close to the action

---

[2] Dom David Knowles, who was a most fastidious (though never a pedantic) historian, took the view that 'There is a possibility (it cannot be called a probability) that Henry left nothing to chance and himself intervened when the bill was about to be presented to the Commons . . .'

as that (he was certainly adroit enough to combine a reasonable posture with veiled menaces), Parliament complied and the Act for the Dissolution of the Lesser Monasteries became law on 4 April. Ten days later, just before the Parliamentary session ended, the Court of Augmentations was officially created, twenty-four hours after Sir Richard Rich was told to drop everything in his portfolio as Solicitor-General and take charge of the new organism. There is plenty of evidence that, once the decision had been made to suppress the monasteries, there was a rider requiring that this be done without further delay and thereafter everything proceeded with great haste.

The preamble to the Act justified it on the familiar grounds of religious decadence.

> Forasmuch as manifest sin, vicious, carnal, and abominable living, is daily used and committed amongst the little and small abbeys, priories, and other religious houses of monks, canons and nuns ... To the high displeasure of Almighty God, slander of good religion, and to the great infamy of the King's Highness and the realm if redress should not be had thereof ... so that without such small houses be utterly suppressed and the religious persons therein committed to great and honourable monasteries of religion in this realm, where they may be required to live religiously for the reformation of their lives, there can else be no reformation in this behalf ...

It further advanced its case on the grounds that 'the Lords spiritual and temporal' as well as the Commons 'by a great deliberation finally be resolved that it is and shall be much more to the pleasure of Almighty God and for the honour of this realm that the possessions of such spiritual religious houses, now being spent, spoiled, and wasted for increase and maintenance of sin, should be used and converted to better uses, and the unthrifty religious so spending the same to be compelled to reform their lives ...' The better uses referred to were resoundingly clarified at the end of the preamble: 'To have and to hold all and singular the premises with all their rights, profits, jurisdictions and commodities, unto the King's Majesty and to his heirs and assigns for ever, to do and use therewith his or their own wills to the pleasure of Almighty God and to the honour and profit of the realm.' And it was perfectly true that the lords spiritual – that is, the bench of prelates who had seats in the upper house – had voted for the Bill to be enacted. Cuthbert Tunstall may or may not have been among them; the Benedictine Abbot of St Mary's, York, certainly was.[3] So were thirty-five other religious of the same rank.

The demarcation line that defined the smaller religious houses isolated those convents with fewer than a dozen monks or nuns 'which have not in lands and tenements, rents, tithes, portions and other hereditaments, above the clear yearly value of two hundred pounds'. For centuries, twelve had been regarded as the perfect number for a coenobitic community living under a superior (who raised the figure to thirteen) and the origin of this prescription was very clearly the twelve Apostles who were with Christ at the Last Supper. The Cistercians, in fact, had decreed it as the essential number at the foundation of any new house of theirs; and when Wolsey decided to suppress St Frideswide's and other communities in order to raise funds for his college-building project, the papal bull which authorised him to do this had stipulated that the houses must be occupied by fewer than a dozen religious. The sum of £200 in income is not so easy to explain and appears to have been arbitrary, based on an assumption that it was what would keep a dozen monks and their superior solvent for twelve months. If so, the assumption was misplaced to some extent. Of the thirty-five Yorkshire religious communities at this time, seventeen had fewer than twelve incumbents, but twenty-four had less than £200 a year.

The number of houses which fell under Cromwell's new interdict was 191 of men and 100 of women (which represented five-sixths of all nunneries) who between them could muster about 1,500 souls; there was therefore an average of between five and six in each community. According to the *Valor* returns, 171 of these had less than half the

---

[3] Tunstall's movements on the day in question are a mystery. He was certainly in London on Sunday 27 February, when he preached a sermon in defence of Henry's new title as head of the Church in England. There is no record of his whereabouts after that until 2 May, when he was back in Auckland.

incomes that put them below the demarcation line, and no fewer than ninety-seven of the 291 could anticipate £50 or less, the nunneries being especially indigent, with thirty-two of them subsisting on £25 a year or less. Most vulnerable among the men were the Augustinians, whose Order of Canons Regular (otherwise known as the Black Canons, because they wore hooded black cloaks over a black cassock and white surplice) had brought their own form of the monastic life to England at the end of the eleventh century, and may have owed their existence to a suggestion by St Augustine of Hippo six hundred years earlier.[4] In 1536, 107 out of their 154 English houses were affected by the new legislation and, of these, no fewer than sixty-four had less than £100 to manage on, with another twenty-nine getting by on less than £150 a year.

Once again, commissioners went forth to conduct an exhaustive investigation of the religious life, and once more the composition of these inspectors was changed. For the visitation of 1536 it was decided to have a mixture of local worthies and Augmentations men, with a total of six appointed for each county or district surveyed: three 'discreet persons' (representatives of the gentry) being balanced by an auditor, a receiver and a clerk from headquarters. The names of Layton and Leigh were not among them though, in Yorkshire, men who had worked as their assistants the previous year were. One of these was William Blitheman, who was down to examine houses in the archdeaconry of Richmond as a colleague of Robert Bowes, lawyer and soldier from East Cowton in the North Riding who, before the year was out, would be leading the rebel host from Cleveland in the Pilgrimage of Grace.

The fate of the houses under investigation was already settled by the new Act, so the purpose of this visitation was not quite like any undertaken before. There were several familiar routine enquiries about the number of occupants, including servants and other dependants,

---

[4] The Augustinian (sometimes called Austin) Canons should not be confused with the mendicant Augustinian Friars (the Order of Hermit Friars of St Augustine) who were created by papal command in 1256. The first professed the traditional monastic life, the second were constantly outside their enclosures, like the Dominicans, the Franciscans and the several other preaching Orders.

about the value of the lead on the roofs and the bells. Inventories were required 'of all ornaments, plate, jewels, household stuff, farm stock &c … with debts owing to and by them'; also what 'bargains, sales and leases have been made'. The Visitors had to find out 'what woods, parks, forests, and commons belong to the same'. And they had to survey 'the demesnes of the house, and certify the clear yearly value, taking account of farms and leases &c'.

But then came the particular questions that could not have been raised if the house had not already been condemned to death. How many of the occupants were priests and how many of them would prefer to be transferred to one of the 'great and honourable monasteries' referred to in the Act; how many would rather 'take capacities', which meant being dispensed from their vows of poverty and obedience? Other instructions to the commissioners were also based on the same premise. They were told to 'command the governor [i.e. the superior] or receiver to receive no rents except for necessary expenses, till they know the King's pleasure'. The superior must be ordered to sow and till the land until further orders. The commissioners must send those monks who wished to remain in the religious life 'to other houses with letters to the governors, and send those that wish to go to the world to my lord of Canterbury and the Lord Chancellor for capacities'; these latter to be given 'some reasonable reward according to the distance of the place appointed'. Again, as in Cromwell's instructions to the *Valor* commissioners, we hear a civilised note of consideration in the midst of so much that was essentially unfeeling and predatory.

The most striking thing about the reports of the commissioners, when they were submitted to the Court of Augmentations, is how much they differed from the opinions expressed by Layton, Leigh and the other Visitors of the previous investigation. Out of the eighty houses in eleven counties for which printed records of the 1536 visitation are still extant – Leicestershire, Rutland, Huntingdon, Warwickshire, Sussex, Hampshire, Wiltshire, Gloucestershire, Norfolk, Lancashire and Yorkshire – only four were condemned as severely as had been the case in the previous year's review, and they were all in Norfolk. Thetford was 'of slender report', only one of its Augustinian canons remaining, supported by sixteen servants, and he asked for a capacity; of the

Premonstratensians at Wendling, it was said that 'their name is not good'; at the Augustinian priory in Weybourne there were but 'two priests of slanderous name as it is said'; and at the Cistercian nunnery of Marham, whence half a dozen sisters had departed since the last visitation, what remained were 'of slanderous repute'. There was also a caveat against the Augustinians of Owston in Leicestershire, where 'religion was not very duly kept for lack of number [only six canons and their Abbot remained] & for because one of them is a very aged man & another not having his wit very well but fantastical & more than half frantic'.

With these exceptions, however, the commissioners had little but commendation for the communities they visited. At Ulverscroft in Leicestershire, the Augustinian Prior 'is a wise and discreet man', leading 'good virtuous religious & of good qualities as writers, embroiderers & painters & living'. Still in the same county, the Benedictine Prioress of Langley 'who is of great age and impotent [is] of good & virtuous living & conversation & so be her sisters, whereof one ... is in regard a fool'. At Polesworth in Warwickshire the Benedictine nuns '& one anchoress of a very religious sort and living, bring up others in virtue very excellent, one of them being upon the point of a hundred years old'. Some houses were singled out for unusual warmth. In Hampshire, the Cistercians of Netley were situated beside the waters of the Solent in a large monastery which was 'to the King's subjects & strangers travelling the same seas great relief & comfort'; as were their brethren a few miles away in Quarr Abbey on the Isle of Wight, which 'is by report great refuge & comfort to all the inhabitants of the same isle and to strangers travelling the said seas'.[5] The Augustinian canonesses of Lacock in Wiltshire were 'to the same [town] and all other adjoining by common report a great relief'.

Not only were the new commissioners more benign than their immediate predecessors, giving a much better impression of the religious life at this level, but they were capable of putting in a good word for some of the communities they examined, and it is difficult to avoid

---

[5] The Cistercians of Quarr maintained a beacon to help mariners avoid the dangerous shoals and rocks off the Isle of Wight.

the conclusion that in many cases they took the view that it would be regrettable if these were closed down: which was a brave thing to be saying to Thomas Cromwell and his sovereign in the circumstances. Henry VIII did not like being contradicted by anyone, least of all by his employees. Nevertheless, the Cistercian nuns of Catesby in Northamptonshire were 'found in very perfect order, the prioress a sure, wise, discreet and very religious woman with ix nuns ... as religious and devout and with as good obedience as we have in time past seen or belike shall see'. The Yorkshire commissioners who visited the Charterhouse in Hull said that its monks were 'well-favoured and commended by the honest men of Hull for their good living and great hospitality'. The Warwickshire Visitors went so far as to beg Cromwell to intercede with the King on Polesworth's behalf, 'for, as we think, ye shall not speak in the preferement of a better nunnery nor of better women'. The commissioners for Northamptonshire boldly reported that in their view the Augustinian abbey in Northampton itself had been undervalued by the officials who had conducted the 1535 visitation there; in other words, it had no business being tallied on the wrong side of the demarcation line.[6] When this intelligence was passed on to the King, he said that the commissioners must have been bribed.

But, in fact, some houses all over the country were spared for the time being. The 1536 legislation contained an escape clause for some communities, though whether they were permitted to take advantage of it depended entirely on the whim of an exceedingly capricious monarch: 'the King's Highness, at any time after the making of this Act, may at his pleasure ordain and declare ... that such of the said religious houses which his Highness shall not be disposed to have suppressed or dissolved by the authority of this Act shall still continue, remain, and be in the same body corporate and in the same essential estate, quality and condition, as well in possessions as otherwise, as they were afore the making of this Act, without any suppression or dissolution thereof ...' As a result, the plea of the Yorkshire com-

---

[6] Although the Northamptonshire reports have not survived in their entirety, some evidence of the commission's findings there is to be seen in *Letters & Papers* Vol. X, documents 858, 916 and 917.

missioners on behalf of the Hull Charterhouse was not made in vain, and in August its Prior, Ralph Malyvere, and his brethren were told that they might continue. That month the Cistercian Abbot of Biddlesden in Buckinghamshire, Richard Greene, was given the same heartening news, as was Elizabeth Shelley, the Benedictine Abbess of St Mary's, Winchester; and in September Christabel Cowper, Benedictine Prioress of Marrick in the North Riding, was also told that she and her sisters would be undisturbed. By the end of the year, some seventy-odd houses of men, almost a quarter of those proscribed by the Act, were still functioning as they had been for several hundred years. So were forty-three nunneries, more than one third of the whole that had been threatened.

Several reasons have been advanced for survivals on such a scale. One is the fact that Thomas Cromwell was an exceedingly busy man in 1536, having not only the legislation and enactment of suppression to supervise, together with setting up the Court of Augmentations, but also the trial of Anne Boleyn and a great deal of legal business connected with the political union of England and Wales.[7] Meanwhile, the Act of Dissolution specifically made provision for the religious whose lives were to be massively disrupted when their houses were closed. Those who chose to live as seculars henceforth 'shall have their capacities, if they will, to live honestly and virtuously abroad, and some convenient charity disposed to them towards their living'; while those who wished to persist in the religious life 'shall be committed to such honourable great monasteries of this realm wherein good religion is observed . . . there to live religiously during their lives'.

Whether or not the Vicar-General had anticipated it, the number of religious who wished to continue their vocations in the 'great monasteries' of their Orders proved in practice to be unmanageable. Something over one thousand souls came into this category, and in some cases the operation would have meant shifting entire communities to other houses which, as often as not, were not big enough to contain the additional numbers. Charterhouses especially would have found it

---

[7] From October, Cromwell also had a huge other problem on his plate, when the Pilgrimage of Grace was stirred up by the inflammatory sermon in Louth.

almost impossible to accommodate extra monks because the very design of their premises – effectively giving each incumbent a small, two-up and two-down house with a walled private garden[8] – strictly limited the population at any given time; and virtually every Carthusian in the houses that fell below the demarcation line (at Beauvale, near Nottingham, and at Coventry as well as at Hull) wanted to persevere in his vocation. The Gilbertines of Sempringham in Lincolnshire (both canons and nuns) also survived for a similar reason, as did every other proscribed house of that Order, seventeen of them in all.[9] Faced with such a predicament on such a scale, reprieve to an unexpected degree was the easier way out of the problem for a government that had overstretched its administration of Henry's ecclesiastical policies.

One other consideration boosted the proportion of survivors, and it was financial. There is no question that some houses, in spite of the fact that their notional income was less than £200 a year, raised enough money effectively to buy their freedom by paying significant fees to the Court of Augmentations, or perhaps even to Cromwell himself. When the transaction was made officially the cost of the necessary licence was generally about the annual figure arrived at by the *Valor* commissioners, though occasionally it was higher. Biddlesden Abbey appears to have got off lightly, however: the *Valor* commissioners put its gross general income at £161 1s 2d, but it secured its continuation by paying £133 6s 8d into the royal treasury – officially, that is. Cromwell's failings notoriously included an appetite for bribes, which was known well enough for him to be approached regularly for favours on the understanding that money would change hands. He could, of course, have defended himself from the charge with the perfectly valid observation that in sixteenth-century

---

[8] At Mount Grace Priory, near Northallerton in North Yorkshire, a Carthusian cell has been completely restored by English Heritage to demonstrate exactly what sixteenth-century living conditions were like in the order.

[9] This was the only purely English religious Order, having been founded in the twelfth century by St Gilbert of Sempringham, who revived the double establishment that had lapsed in the seventh century. Its canons followed the Augustinian Rule, while its nuns were professed as Benedictines. In 1536 the Order had twenty-four houses all told, of which ten were occupied only by canons, the rest by men and women living adjacently.

England most favours were, in some way or other, bought.

Occasionally the transactions were deviously complex, and it was not entirely clear into whose pocket monies were being transferred. The Cistercian Fountains Abbey in Yorkshire provided a case in point in March 1536, when a new Abbot, Marmaduke Bradley, wrote to Cromwell, thanking him for his promotion from the ranks, as it were. He referred to the recent visitation by Richard Layton, who had ordered his predecessor to draw up the accounts for his period in office, and to pay 'all such goods as remained in his hands' before he could receive the pension that was allotted to the superiors of suppressed houses.[10] Not only had the former superior failed to do this, said Bradley, but the man intended to keep all the goods, worth more than £1,000, which was approximately what was owed to the King in first fruits, in addition to which the abbey was shortly expected to find the £100 due in the annual tax of the tenth. 'We therefore beg your interference', he told the Vicar-General. There can be no doubt that interference followed swiftly; certainly Fountains continued its Cistercian existence for another three years which, as one of the formerly exempt houses which had also been singled out for attack beside the smaller convents, it had no right to expect.

But by the end of 1536, 244 houses had been confiscated, their buildings demolished, their lands appropriated, anything portable removed from the premises, their occupants scattered abroad in what must have been a traumatic upheaval for most of them. These were people, it should be remembered, who had spent their whole lives, from the cradle onwards, nearby or inside their local convent; and now they were required, in many cases, to live in distant parts of the country among total strangers. And the religious were not the only people whose lives were disrupted by suppression; there was also the very considerable number of lay people who were attached to every community. These were the layfolk who acted as servants of the religious, working in and

---

[10] Clause VIII in the Act of Suppression declared that 'his Majesty is pleased and contented of his most excellent charity to provide to every chief head and governor of every such religious house during their lives such yearly pensions or benefices as for their degrees and qualities shall be reasonable and convenient . . .'.

around their houses in a number of capacities; they also included the 'corrodians', who were men and women living within the precincts in an act of monastic charity or else in return for money. Their numbers were much more difficult to estimate than those of the religious, but one attempt has been made after a scrutiny of papers relating to fifty-two communities of both men and women, scattered across a dozen different counties.[11] In the ten nunneries examined (which had a total income of £1,650), containing 143 sisters, 242 lay servants were employed. In the forty-one men's communities, which contained 487 monks and canons (and had a total income of £12,700) the religious employed 1,685 servants. All the dependants of the nunneries were threatened by the 1536 legislation; so were most of those who lived off the male communities.

Some areas were hit harder than others in the great clear-out, and Lincolnshire was one of the biggest losers (which is the principal reason why the sermon that started the Pilgrimage of Grace was preached there). The largest county in England after Yorkshire, covering 2,600 square miles, it contained nine large abbeys before the First Act of Dissolution and thirty-seven smaller communities. By the end of the year it had lost thirty-four of them. East Anglia was also badly mauled, Norfolk losing eighteen out of twenty-six houses and Suffolk ten out of fourteen. In the eastern half of Yorkshire, where there had been forty-four houses in 1535, fourteen women's communities and ten of men were lost. This meant that eastern England as a whole above the Thames lost more than two-thirds of its conventual establishments. The western side of the country got off much more lightly than that: in the seven neighbouring counties of Berkshire, Hampshire, Dorset, Somerset, Wiltshire, Gloucestershire and Worcestershire, which contained forty-six great abbeys and seventy-five houses in all, only twenty-five communities were suppressed.

There appears to be no very obvious reason for this inequality, though one particular factor may be relevant. Time after time, in the *comperta* of the various commissioners who swept back and forth across England in these years, monks can be found complaining in different places about the laxity of their superiors, about the lack of ascetic rigour in their com-

---

[11] See Savine, pp. 221–4.

munities; but this tendency is most noticeable in the southern counties, where superiors who refused to acknowledge the Royal Supremacy were almost always informed on by someone in their community. The example at Fountains Abbey quoted above is one of the very few occasions when similar tale-telling occurs in the northern shires. From which it has been concluded that in the North 'The abbots and their subordinates almost invariably supported each other, and their loyalty to the Old Faith and their hatred of those who tried to disestablish it, gave the Commissioners a far harder task in the north than in the south'.

In the southern shires people were readier, on the whole, to accept the new version of Christianity; and so, it can be argued, it was necessary to take a tougher line in the dissident areas, to close down monasteries which might otherwise have been allowed to stay open for a while longer, as in the more complaisant parts of the realm. The fact that the Pilgrimage of Grace occurred when and precisely where it did lends some support to this theory; though whether the rebellion might have spread south had Henry and the Duke of Norfolk not talked their way out of potential disaster in Doncaster at the end of October 1536, can never be more than a conjectural likelihood; and perhaps it cannot even be more than a possibility. It is certainly possible that Thomas Cromwell, who was above all things an extremely calculating man, factored into the equation he had created in order to increase his master's wealth and enforce a reformed version of Christianity, the regional discrepancies in behaviour and belief that were to be found within as well as beyond the religious life.

Chapuys was right when he told the Emperor at the beginning of April that the already well-to-do would improve their estates even more, following their sovereign's great cull of monastic properties: 'All these lords are intent on having farms of the goods of the said churches, and already the Dukes of Norfolk and Suffolk are largely provided with them', he had written.[12] The Earl of Westmorland was another

---

[12] Thomas Howard, 3rd Duke of Norfolk, was uncle to both Anne Boleyn and Catherine Howard, Henry's two most unfortunate wives, who were not only discarded but finished up on the scaffold. Charles Brandon, Duke of Suffolk, was a boyhood friend of the King's and subsequently his brother-in-law.

who watched the suppressions with a gleam in his eye, which was fixed on the Blanchland abbey of the Premonstratensians the moment he realised it fell below the income level necessary for survival; but, unfortunately for him, it was reprieved in January 1537 and was not dissolved for another two years, what time a Mr William Green (a receiver for Westmorland, Cumberland and Northumberland) had also put in a bid for it, which was accepted in May 1541, together with others he made for the rectories of Kirkharle, Heddon and Bywell St Andrew. Then there was Lord Thomas de la Wane, who wanted to farm the Benedictine priory at Boxgrove in Sussex, 'if it must go', and Lady Oxford, who wished to farm the nunneries at Blackborough or Shouldham in Norfolk, which were 'not far from her home'.[13] Sir Piers Edgecumbe wanted 'something out of Totnes', where there was another Benedictine priory. Archbishop Cranmer wanted the Augustinian house at Shelford in Nottinghamshire for his brother-in-law. A certain John Whalley sought the home of the Austin canonesses at Burnham in Buckinghamshire or, failing that, the Folkestone priory of some Benedictine monks who were facing eviction; and he wanted them 'at a reasonable rent'.

Nor was William Green the only official in the apparatus of suppression who made the most of his position: John Tregonwell sent his boss a list of nine abbeys and said he would be content with any of them. All these people had expressed their hunger for monastic property before 1536 was out, and some were prepared to abase themselves to an extraordinary degree in order to satisfy it. Lord Lisle, the former penitent, sent a despatch to Cromwell from Calais, where he was serving as the King's Lord Deputy, 'beseeching you to help me to some old abbey in mine old days'. Before long, monastic lands were being traded by those who had first secured them, and inflation had set in. 'Two gentlemen of substance in Yorkshire' in August 1537 were offering Lord Scrope of Bolton Castle £1,000 for St Agatha's Abbey at Easby, on the banks of the River Swale near Richmond, which milord had acquired for £400. Not far away, on the North Yorkshire Moors, the

---

[13] A farmer in the context of land transactions was someone who paid the Crown an agreed sum in order to enjoy the revenues of a property, quite often in perpetuity.

demesnes which had formerly belonged to the Cistercian nuns of Rosedale were being farmed at well above the original rate settled on them by Augmentations; at Merten, what had been worth £28 per annum was now bringing in £260, at Arden £8 had shot up to £140, at Melsby someone was farming for 100 marks what he had come by for £12 a year.

Such appetites did much to improve the state of Henry's finances, either in that year or not very long afterwards. Between 24 April 1536, when the Court of Augmentations opened its accounts, and September 1538, Cromwell's receivers unloaded £27,732 2s 9 3/8d in revenue from the lands of the suppressed houses: just one of these officials, John Freeman, brought in £8,756 11s 9 3/4d in the first six months of the Court's existence alone. In addition to the revenue, £6,987 8s 11 1/8d was received from the sale of various movable things, from lead and other base metals, from stone, from plate, from jewels, from ornaments. Land sales brought in another £29,847 16s 5d and smaller sums also came in from leases and various other fines. When everything was accounted for in that period, £71,616 16s 11 1/2d had come into Augmentations, which had to be offset by some £19,883 in expenses of various kinds. More than £50,000, therefore, was available for government spending on Henry's orders, or went straight into the King's own treasury. This was not an astronomical sum, even in the sixteenth century; but it would be vastly increased in the next few years.

There is no reason to believe that in 1536 Henry had thought much beyond this point and he was, in fact, perversely about to sanction two new communities of religious, whose express purpose was to pray for him and his third Queen, Jane Seymour. One involved the transfer of the Benedictine Abbot and fourteen monks from the suppressed abbey at Chertsey to the suppressed house of Augustinians in Bisham; the other was the similarly bizarre shipment across Lincolnshire of Benedictine nuns from their old home at Stainfield to the priory of Stixwold, from which Cistercian sisters had lately been evicted: both these transfers were effected in July 1537. The fate of the greater religious houses at the end of 1536, however, was still undetermined. Yet no superior could have been in any doubt that henceforth anything might lie in store for his or her community, depending entirely on which direction their unpredictable sovereign decided to propel them in. They did the only thing possible in the circumstances: they simply carried on as they and their predecessors had always done, applying themselves to their particular tasks in the convents, saying their offices dutifully in quire, from Mattins to Compline every day, getting on with the *Opus Dei*, ever mindful of St Benedict's injunction that nothing at all must be put before the Work of God. And they kept vigil. Now, more than ever, they did that.

THE FURNESS EXAMPLE

✠

> '*I thanked him [the King] for being content to give us Lewes, if we might conclude the bargain ... and saying I was content you should have two parts. He said ... he thought it well bestowed*'.
>
> THOMAS HOWARD, DUKE OF NORFOLK,
> TO THOMAS CROMWELL, 4 NOVEMBER 1537

In Durham, Hugh Whitehead and his brethren were not isolated from these events, even though they themselves fell well outside the terms of the 1536 Act. They were, in fact, visited by Drs Layton and Leigh during the winter excursion through the North of England which had started in Lichfield at the end of 1535 and finished at Chester two months later, whose purpose was to accumulate evidence to justify suppression; and also to intimidate. It isn't clear when the two Visitors turned up on Wearside, though it was certainly sometime between the 20th and the 26th of January, because they were in Richmond on the first of those dates, in Newcastle on the second. Beyond that, all we know is that Cromwell's men inspected both the monastery and Cuthbert Tunstall's household, and that they left Durham in high good humour.

On the 26th, both Doctors wrote separate letters to their employer from Tyneside, which conveyed more or less the same intelligence. They had been especially impressed by the Bishop, of whom Layton declared that in anything that required 'high judgement, Parliament matters &c, he is not living that would advertise you more for your honour and prosperity'. The country round Durham 'is substantially established in the abolition of the bishop of Rome and his usurped power', he said, adding that the Vicar-General ought to send for the Bishop and hear his advice 'for the extirpation of the said power and how it might be extinguished for ever. I thought myself to have known a great deal and all that could be said in the matter; but when I heard his learning, and how deeply he had searched into this usurped power, I thought myself the veriest fool in England.' Layton was, of course, speaking of his uncle; but his colleague's despatch was also warm about Tunstall's merits. As a result of the Bishop's preaching 'to the utter abolishment of the bishop of Rome', Leigh announced, 'no part of the realm is in better order in that respect, all through his handling, whom if it pleased you or the King to move to make a book in this matter he would do it excellently, especially as many learned men hang much upon his judgement'.

But Leigh gave away another reason for all this effusion. 'It would be too long to tell you the gentle and lowly entertainment of the bishop of Durham', he wrote, 'meeting us at our entry into his diocese three or four miles from his house with a great company of his servants, and on our leaving him conducting us from Auckland more than half way to Durham Abbey.' A man who, if John ap Rice is to be believed, could be very unpleasant when people didn't put themselves about to welcome him, was always going to be impressed by such a measure of hospitality; and maybe Cuthbert Tunstall had heard of Leigh's reputation, and had decided that nothing must be left to chance, that he must err on the side of extravagance for safety's sake: his bruising encounter with Cromwell's methods four years earlier would have prepared him accordingly. But there was another thing that had impressed the official Visitor. 'Both we, our servants and our company', Leigh told his superior, 'had large rewards, thus setting an example to the people, and especially to the abbots, of their duty towards their Prince, and how they ought to accept him as their Supreme Head.'[1]

---

[1] Two other considerations should be borne in mind when reading this correspondence, as well as the fact that Layton was the Bishop's nephew. Tunstall had just placed him in the benefice of Sedgefield, on 22 November; and he had made Leigh the Master of Sherburn Hospital on 14 September. Within another six months, on 1 July 1536, he would hand over to the King the Thameside Durham House, which had belonged to the Prince Bishops for centuries.

Hugh Whitehead did not receive any such applause: only a comment that he may well have been happier with than anything more personal that might have come his way. 'Your injunctions', Layton told Cromwell, 'can have no effect in Durham Abbey in some things; for there was never yet woman in the abbey further than the church, nor they [the monks] never come within the town.' His obsessions had not deserted him on Wearside, but only in one instance were they gratified. When, at the conclusion of their northern tour in February 1536, the two officials reported to Cromwell their findings on the 122 places they had visited, starting with Lichfield Cathedral and finishing with the College of St John the Baptist in Chester, they made this observation about two members of Cuthbert Tunstall's household. '*Phillipus Dacre in manifesto incestu cum filia uxoris, Cuthbertus Conyers in manifesta fornicatione cum quadam Layton solute*.[2] These have been frequently admonished by the Bishop to desist, but persevere.' Of the Priory, they simply reported 'Founder, the Bishop. Rents £2,115. Here they have the bodies of St Cuthbert and St Bede, and the Cross of St Margaret, supposed to be good for those lying-in.' This was a very temperate message compared to some that Layton and Leigh were sending to Westminster. Much more typical was their verdict on the Cistercians of Rufford Abbey in Nottinghamshire: '6 sod. Incontinence, Thos. Doncaster, abbot, with 2 married women, and 4 others; 6 seek release. Superstition: Virgin's milk. Founder, Mr Henry Norres. Rents £100; debt £20.'

Life in Durham thereafter continued along its familiar patterns. Dutifully the monks filed into the Cathedral for the offices each day, taking their appointed places in the quire, whose floor was strewn with rushes which had been cut from marshland at Ferryhill, a few miles south. Daily, Masses continued to be said at the chantries of Bishop Hatfield, Lord Neville and others, each one served by a different monk whose duty this was for a month before it passed to one of his brothers, and from which only Hugh Whitehead himself, the sub-Prior, the Terrar and the Sacrist were excused. As always, when midnight came

---

[2] 'Philip Dacre in open incest with his wife's daughter, Cuthbert Conyers in open fornication with a Layton woman who is not married.'

and Mattins began, four men rang the bells in 'the Galilee Steeple' to announce the hour: the one dedicated to Bede, another to St Oswald, a third which had been given by Prior Fosser two hundred years before, and 'a Long bell, which was a narrow skirted but well-tuned bell'. Every Sunday morning fresh water was poured into a piscina beside the south door of the church, which was for the use of the Prior and his community, and another beside the door opposite, which the laity who attended divine service could dip their fingers in; 'wherein one of the monks did hallow the said water very early in the morning before Divine service'. The liturgical seasons followed each other as they had done for five hundred years in this place, with their different moods of anticipation and joy, celebration and despair, penitence and hope and pensiveness; with their changing vestments, their distinctive services, their unvarying rituals, and those that shifted as the seasons came and went. From Ash Wednesday (which fell on 1 March in 1536) until Easter Day (16 April) Lent was marked by a short devotion at the end of each office except Mattins, in which two of the psalms for that day were said by the monks prostrate on the floor. Durham was not unique among the English religious houses in this respect, though it could generally be relied upon always to take the stricter course if canon law and liturgical custom admitted alternatives: Cuthbert again, Cuthbert still, Cuthbert ineluctable.

Maundy Thursday's heartbreaking significance was heightened – after the reception of penitents and the consecration of the oils – when the monks took themselves to the south side of the cloister; and there they ministered to the children of the almonry, who sat on a stone bench in a row:

Where all the whole convent of monks ... had every one of them a boy appointed them sitting upon the said bench, where the said monks did wash the children's feet, & dried them with a towel, which being done they did kiss the said children's feet, every one of those he washed, giving to every child xxxd in money and vii red herring & iii loaves of bread, and every one certain wafercakes, the monks serving every child with drink themselves, the godly ceremony thus ended after certain prayers said by the Prior & the whole convent, they did all depart in great holiness.[3]

Hugh Whitehead alone performed exactly the same service for thirteen 'poor aged men' who had also been told to come to the cloister that day 'at ix a clock or thereabout', and who were rewarded with the same money, the same red herrings, the same loaves of bread that the children had been given. Then came the stripping and the washing of the altars before the desolation of Good Friday began.

Scholarship continued, as it had done since Bede's time. After dining each midday, the entire community made its way to the cemetery, where they stood bare-headed and prayed for the souls of their departed brothers 'and when they had done their prayers then they did return to the cloister, and there did study their books until three of the clock that they went to Evensong'. The novices studied at desks set along the west side of the cloister, near the treasure house containing most of the Priory's portable wealth ('it hath a very strong door with two strong locks upon it'), where Richard Crosbie, their Master, 'had a pretty stall or seat of wainscott adjoining', and where a porter, Edward Pattinson, was stationed to make sure that no stranger, wandering into the cloister, would distract the young scholars from their books: this was always a possibility, when merchants were allowed to trade in the slype, the barrel-vaulted passage which separated the chapter house from the church.

Much was expected of these young men, whether or not they were destined for Oxford: they were required to learn by rote the Psalter and the canticles, the Hymnal, St Benedict's Rule, all the Invitatories (which preceded prayers, and were almost innumerably varied), all the responses, all the antiphons; and they were all but required to know their Gospels by heart. The professed monks had carrels along the north side of the cloister; 'and in every Carrell was a deske to lye their books on ...' with cupboards set against the church wall containing 'great store of ancient Manuscripts to help them in their study, wherein

---

[3] Wafercakes were made specially for Maundy Thursday in Lincoln as well as in Durham. Wheat flour was used.

did lie, as well as the old ancient written Doctors of the Church ... with diverse other holy men's work, so that every one of them did study what Doctor pleased them best, having the library at all times to go study in beside their Carrell'.[4] Cerebration was not interrupted in Durham Priory by the growing turmoil outside.

Nor were the other and mundane things that characterised this community. Recreation still punctuated the *Opus Dei* in the long tradition of the house, and a great deal of it was enjoyed out at Bearpark. In spite of the fact that the Prior's Lodging was palatial in size and in its facilities, the Durham superiors had always repaired to this country estate at regular intervals, in retreat from the everlasting busyness of the monastery, and also for a degree of self-indulgence that would not have been thought seemly within the precincts of the enclosure. There, amid water meadows beside the Browney stream, a tributary of the Wear, stood a substantial manor house containing two chapels, a great hall which accommodated five dining-tables, a buttery, a kitchen and two other chambers. Outside it were 400 acres of good pasture, on which the Prior maintained a stud of horses and the Bursar some cattle and sheep. The Priors of Durham had other manors which were used as places of retreat, notably at Wardley on the south bank of the lower Tyne, at Bewley, and at Pittington, a few miles to the north-east of the monastery, but Bearpark was always the principal diversion, the place where they were most likely to be found if they were not in the mother house, largely because it was the nearest and most accessible.[5]

They also shared it with their brethren at the so-called and elusive Prior's games *(ludi)* which were normally held four times a year, on the

---

[4] The 'cupboards' were, in fact, large boxes divided into compartments, whose contents were visible behind transparent windows made of horn (or possibly pressed parchment) which could be slid open for access to the documents inside. One or two have survived and still contain muniments in the Durham archives today.

[5] Other monasteries had similar refuges, where their superiors were often found. The Prior of Worcester took himself off to Battenhall where, at about this time, he spent only nine weeks of the year in his monastery. In the late fourteenth century, the Durham superiors were to be found in the Prior's Lodging for no more than one third of the year.

feasts of the Purification, Easter, St John the Baptist and All Saints, and which lasted for a couple of weeks or more at a time. Even though the *ludi* are something of a mystery, we do know that the usual Benedictine dietary regulations were then waived. Among the expenses incurred during the event in 1531–2 were 'the price of 40 lambs 33s 4d, of 9 pigs 45s, of 2,000 red herrings 18s. Item 4lb of pepper. Item 2lb of mace and cloves. Item 4lb of dates. Item 4lb of sanders [sandalwood, which added colour to certain dishes]. Item 24lb of amigdalarum [almonds]. Item 6lb of rice. Item 8lb of racemorum correnc' [Corinthian raisins or currants]. Item 16lb of raisins. Item 24lb of figs. Item 48 dogdrave. Item 24 salt salmon ...'

We also know that other forms of relaxation were allowed. Hugh Whitehead himself lived more austerely than had some of his predecessors, but he recruited minstrels for the *ludi*, in a tradition which had been maintained since 1278 at least and, when the Countess of Derby came on a pilgrimage to Cuthbert's shrine in 1532, provision for a bear and a monkey-keeper subsequently made its appearance in the Bursar's Roll. It is very likely that the Prior also brought players to Bearpark to act out dramas with a spiritual significance. But there is no evidence that he ever employed a jester in his household, as some past superiors of Durham had, and he certainly did not indulge himself as freely (and dangerously) as Thomas Melsonby had done in the thirteenth century. Prior Melsonby sanctioned the appearance of an acrobat within the precincts of the monastery, and even gave his permission for a tightrope to be fastened between the two western towers of the Cathedral, from which the man fell and broke his neck while attempting to walk across it; which gave Henry III a golden opportunity to hit back at the Durham Benedictines for choosing Melsonby as their superior in preference to his own candidate. The Prior was charged with homicide because, said the King, he ought to have prevented the acrobat's sacrilege, and was so held accountable for the unfortunate fellow's death.

There was entertainment on a much more modest scale than at Bearpark in the monastery itself. Beside the warming-house, where the monks were permitted the luxury of a winter fire, was the garden and the bowling alley which the novices used, with 'the Master standing by to see good order kept'. In the cloister were some benches with notches cut into their upper surfaces, so that nine-holes could be played by rolling small balls into them competitively, each with a different scoring value; and there was another pastime called fox and geese, which required a similar surface with holes into which pegs could be put.

It is probable that, as well as the novices, the Cathedral choristers made the most of these opportunities when they were not otherwise engaged in the church or in the song school which was attached to the south side of the apse and its nine altars: a long room, 'builded for to teach vj children for to learn to sing for the maintenance of God's divine service in the abbey church, which children had their meat and their drink of the house cost among the children of the Almery'.[6] Its walls and floors were boarded for warmth, and it housed a desk which extended from one end of the building to the other, on which the pupils could rest their chant books, with 'long forms set fast in the ground for the children to sit on'. There had been choirboys here for well over a hundred years, performing under the direction of the Cantor at certain services, such as the Jesus Mass, when they sang in harmony with the monks from the organ loft situated between two pillars on the north side of the nave; and, when the Mass was concluded, they came down from the loft to kneel before the high altar and to sing an anthem by themselves.

The Cantor since 1535 had been John Brimley, a man in his early thirties when appointed, and his contract gives a clear idea of how seriously music-making was taken by the Durham Benedictines. He had to instruct certain monks (presumably the ones with the best voices and the finest ears for a key) and the eight choristers 'in singing plain chant and singing with organ accompaniment, namely *plainsong, pricknote, faburdon, descant, square note* and *countre;* to teach organ-playing as well as plain and accompanied chant to the monks and one or two of the boys whom he (the said John), the prior and the precentor

---

[6] The choristers were on the strength for what they could add to the singing of the monks: six of them for most of their history, though by 1537 certainly their number had risen to eight.

judge capable; and to teach the said monks and eight boys diligently (&c) every usual day . . .'. In addition, he himself had to be present 'in person, barring legitimate excuse, from beginning to end, at all masses, vespers and *Salve regina* to be celebrated in the cathedral or elsewhere in the monastery's precincts . . . playing the organ if need be and singing the vocal part most suited to him . . .' He had to be present at the St Mary's Masses in the Galilee, at the Jesus Masses in the nave every Friday, 'and to play or sing the anthem on Friday afternoons in the same mass, also the anthem accustomed to be performed in times past in God's honour'. He had also 'each year during his life, so long as able, to compose a new four or five-part mass, or another equivalent work as should seem fit to the prior and the precentor, in honour of God, St Mary and St Cuthbert'. For these duties, Brimley was paid £6 per annum in instalments which fell due at the Invention of the Holy Rood, Lammas, All Saints and Christmas 'along with three ells of cloth of the livery of the gentlemen clerks' every Christmas; 'also that for his sustenance John will have food and drink with the prior's fellow monks where they should happen to be sitting, and in the hall of the monastery's lodging, called *"le gheste hall"* in the absence of the prior from the monastery'.

So the monks of Durham carried on the traditions of their house, blending the busyness of practical necessity with the stillness of prayer and meditation, in a paradox of vibrant tranquillity. In the cloister garth was the great marble laver bowl with its twenty-four little brass spouts, from which springwater flowed for the brethren to wash their hands in. Above the doorway which separated the south transept from the parlour and the chapter house, the elaborate mechanical clock which Prior Castell had installed to replace one that kept breaking down, still told the hours. After the prayer for peace in the Mass, the celebrant kissed the corporals, the chalice and the altar, then his deacon passed round to all present the richly illuminated copy of the Gospels which had just been read aloud, for each monk to kiss in the traditional *pax*. All appeared to be as it so familiarly had been for centuries, quietly purposeful, utterly assured of its place in the firmament, absolutely immutable. But in the world outside, the religious life was subsiding into chaos, and the monks of Durham were all too well aware of this.

For the Pilgrimage of Grace had not only swept into their enclosure, the rebels taking St Cuthbert's banner from his shrine in order to brandish it before the King's soldiery: it had also left in its wake a detritus of newly broken religious houses. After the carnage outside Carlisle and after the executions which followed the disastrous attempts by the fantasist Sir Francis Bigod and the tragic Sir John Bulmer to reignite the rebellion, a number of monasteries paid the full penalty for having lent themselves in varying degrees to the uprising. Two Cistercian houses, at Whalley in Lancashire and at Kirkstead in Lincolnshire, were the first to go, together with the Premonstratensian abbey of Barlings just north of Lincoln. At Whalley, Abbot John Paslew and two of his monks were executed in the customary way for those convicted of treason, by hanging, drawing and quartering, and their parts were then hung from the abbey's gatehouse as a warning to all comers. At Barlings, Abbot Matthew Mackerell and six of his canons were also done to death for having provided the Lincolnshire rebels with victuals. At Kirkstead, too, the Abbot and three of his brethren perished on the scaffold. All these executions took place in March 1537 and shortly afterwards Adam Sedbar, Abbot of Jervaulx, met the same fate after leaving his name carved pitifully on the wall of his cell in the Tower of London. His fellow superior at Sawley on the other side of the Pennines, Thomas Bolton, had been taken at the end of February after going into hiding, but we do not know what happened to him after that; he was a sick man at the time of his capture and he may have died on his way to or even in the Tower. These, however, were only the most gruesome consequences of ill-starred rebellion.

Of much greater significance was a legal measure which was applied at this time and resulted in the loss of the monasteries themselves, together with all their possessions. The Act of Treasons which had been passed in November 1534 specifically to discourage criticism of the Boleyn marriage and of Henry's new status as head of the English Church, also included a clause which held that the head of any corporate body who had been found guilty of treason would forfeit to the Crown that corporation's property as if it were his own: in other words, a religious superior who had offended the law in this way, would bring his entire community crashing down in the wake of his personal predicament. There was not the slightest justification for this wayward definition of ownership in either canon law or in the Rule of any religious Order, and it reeks of Thomas Cromwell's extremely supple lawyer's mind.

The clause was enforced for the first time as a result of the failed northern rebellion; and so the convictions and executions of Paslew, Mackerell, Sedbar and other superiors was swiftly followed by the ejection of their brethren from each house, whether or no they were implicated in the same offence, by the removal of all its valuables, by the seizure of all its lands, and by the demolition of its buildings for the stone, the roof lead and the other marketable fabric of the monastery. John Paslew was executed in Lancaster on 10 March, and on the 24th Whalley Abbey's goods were already being inventoried by the Augmentations men. Having swollen his sovereign's purse by suppressing some small convents which failed to pass a means test, the Vicar-General had now devised a further source of royal income by introducing treason as a means of achieving the same result. One other lucrative idea was by now taking shape in his mind and before long it, too, would be added to his repertoire.

Meanwhile, the smaller suppressions were resumed. They had been suspended because the government was too busy coping with a crisis that threatened to destroy it, to have time for any other business between the autumn of 1536 and the spring of 1537: the Pilgrimage brought official affairs to a standstill throughout the land, and no Augmentations man's life would have been worth a farthing if he had ventured into the North during those months. But from the summer of 1537, the culling of the houses caught in the means test continued; and for the first time Durham was violated, too. The mother house itself was still safe for the time being, but its dependent cells were another matter. The 1536 *compertus* had noted that the combined incomes of Finchale, Jarrow, Wearmouth, Lindisfarne, the Farne, Lytham and Stamford, together with that of the Benedictine nuns of Neasham (south of Darlington, who had nothing to do with the Priory but were also in the bishopric of Durham) amounted to no more than £343 12s 9d. The dependencies ought nevertheless to have been exempt by virtue of their attachment to a wealthy convent, as Clause XV of the Act made perfectly clear. But Cromwell – normally so very careful to stay within the strict letter of the law, even if it meant that fresh legislation had to be forced through Parliament in order to justify a new policy – had made up his own rules for this operation and they were treated as individual entities. The Prior of Finchale, William Bennett, was back in the mother house (where his brother Robert was the Bursar) by the middle of the year, which signified the end of his own small community further downstream. And though there is no surviving documentary evidence of the processes by which Finchale and the other dependencies were suppressed, the fact is that all appear to have ceased functioning by the end of 1537.

It seems very likely that sometime during the autumn of that year, maybe in October, Cromwell made a decision about the next stage of his master plan, which he must have been considering for several months before. Indirectly, this was yet one more consequence of the Pilgrimage of Grace. Another of the northern monasteries implicated in the rising was the Cistercian abbey of Furness, tucked away in a narrow little valley on the north-eastern edge of Morecambe Bay. Its Prior, its Cellarer and one or two other monks openly sided with the rebels and actually threatened some of their tenants with the burning of their homes if they did not get into harness and join one of the main hosts marching towards Doncaster to confront the King's army.[7] They also put some money into the war chest of the local rebels. Abbot Roger Pyle, however, an exceedingly nervous and ambiguous man, ducked out of the crisis by taking refuge with the Earl of Derby while simultaneously telling his monks to co-operate with the insurgents. He returned to the community a month later, in November, so intimidated by the atmosphere there, he said, that he was too frightened to go into the church alone at night; and now he told his brethren that they ought to obey the injunctions that Drs Layton and Leigh had left

---

[7] Harness was rudimentary body armour, which every male in the land between the ages of sixteen and sixty was supposed to keep and maintain against the day when he might be called up in the King's service for national defence or any other purpose the sovereign had in mind. The royal army which faced the Pilgrims at Doncaster consisted of such men.

behind earlier in the year. Two of Pyle's monks in particular were brazenly hostile to the King, and denunciations of the community by people who favoured the Crown and Henry's new ecclesiastical policies had already begun to spread throughout Furness and beyond, leaving the wretched Abbot uncertain about his own safety, about the reliability of his monks, about the future of the house for which he was responsible before his own Benedictine superiors and before God. This was a man who didn't know whether he was coming or going in these circumstances: he was a perfect prey for the next tactic in the government strategy.

In the North-west, in the spring of 1537, Robert Radcliffe, 1st Earl of Sussex, had been charged with ensuring retribution against everyone connected with the Pilgrimage in the region, acting under orders from Thomas Howard, Duke of Norfolk, whom Henry had appointed executioner-in-chief for the whole of the North. By the end of March, Sussex had come to the conclusion that there was not enough evidence to justify the suppression of Furness on the grounds of its superior's treason ... and then he had a brainwave that might achieve the same end differently. A couple of weeks after John Paslew's execution, he summoned the Abbot of Furness to his headquarters, which had been set up in Whalley Abbey, whose gatehouse was deliberately festooned with the butchered remains of three Cistercians. Pyle was questioned further about his behaviour when the rebels were in his vicinity and Sussex found no reason to revise his own earlier opinion; which meant that there was no way in which Furness Abbey could be acquired in the same fashion as Whalley; but there was an alternative. Why not, he suggested pleasantly, simply surrender it to the Crown as a gesture of goodwill, by which the slate would be wiped immaculately clean for ever, and all the awful pressure on the Abbot would be eased?

The by now thoroughly terrified Pyle probably didn't even stop to think before he agreed to this proposition. And so a great transferring document was drawn up – redrafted more than once to ensure that there were no loopholes in it that would encourage legal challenges later on – and on 9 April 1537, Roger Pyle and twenty-eight of his brethren signed away their abbey and handed it and all its possessions over to the Crown. Sussex had created legal history in obtaining the forfeiture of a monastery by voluntary conveyance instead of by attainder. Henry had acquired more plunder by intimidating a community to the point of surrender; and such a piece of plunder it was, bringing with it great flocks of sheep, a thriving salmon fishery, a smelting manufactory, and even its own ships for the export of the finished iron. The *Valor* had assessed Furness's income at £946 1s 10d, which made it the second wealthiest Cistercian house in the country after Fountains. Even more valuable than this to the sovereign, however, was the fact that he and his Vicar-General had established a new precedent: the transfer of wealth merely by talking people into it.

Seven months later, the Cluniac priory of St Pancras at Lewes in Sussex followed where Furness had led, taking with it a dependent cell at Castle Acre in Norfolk; and here yet another precedent was created.[8] In all the suppressions so far, ejected religious had been offered alternative futures either with larger houses of their Orders or with capacities to re-enter the secular world, the affected superiors alone being granted pensions to compensate for their sudden loss. But at Lewes a more ample compensation was negotiated, in which all the monks were given a down payment of £2, followed by quarterly pensions. Just after Christmas, the Premonstratensian Titchfield Abbey in Hampshire was also surrendered, and there the Abbot received a pension of 100 marks, eight priests £613s 4d apiece, and the three novices £5 each. Thus, yet another phase in the policy began, a form of bribery which immediately produced further dividends. December 1537 yielded the Cistercian abbey at Warden in Bedfordshire, too; while January brought in the Westacre Priory of Augustinians in Norfolk, with monasteries at Peterborough, Ramsey, and St Albans (all Benedictine) plus Sawtry (Cistercian) lined up for surrender as well.

Lewes was surrendered on 16 November, yet well before that date private arrangements were already being made to share the loot.

---

[8] The Cluniacs were the senior Order of monks after the Benedictines, founded at Cluny in Burgundy in 910 (two centuries before the Cistercians appeared). They changed the essentials of Benedictine life but fractionally, and were most notable for the incomparable splendour of their churches. They came to England in 1077 and Lewes was the first of the thirty-two priories that still flourished here in the sixteenth century.

Cromwell and Thomas Howard, Duke of Norfolk, may well have begun to discuss in October or even earlier which of them should get what, in anticipation of its fall; certainly by 4 November, Howard was writing to the Vicar-General from Hampton Court, telling him that he had discussed the matter with the King, who had approved a proposal whereby Cromwell would get two-thirds of whatever was coming from Lewes, and Howard the remaining piece. Henry's two principal henchmen were supposed to be sworn enemies yet in this they were as one, and quite clearly a degree of wider harmony existed between them at this time, judging by the letter, which began with Norfolk thanking Cromwell 'for your venison'. Nor were they by any means the only people whose acquisitive appetites were roused by what was going on.

'The pears', as Dom David Knowles once memorably observed, 'were falling off the wall one by one'. And wherever they dropped, eager hands were outstretched and ready to grab.

X

BUYING TIME

☩

'... *our now most dread Sovereign Lord* ...'

THE SECOND ACT OF DISSOLUTION, 31 HENRY VIII C 13

Durham's time, however, had not yet come, and Prior Whitehead was buying as much more of it as he possibly could by following his Bishop's lead. The two men had a great deal in common, both theologically and in their approach to political events when these unavoidably required a response. Cuthbert Tunstall's position as a national figure who was continuously in consultation with his sovereign and with the government's chief minister meant that his reactions to everything from the Aragon divorce to Henry's separation from Rome were publicly on record. Everything he said, every move he made, served to mark him as an essentially moderate man whose principles were liable to bend if sufficient pressure was applied: his opposition to the notion of Royal Supremacy in the Convocation of May 1531 and his subsequent renunciation of all foreign jurisdiction over the English Church in March 1535, were simply the most obvious example of this weakness. The Bishop of Durham was not, in truth, the stuff of which martyrs are made and his hurried departure to the safety of Norham Castle when the northern rebels – who might reasonably have expected his theoretical support in their cause – threatened to ransack his Auckland home as effectively as Cromwell's agents had done three years earlier, was the clearest possible indication that here was a thoroughly decent but equivocal and rather timid man.

Hugh Whitehead's profile was much less visible except in Durham and its northern hinterland, but from extremely limited evidence it is apparent that he resembled Tunstall in many ways. When twenty-two religious superiors, together with other leaders of the English Church, wrote to the Pope in 1530, effectively threatening him with the possibility of separation if he did not grant Henry's petition for a divorce, Whitehead's signature was conspicuously missing from the document; but within a few months he had joined the multitude which acknowledged in Convocation the King as Supreme Head of the Church. As telling as anything, perhaps, is the fact that Whitehead's relations with Tunstall were never less than harmonious, which was far from being an invariable in the historical association of the Priors and Prince Bishops of Durham. And Hugh Whitehead, like Cuthbert Tunstall, had a powerful instinct for survival.

Both men had gone out of their way to be agreeable to two of Cromwell's most odious Visitors in January 1536, to a degree which some might regard as only just short of sycophantic. Long before that, however, Prior Whitehead had recognised the manner of man he must deal with in the hazardous years that were unfolding, and he had reacted accordingly. The first recorded sign that he well understood his position and how he must behave if he and his community were not to be imperilled by the new ecclesiastical policies and the Vicar-General's implementation of them, came as early as August 1534, when he wrote to Cromwell to say that he was sending him, by special courier, the 'grant of an annuity of £5 ... under the conventual seal, and requests him to continue his kindness towards St Cuthbert's monastery'.[1] He added that he had also spoken to the Herald about the Vicar-General farming the parsonage of Giggleswick in the West Riding of Yorkshire, which was in the Prior's gift and which the King himself had evidently urged Whitehead to grant the chief minister. Just over two months later, on the last day of October, the Prior wrote to Cromwell again. When Carlisle Herald had arrived in London with

---

[1] The courier was Carlisle Herald, one of that band of functionaries whose duties included acting as King's messengers and proclaiming royal intentions throughout the land, when greater impact was required than local agents of the Crown could be expected to produce. Thomas Miller, the Lancaster Herald who was roughed up in Durham at the end of 1536, was another of them.

Durham's £5, the Vicar-General was elsewhere and so the messenger had brought the money back to the North: that at least was the bagman's story, though we may well wonder whether Cromwell had simply indicated that the sum was not enough and told the fellow to transmit the information that his price was higher than that. Whatever the truth of the matter, this caused the Prior to revise his first calculation of the gift, which on reflection he thought 'too small, and sends him [Cromwell] a grant of an annuity of £10 for life for his kindness towards St Cuthbert's monastery'.

And Hugh Whitehead *was* a calculating man, who played his very limited number of cards deftly from first to last. He kept the Vicar-General waiting as long as possible before the parsonage in Craven was gifted to him, doubtless seeing this course as a small leverage in obtaining the best terms possible for himself and his community, when the monastery could do almost nothing to defend itself against the depredations of the Crown. Not until 31 January 1539 was a grant actually made 'by Hugh prior and the convent of Durham to Thomas Cromwell, knight, lord Cromwell and keeper of the privy seal, and Gregory Crumwell (*sic*), his son and heir, and their assigns, of the next presentation to the vicarage of Giggleswick'. That was just about the last possible moment when the transfer could have been made as an act of goodwill rather than forfeiture; before the year was out, it would probably have come to Cromwell anyway in the due processes of Dissolution. But between the first mention of Giggleswick and its disposal, several other transactions had taken place between the two men. On 2 November 1536, Cromwell accepted a fee of £10 from the Priory and on 1 September 1537 his agent Richard Bellasis collected another £10 from 'prior of Durham ... due Mich[aelmas] last' with a similar sum accruing on 2 October the following year.[2] Bellasis was also the intermediary in a further cash transfer in January 1539, when he collected 200 marks from the Prior on another trawl which simultaneously netted £20 from Cuthbert Tunstall.

Meanwhile, in November 1537, Cromwell had written to Whitehead

---

[2] These were obviously part of the original deal, though the irregularity of the dates is intriguing.

asking 'for the promotion of Sir Wm Ressley to the vicarage of Billingham, on the resignation of Sir Thos Bentley', but on this occasion he was to be disappointed: the Prior had already granted the benefice to Dr Hyndmer, the Bishop of Durham's Chancellor. Four months later, it was Whitehead writing to Cromwell for help with a particularly tricky problem because it involved the King himself. Henry had called for the preferment 'of his Grace's servant, Stephen Brakenburie, to a ground called Rylley, which has always been in the use of the monastery and never leased. The lack thereof', said the Prior, 'would diminish hospitality. Begs Cromwell's mediation to excuse compliance.' There appears to be no record of the outcome, but Hugh Whitehead was certainly doing his best at this time to mollify all who might be in a position to influence his community's future. November 1537 was, as we have already noted, also the month when another prominent member of the government, Thomas Wriothesely, received a £5 annuity from Durham Priory.

And the strategy appeared to be successful, while the momentum of the government's programme gathered pace all over the country. The next significant moment in Henry's campaign came at the end of January 1538, when the Cistercian abbey at Boxley, near Maidstone, was surrendered, because for the first time this involved a shrine of national importance. Boxley was an offspring of St Bernard's great foundation at Clairvaux, and had flourished since *c.* 1146, some thirty years after the establishment of the mother house near the headwaters of the Seine. It sheltered the Holy Rood of Grace, which attracted pilgrims and their donations from much farther afield than Kent because it was, as Archbishop William Warham of Canterbury once told Thomas Wolsey, 'so holy a place, where so many miracles are showed', the chief of which was probably the rotating eyes which were activated by a piece of clockwork at the back – 'certain engines and old wire, with old rotten sticks', which the Abbot and his senior monks said they were completely unaware of.

A number of monasteries had national reputations almost entirely because of the corpses and other relics in their custody, like Durham itself (on account of Cuthbert and Bede), Winchester (St Swithun), Bury (St Edmund) and Hailes (the Holy Blood), some of which were more obviously spurious than others: when analysed, the blood preserved in a phial at Hailes turned out to be that of nothing more sacred than a common duck. Even below this widely celebrated level in the pecking order of veneration, however, virtually every religious house in the land had something that attracted devout people who needed above most things a tangible focal point for their entreaties, their generosity and their adoration. The most obscure figure could mean the difference between solvency and destitution to the religious promoters of such a memory: as was the sixth-century Welsh St Derfel Gadarn, a giant of a man in life, when he was a warrior at King Arthur's court, and a prodigious object of veneration ever since in Merioneth, because he was strong enough to rescue souls from hell by sheer strength, so that his image attracted five or six hundred people in a single day according to Cromwell's commissioner Elis Price, reporting to his boss in April 1538.

The relics could be even more bizarre than the supposedly divine blood of Hailes and were frequently invoked for intervention in the most arcane circumstances. The Augustinians of Repton had a bell which quite possibly had belonged to the teetotal saint Guthlac, who tried in the seventh century to imitate the eremitical ways of the Desert Fathers, which was said to cure cranial disorders. The Benedictines of Suffolk not only had St Edmund at their disposal but also the skull of St Petronilla (feast day 31 May, which nicely balanced that of their major saint six months later on 20 November) for the relief of those in a fever. Nuns of the same Order at Arden Priory in the North Riding of Yorkshire exhibited an image of St Bride, which was especially attractive to the local farming community because it could work wonders in the healing of sick cows, or the recovery of those that had strayed. The Cluniacs of Pontefract possessed a felt hat which had been worn by a disgraced but pious Earl of Lancaster until he was beheaded in 1322, after which he worked miracles. Little more than a cockstride from Durham, the Premonstratensians of Alnwick made the most of Simon de Montfort's foot, which had fetched up fortuitously in Northumberland after the Battle of Evesham and after doing heroic service during the Fifth Crusade. There were so many girdles allegedly worn by the Virgin Mary (very efficacious if touched by women approaching childbirth) that they might easily have encircled more than one religious house, if not quite stretching the distance from Canterbury to Bethlehem.

Such shrines and the superstition that too often attended them were the weakest point of the old faith and they provided Henry and Cromwell with a rationale for the renewal of suppression, which equalled the corruptions that had crept into the religious life and had been used as a justification of reform three years earlier. Having attacked the monastic life at the outset of its campaign, the government now turned to another version of the religious life with a sustained drive against the friaries, whose occupants pursued a significantly different form of vocation from that of monks. The life of every monastery was in its essentials withdrawn from society and inward-looking, whereas friars professed the opposite, by going out into the world and embracing it as preachers and as mendicants, who subsisted largely on alms rather than on landholdings and other reliable sources of income. They roused people to surpassing fervour, they incited them to veneration, they encouraged them to hold fast to those verities which had been handed down through the generations, without attempting to discriminate between what was authentically holy and what was authorised but godless. The friars were a different and generally more potent threat to reform than were monks who simply prayed for the salvation of souls. An example had been made of the Friars Observant who were executed in 1534, their houses suppressed, because they were regarded as the most virulent form of the species; now it was the turn of the less audacious but still pernicious remainder of their kind.

A week after Boxley and its precious Rood were surrendered, Richard Ingworth, the suffragan Bishop of Dover – Thomas Cranmer's auxilliary, who supervised the diocese of Canterbury in the Arch-bishop's all too frequent absences at Lambeth and wherever Henry was holding court – was commissioned to visit every English friary and correct any abuses he found there. Ingworth was very carefully chosen for this operation because he had lately been Prior Provincial of the Dominicans and, as such, knew as much as anyone about the profession and function of the friars. He also retained some sympathy for them, reporting to Cromwell that 'in every place is much poverty', which was no less than the truth. The Augustinian friars of Stafford possessed no jewels and their only silver was a small chalice, their rents amounting to a pitful £2 11s 8d a year; their Franciscan neighbours in the town collected only £1 6s 4d in rents, the rest of their wealth consisting of a chalice and six spoons. The Dominican house in New-castle-under-Lyme managed on a mere £2, with only thirteen ounces of silver plate also standing between its occupants and absolute des-titution, whereas the Prior and two Irish friars who alone kept the Augustinian house in Shrewsbury going had not even a chalice to fall back on, and would have raised no more than £1 6s 8d if they had sold off all their furnishings. Such was the extent of mendicant penury wherever Ingworth and his commissioners went in 1538.

One of the more recent recruits to the Court of Augmentations, now making a name for himself among the friaries, was Dr John London, an erudite man who had been Warden of New College, Oxford and Treasurer of Lincoln Cathedral, fifty years old or there-abouts at his appointment as commissioner, and a zealot who has often been bracketed with Thomas Leigh and Richard Layton for his efficiency and much else. He was particularly vigorous in his attack on superstition and all its manifestations, with a growing reputation for the destruction of shrines and any furniture that was found in them. At the Augustinian cell at Caversham he broke up the shrine of Our Lady, sending the image itself up to London in a barge from Reading and smashing all else, including lights, shrouds, jewels and images of wax. At Reading itself, where the Franciscans had a house, he removed from their church all the screens and altars and was instrumental in its conversion into a new town hall, to replace the old one, which was so exposed to the clamour of the adjacent streets that juries could not hear the charges being read out during their attendance at Quarter Sessions. Yet he could be kind – where Leigh and Layton showed consideration only when there was something in it for them – as he was in obtaining a substantial pension for the Benedictine Abbess Katherine Bulkeley of Godstow and somewhat smaller portions for her nuns, after she had denounced him (rather hysterically) to Cromwell for having 'borne me great malice and grudge, like my mortal enemy' and had pleaded with the Vicar-General 'to direct your honourable letters to remove him hence'. Yet in a report to his superior the following day, when he could not possibly have known of her attack on him, London merely observed rather mildly that 'I perceive my lady to take my coming something pensively ... [and] I beseech your lordship to admit me an humble suitor for my lady and her sisters and ... be good lord unto them'. The pension of £50 followed without much delay, her prioress receiving but £4, the other nuns no more than £3.

The procedures which Richard Ingworth and his men adopted were clearly established in Gloucester, where the Bishop himself was the Visitor and where all fifteen friars in the town – a mixture of Dominicans, Franciscans and Carmelites – were mustered to hear his adjudication in front of Mayor William Hasard and three of his aldermen – William Matthew, Thomas Bell and Thomas Pane. These four worthies themselves reported to Cromwell that the said friars had been put

> at their liberties, whether they would continue in their houses and keep their religion and injunctions according to the same, or else give their houses into the King's hands. The injunctions he [Bishop Ingworth] there declared among them, the which were thought by the said mayor and aldermen to be good and reasonable, and also the said friars said they were according to their rules, yet as the world is now they were not able to keep them and live in their houses, wherefore voluntarily they gave their houses into the visitor's hands to the King's use. The visitor said to them 'think not, nor thereafter report not, that ye be suppressed, for I have no such authority to suppress you, but only to reform you, wherefore if ye will be reformed according to good order, he may continue for all me'. They said they were not able to continue. Wherefore the visitor took their houses and charitably delivered them, and gave them letters to visit their friends, and so go to other houses, with the which they were very well content, and so departed.

The religious were, in short, now being coaxed into surrendering their houses in spite of the fact that the official excuse for the Bishop of Dover's expedition was the reformation of the religious life rather than its suppression.

Ingworth seems to have been reproved by Cromwell for his lenient approach to his co-religious, because within a few weeks of being charged with visiting the friaries he was writing defensively to his superior in the following terms:

> And where that it hath pleased your lordship to write to me, as ye judge, that though I have changed my habit I have not changed my friar's heart, good my lord judge me not so, for God shall be my judge, my friar's heart was gone 2 years before my habit, saving only my living; but the favour that I have showed hath not been for my friar's heart, but to bring all things with the most quiet to pass; and also till now that your honourable letter came to me, I never could perceive anything of your pleasure, but forever feared that if I were to quake, that I should offend your lordship, the which I would not by my will for all that I am able to make in the world.

Nothing illustrates more clearly the philosophical distance that sometimes existed between the begetters of the new ecclesiastical policies and those who were obliged to enforce them in the field. Henry and Cromwell didn't much care what havoc they wrought, so long as their bidding was obeyed. Some of the commissioners – perhaps even a majority of them – tried as best they could to make the transition as painless as possible for the men and women who were on the receiving end of it all.

And while the friaries were being dealt with, the enforced surrender of monasteries was resumed even more intensely that year, which also saw yet another new departure in policy and, like the award of pensions, an agreeable one. In May 1538, the government turned its attention to the Priory cathedral of the Holy Trinity in Norwich, a Benedictine foundation since 1096, two years after the principal East Anglian see had been transferred there from Thetford. It had functioned ever since in the same fashion as Durham and several other houses following Benedict's Rule, which were each simultaneously a monastic community and a bishop's spiritual base in his diocese. Norwich's case was peculiar partly because Henry's treatment of the religious houses was so heavily motivated by his avarice.

Ten miles north-east of the city stood the monastery of St Benet of Holme, which was in a sorry state by the time the new ecclesiastical policies were devised: many of its monks were barely literate, and there had been local complaints about the number of dogs running loose around the premises, eating food which had been intended for the poor. Cromwell (and what followed clearly bears his calculating imprint even more than his sovereign's) had discovered that the Bishop of Norwich's income was much greater than that of St Benet's, and manipulated these finances accordingly. William Rugg, the Abbot of St Benet, was promoted to the see of Norwich in 1536, his abbey's endowments being transferred with him under the recent legislation which held that a religious superior was personally accountable for all the property and monies belonging to his house; at the same time, however, he was considered still to be Abbot of St Benet's. This astute tactic was completed by appropriating the existing episcopal revenues after switching them nominally to the abbey, where they could be acquired in due course without too many more legal niceties.[3]

The treatment of Norwich was unprecedented in one other way, and in the light of later events it is tempting to see it as an experiment, a tentative step towards Henry's vision of a reformed Church: insofar as he had a vision, that is, for this King acted impulsively when opportunities presented themselves far more frequently than he ever carefully planned anything. Cromwell was the schemer, his sovereign a much more primitive man. Not until 1539 would the government's great new future for the English bishoprics and colleges be unveiled, and not until 6 April in that year would Norwich be surrendered to the new order, but it was in the previous May that its future was settled in what has the appearance of a trial run for the major transition that eventually followed. On the 2nd of that month a charter was drawn up, which transformed the Priory cathedral and its monastic incumbents into a deanery and chapter on the following lines:

---

[3] Another result of this singular arrangement was that St Benet's was never, in fact, authentically suppressed, though it did eventually pass into secular hands and in time became the fragmented ruins visible beside the River Bure today. It was the only religious house in the country to escape all the legalised processes of Dissolution; and the Bishop of Norwich is still, even now, the titular Abbot of St Benet's.

The present prior, Wm Castelton, to be dean, and Walt. Gryme *alias* Crowmer, Wm. Harydans, Henry Manuell, Edm. Drake *alias* Norwiche and William Thurkyll *alias* Attiburgh, monks of the said house, and John Sarisburie, bishop of Thetford, to be prebendaries of the said cathedral, and Robt. Twahaytys, Stephen Roper *alias* Darsham, Thos Leman, Robert Bowgyn *alias* Woorsted, Robt. Benneys *alias* Catton, Francis Atmere *alias* Norwiche, Robt. Grene *alias* Trows, Robt. Stanton, Geo. Bawcham *alias* Hanwurth, Fras. Yaxley, John Sherene *alias* Kyrby, Thos. Jolye, Wm. Kegell *alias* London, Adam Barker *alias* Sloley, Botulph Parker and Andrew Tooke, likewise monks, to be secular canons. Also licence to the said Wm. Castelton to hold two, and each of the prebendaries and canons one other benefice and be non-resident.[4]

The Prior and other monks of Norwich therefore had a potential future under this arrangement, whatever that might or might not be worth in the hands of Henry VIII and his chief minister. Other religious were not so fortunate as 1538 turned into a new year. At the start of the renewed *putsch*, the Observant friar John Forest was roasted alive over the flames which destroyed the image of St Derfel Gadarn, 'on heresy charges which amounted to the orthodoxy of a decade before'; as it gathered pace, walls literally came tumbling down throughout the land, monasteries and other convents were looted as never before, their occupants pensioned off from the only life they had known since puberty, and sometimes left even more bereft than that. By 1539, surrender had become the normal method of acquisition by the Crown, instead of the novelty that was thought up on the spur of the moment at Furness two years earlier. If you lean on people hard and long enough they do (most of them, at any rate) eventually give way...

There was a pause in the due processes early in that year and it is

---

[4] A prebendary was one who held a prebend (Latin *praebenda*, a stipend or pension), a canon (Latin *canonicus*, one living under canons or statutes) a slightly different form of income, though the distinctions also involved seniority and consequent precedence, as well as historical evolution and the functions of each within the Cathedral community. All these priests formed the Chapter, which took collective decisions under the leadership of the Dean on everything affecting the Cathedral's existence.

quite possible that this was partly occasioned by nothing more (or less) than the fact that the concentration of both Henry and Cromwell was then being more wholeheartedly applied to the matter of finding the serial husband a new wife to succeed the tragic Jane Seymour, who had died giving birth to the future Edward VI. Europe was being scoured for another Queen, Hans Holbein was running from one Continental palace to another in order to portray all possible candidates, so that the widower could make a more informed choice from an array of women he had never met. Eventually, in October 1539, a treaty was concluded with a Rhineland prince for the hand of his daughter, Anne of Cleves, in a marriage which was to be an unconsummated disaster from the very beginning, and for which Thomas Cromwell would in due course be dismissed and eventually pay with his life, because Henry VIII did not like being made a laughing stock in front of his people, and the subject of ribald jests across the length and breadth of Europe.

Or perhaps the moment of inactivity resulted from Cromwell's immediate preoccupation with a great swither of new legislation, all of it to do with the future of the Church in England, whose preparation he supervised much more closely than Thomas Wolsey had ever done when he enjoyed similarly overriding powers. Certainly the interlude occurred when Parliament was sitting to consider these proposals. The most remarkable new statute, given that Henry and Cromwell had been progressively rejecting everything to do with Roman Catholicism since the failed divorce petition of 1527, was the Act of the Six Articles, which was officially reckoned to enforce uniformity in religion and whose eponymous clauses considered

whether, in the most blessed sacrament of the altar, remaineth after the consecration the substance of bread and wine or not ... whether it be necessary by God's law that all men should be communicated with both kinds or not ... whether priests (that is to say, men dedicated to God by priesthood) may by the law of God marry after or not ... whether vows of chastity or widowhood made to God advisedly by man or woman, be by the law of God to be observed or not ... whether private masses stand with the law of God and be to be used and continued in the Church and Congregation of England, as things whereby good Christian people may and do receive both godly consolation and wholesome benefit or not ... whether auricular confession is necessary to be retained, continued, used and frequented in the Church, or not.

In fact, the conclusions promulgated in this Act reflected Henry's own innate religious conservatism much more than anything in Thomas Cromwell's philosophy: the King didn't want anything more to do with Rome but he continued to regard himself as a good Catholic. It was declared that 'there remaineth no substance of bread and wine, nor any other substance, but the substance of Christ, God and man'; that 'communion in both kinds is not necessary ... as well apart, as though they were both together'; that 'priests ... may not marry, by the law of God'; that 'vows of chastity ... ought to be observed by the law of God'; that 'private masses be continued and admitted in this the King's English Church and Congregation, whereby good Christian people, ordering themselves accordingly, do receive both godly and goodly consolations and benefits', and that 'auricular confession is expedient and necessary to be retained and continued, used and frequented in the Church of God'. Rigorous Protestants were to regard this document as 'the bloody whip with six strings', and it became a great matter of contention between the opposing factions which now were attempting to shape the future of the English Church.

The government also pushed through a Bishoprics Act, which would enable Henry to refashion the episcopacy in any way he chose. And then there was the measure that would end the conventual life in England for centuries in its traditional form: it was passed by a House of Lords which included seventeen abbots, who did not demur at any of its provisions.[5] The measure would be calendered as the Suppression of Religious Houses Act and it gave the process of surrendering any monastery or other convent a thoroughly legal basis that it had not previously enjoyed. This included a clause which validated

---

[5] There had been twenty-eight abbots in the Parliament which passed the Act that led to the suppression of the smaller religious houses in 1536; and they, too, had nodded the legislation through.

the Crown's acquisition of all monastic properties and possessions surrendered since the first Act of Suppression in 1536 – and all such acquisitions which might be made in future. The new Act reflected on what had been accomplished in the earlier purge of religious houses and promised that 'in the reign of our now most dread Sovereign Lord ... all other monasteries, abbacies ... which hereafter shall happen to be dissolved, suppressed ... shall be vested, deemed and adjudged by authority of this present Parliament in the very actual and real seisin [freehold] and possession of the King our Sovereign Lord, his heirs and successors, for ever, in the state and condition as they now be ... shall be in the order, survey and governance of our said Sovereign Lord the King's Court of Augmentations of the Revenues of the Crown ...'.

The Great Seal of England was affixed to this document, and transformed the existing situation with one impress of wax. What had previously been a cavalier and freebooting exercise by a petulant and greedy sovereign with no legal validity whatsoever, had now become the unchallengeable right of a King who was increasingly uncontrollable by his Parliament or any other force.

XI

A GREAT VIOLATION

✠

> 'If all the water in the Thames were flowing gold and silver, it were not able
> to slake their covetousness.'

THE ABBOT OF COLCHESTER, ON HENRY VIII

AND HIS COUNCIL, NOVEMBER 1539

As 1539 dragged on and the passive surrender of religious houses continued with frequent regularity, yet more executions were added to the price that had already been paid by the most tenacious adherents of the old ways. Martyrdom, as we have seen, had occurred quite early in the alteration (as the government chose euphemistically to phrase it) of the Church; and there had been others who were put to death for their defence of the old faith in the aftermath of the Pilgrimage of Grace. The northern rebellion had, in fact, two tremendous consequences for the religious houses of England and Wales, for it sealed the fate of those that had been spared the initial cull of 1536, and the punishments that followed it had so frightened everybody that almost all communities were prepared to take the easy way out of their predicament by emulating Roger Pyle of Furness and simply giving up under pressure. No religious had been brave or stubborn enough to go to the block since then because he or she was prepared to defy authority unto death when it prepared to close down a community. Even now, in 1539, only one superior was executed for precisely that reason; while two other abbots were condemned and suffered for other forms of defiance.

The first to mount the scaffold was Hugh Cooke, the Benedictine

Abbot of Reading, who had been chosen by the King to sing Mass on the fourth day of mourning at court for the deceased Jane Seymour, and who in other ways had enjoyed royal favour over the years. He was a man with a mind of his own, however, which had meant that in 1533, when Henry was still arguing that his marriage to Katherine of Aragon was invalid because she was his brother's widow, Cooke was one of sixteen theologians who took the contrary view at the risk of catastrophically offending the King. But in due course he accepted the Royal Supremacy even though, rumour had it, he continued to offer a Mass for the Pope every week in his monastery. This was plausible, when he maintained a friendship with Henry Courtenay, Marquess of Exeter, and with Henry Montague, both of whom were beheaded in December 1538 for their connections with the renegade (in Henry's eyes) Cardinal Pole and for their supposed conspiracy to dethrone the King by assisting an invasion by European powers in alliance with the papacy.

It is entirely possible that this friendship led to the Abbot's own downfall. But it would not have helped his case that towards the end of 1537 rumours were rife in Reading that the King was dead, when to speak of such a thing was held to be close to a treason in itself. Cooke had been one of many local people, together with his servant Nicolas Wilkinson, who were examined at the Bear Inn just before Christmas about the origin of this story; and though no one suffered the extreme penalty, Edward Lyttelworke, fuller, was punished for spreading the falsehood by being set in the pillory for an hour on market day, 'his ears fast nailed, and after to be cut off by the hard head, and then he to be tied to a cart's arse, and to be stripped naked to the waist of his body, and so to be whipped round about the town ... and at Reading he remaineth in gaol still until the King's pleasure be known'.

According to Cromwell's man John London, who visited Reading in the summer of 1538, and sent to his employer 'the principle relic of idolatry in England, an angel with one wing that brought to Caversham the spear's head that pierced our Saviour's side upon the Cross', Cooke had said 'as they all do [that] he was at the King's command', with the ominous rider, 'but loth they be to come to any free surrender'. At that stage, Cooke was doubtless buying time, just as Hugh Whitehead was doing at Durham, and it would be quite consistent with such behaviour that as late as 15 August the following year, when Reading was on the verge of dissolution, it was reported that 'the abbot, preparing for the same, sells sheep, corn, woods etc, to the disadvantage of the king and partly also of the farmer'.

Many superiors were concealing or prudently rearranging their assets before the Augmentations men could get their hands on them; Whitehead, too, may have been doing so, and we shall come to that shortly. At Reading, the King's men led by Thomas Moyle (who would one day be director of Augmentations) took possession of everything, which Moyle meticulously described in his report to Cromwell on 8 September. 'There be seven feather beds and four of them furnish four trussing bedsteads hung with silk like bawdekin [which had gold thread worked into it and originated in Baghdad]. In the church are eight goodly pieces of tapestry ... 13 copes of white tissue and 10 of green ...', and they had come across 89 ounces of gold and 'the silver, gilt, and not gilt, 2,645 $^1\!/_4$oz'. The abbey was suppressed, its contents confiscated, within the seven days from 12 to 19 September, by which time Hugh Cooke had been arrested and was being referred to as 'the late abbot'.

The indictment read out at his trial accused him of contradicting the King's claim to be Supreme Head of the Church in England, and alleged not only that he regularly prayed for the Pope but had declared 'I will say there is a pope as long as I live'. However, a communication from Charles de Marillac, the French ambassador in England, to Francis I at the end of November is more suggestive. In it, the envoy said that although he hadn't been able to find out what the particular charge was, he believed that the Abbot was part of the price exacted by the government for the failure of the Exeter conspiracy; and that, too, is plausible. In spite of pleading not guilty to the charge of treason brought against him, Hugh Cooke went to the gallows on 14 November, accompanied by John Eynon, the parish priest of St Giles, Reading, and by John Rugge, a former prebendary of Chichester who was spending his latter years in the Berkshire abbey. Rugge had been interrogated about writings found in his possession which were against the King's Supremacy and his divorce; also 'he had a relic named St

Anastasius' hand at Reading, knowing that his Majesty had sent visitors to the said abbey to put down such idolatry'.

Of much greater moment were the events leading to the execution of Richard Whiting, because he was the Abbot of Glastonbury. Only the shrines at Canterbury and Walsingham attracted more pilgrims than did his monastery, not merely because it was supposed to contain the remains of both King Arthur and St Dunstan, but because of the legend associating it with Joseph of Arimathea, who asked Pilate for Christ's body after the Crucifixion and who was said to have come to England with the Holy Grail and to have founded the very first church on English soil there. St Mary's Abbey, as a result, was one of the wealthiest foundations in the land, with an income of £3,642 3s 3/8d according to the *Valor Ecclesiasticus*. It was not, however, a particularly happy community, its thirty-two monks being sharply divided between the older traditionalists, of whom the Abbot was distinctly one, and about a dozen young religious who for reasons that can only be a matter of speculation were in a state that was verging on the mutinous and certainly disloyal to their elders. For twelve months and more they had not scrupled to lodge complaints with Cromwell's office, to the effect that certain new decrees were not being obeyed, that there had been some fiddling of the accounts, that the house lacked both a library and the books to put in it, that not enough time was allotted for the study of Scripture, that some of the seniors spent much time dicing or playing cards, that the church services were too tedious, that the place was 'much grieved with many processions and other ceremonies'. Richard Whiting and his Prior were picked out for particular criticism.

Whiting was an ailing old man who had been made Abbot by Thomas Wolsey fourteen years earlier and since then appeared to have done everything possible to stay out of trouble: while disliking the royal divorce he had petitioned the Pope against Henry's marriage to his brother's widow, he had subscribed to the Royal Supremacy and nowhere had been heard to utter anything remotely treasonable. Like Hugh Whitehead, he had gone out of his way to obtain Cromwell's approval by a judicious deployment of sweeteners. And he must have thought that these gratuities were having an agreeable effect when he was told by the Vicar-General himself in March 1538 that the King 'would not in any wise interrupt you in your state and kind of living' and that 'no man's words nor any voluntary surrender made by any governor and company of any religious house ... shall put you in any doubt or fear of suppression or change of your kind of life or policy'. Henry was also supposed to have declared that he would not attempt 'to trouble you or to devise for the suppression of every religious house that standeth, except they shall either desire of themselves with one consent to resist and forsake the same, or else misuse themselves contrary to their allegiance, in which case they will deserve the loss of their lives as well as of their possessions'.[1] Long before these weasel words were uttered, and after the commissioners had visited him in 1535, Whiting had actually earned the commendation of Richard Layton, who later made a grovelling apology to the Vicar-General for his unauthorised sympathy.

'I am a man', he wrote, 'and may err and cannot know the inward thought of a monk, fair of outward appearance but inwardly cankered ... I beg you to pardon my folly and henceforth I shall be more circumspect whom I shall commend to his Grace or you.' Then he returned to Glastonbury with Thomas Moyle and with Richard Pollard, who was another coming man in the government's apparatus for the increase and maintenance of royal wealth: he would later become General Surveyor of Crown lands. Now, on 22 September 1539, these three reported to Cromwell how they had arrived in Glastonbury the previous Friday at 10 o'clock in the morning to interview the Abbot at his lodging in Sharpham, about a mile from his monastery, 'and examined him on certain articles'. We can assume that this interview was not conducted amiably; for 'As his answer was not to our purpose [we] advised him to call to mind what he had forgotten and tell the truth'.

The Visitors went to the abbey itself and searched Whiting's study, where they found a book which argued against the King's divorce, 'and divers pardons, copies of bulls, and the counterfeit life of Thos. Bequet

---

[1] The evidence for this transaction between Cromwell and the Abbot of Glastonbury can be no more than a strong possibility, however. See Bernard, p.451 and a footnote to LP XIII (1) 573.

in print; but could not find any letter that was material'. They examined the Abbot again 'on the articles received from Cromwell. His answers ... will show his cankered and traitorous heart. And so, with as fair words as we could, we have conveyed him from hence unto the Tower, being but a very weak man and sickly'. They then proceeded to discharge the monastery's servants and its monks, reporting that they had found £300 on the premises 'and how much plate precisely we cannot yet say. Have found a gold chalice and other articles which the abbot hid from previous commissioners, and as yet he knows not we have found them'. They asked their boss to whom they should deliver the monastery itself which, they declared, 'is the goodliest house of the sort we ever saw – meet for the King and no man else; and we trust there shall never come any double hood within it again'.

A few days later, and the three commissioners were reporting that they had found money and plate concealed in walls, vaults 'and other secret places', with other valuables hidden elsewhere in the country, though they expected to uncover more if they stayed in Glastonbury for another fortnight. By now, Richard Whiting wasn't the only person in serious trouble. 'Have committed to jail, for arrant robbery,' Layton and his colleagues wrote, 'the two treasurers of the church, monks, and the two clerks of the vestry, temporal men.' They enlarged on the wiliness of those responsible for hiding Glastonbury's wealth, claiming that when they first entered the monastery's treasury and vestry they hadn't even found enough jewels, plate or ornaments 'for a poor parish church, but recovered it by diligent enquiry and search'. They hadn't yet weighed everything but they were sure it was very valuable indeed and it was clear to them that 'the abbot and monks have embezzled and stolen as much plate and ornaments as would have sufficed for a new abbey'. They asked whether it was the King's pleasure that justice should be executed on the four new captives. They said they had discharged the servants with half a year's wages, 'the monks also, with the King's benevolence and reward, and have assigned them pensions'.

The Visitors also expanded on their initial enthusiasm for the premises of Glastonbury. 'The house', they said, 'is great, goodly, and so princely as we have not seen the like, with four parks adjoining, the furthest but four miles from the house; a great mere of five miles compass . . . well replenished with great pikes, breams, perch and roach, four fair manor places belonging to the late abbot, the furthest but three miles distant, and one in Dorsetshire, twenty miles distant.' They intended to sell the monastery's cattle and let the pastures. On 2 October they were writing again to their superior, this time much more ominously. They claimed to have discovered treasons committed by Abbot Whiting in the four days since their last communication; and they enclosed 'a book thereof, with the accusers' names'.

Who these accusers were we do not know, for the relevant document has not survived. Nor can we be sure how Thomas Cromwell justified the charge of treason against Whiting, for the customary account of the trial is missing, too. We are therefore left wondering whether the 'treason' was nothing more than the fact that this Abbot was more obdurate than some who were surrendering their houses with little or no protest; though there is, again, no direct evidence that Whiting refused to abandon either his principles or his charge. What we do certainly know is that the Vicar-General was carefully totting up the loot as soon as the Abbot was in the Tower but before he was put on trial, with the air of a man well satisfied with what was already accomplished, noting 'The plate from Glastonbury 11,000 oz and odd, besides gold. The furniture of the house of Glastonbury. In ready money from Glastonbury, £1,100 and odd. The rich copes from Glastonbury. The whole year's revenue of Glastonbury.' We can almost hear the smacking of lips as Henry's Vicar-General contemplated this loot.

We also know that 'on Thursday the xivth day of this present month the abbot of Glastonbury was arraigned, and the next day was put to execution, with two other of his monks, for the robbing of Glastonbury church . . .' The letter conveying that intelligence to Cromwell was written by Sir John Russell, who had been in the King's negotiating team which hoodwinked the northern rebels into laying down their arms at Doncaster in October 1536, and who was about to be made Admiral of England for a couple of years in the early 1540s. He had now been charged with disposing of Richard Whiting, and his despatch graphically described what happened to the Abbot, who was dragged on a hurdle from his abbey to the nearby Tor Hill, where he was hung, drawn, quartered and beheaded on the day after Hugh Cooke was put to death in Reading, his four body parts then being sent to Wells, Bath, Ilchester and Bridgewater for public display, the severed head being stuck upon the abbey gate. 'And as concerning the rape and burglary committed, those parties are all condemned, and four of them put to execution at the place of the act done, which is called the Were, and there adjudged to hang still in chains to the example of others.'

Also present at the execution and dispersal of Whiting's remains was Richard Pollard, who informed Cromwell that the Abbot 'asked God mercy and the King for his great offences towards his Highness ... that we should desire the King's Highness of his merciful goodness and in the way of charity to forgive him his great offences by him committed and done against his Grace, and thereupon took his death very patiently ... and likewise the other two monks desired like forgiveness, and took their death very patiently, whose souls God pardon'. The Abbot, said Pollard, had been examined 'on divers articles' before his execution, '... but he could accuse no man but himself of any offence against the King's Highness, nor he would confess no more gold or silver nor any other thing more than he did after your lordship in the Tower'.

The third superior who had to settle for martyrdom was Thomas Marshall (or Beche), the Abbot of Colchester, who went to the block at the beginning of December; and in his case, again, there is evidence that information was laid against him to Cromwell by a number of people. Marshall was a scholar who had been elected Abbot in 1533, less than twelve months before one of his monks reported to the authorities that the sub-Prior of Colchester had castigated the Vicar-General, the King and his whole Council as heretics, implicitly with the Abbot's approval. The charge seems not to have been pursued, however, and the entire community in Colchester went through the motions of accepting the Royal Supremacy in July 1534. Then reports began to emerge that the Abbot of St John's was anything but sympathetic to the way things were going in England.

A Colchester glovemaker, Robert Rouse, told the authorities that Marshall was sympathetic to the Pilgrimage of Grace and reviled those responsible for putting it down and destroying the abbeys of Jervaulx,

Sawley and Whalley in punishment as 'tyrants and bloodsuckers', that he regarded Bishop John Fisher of Rochester and Sir Thomas More as heroic martyrs. Another fellow pursuing the same trade in the town whilst also attending the abbey in the role of physician, Thomas Nuthake, reported much the same thing, adding that the superior had declared his devotion to the Pope, 'the only supreme head of the church by the laws of God, next under Christ'. One of the abbey servants, Edmund Troman, said his employer had remarked during the Pilgrimage of Grace that 'I would to Christ the rebels in the north country had the bishop of Canterbury, the lord chancellor and the lord privy seal amongst them and I trust we should have a merry world again'; and had described the King's greed as such that could not be slaked by all the waters in the Thames. One of Cromwell's officials, Sir John St Clair, reported to his boss how the Abbot had vowed that 'the king shall never have my house but again my will and again my heart, for I know by my learning that he cannot take it by right and law wherefore in my conscience I cannot be content nor he shall never have it with my heart and will'.

Marshall then made the mistake which, compounded with all these insubordinate opinions, would have settled his fate. In November 1538 Thomas Leigh and another of the government's men, William Cavendish, were ordered to close down the neighbouring monasteries of St Osyth and Colchester, the one an Augustinian house, the other Benedictine. The first of these obediently surrendered, the second did not. And so the Abbot of Colchester was sent to the Tower for examination before trial – at which point his nerve appears to have failed and he denied a great deal that had been said about him, equivocating on much else. He said he had not criticised the Royal Supremacy, had not accused his sovereign of unbridled covetousness, had declared that if the suppression of monasteries was God's will then he accepted such procedures. Being well aware of the appalling death that awaited men convicted of treason, he attempted to minimise the offence he had caused in refusing to give up St John's to the commissioners, by saying that 'I thought somewhat to stand in it, for that I would my pension should be the more'. This was a hopeless defence, as he probably realised while he was desperately uttering it.

On 1 December, 1539, Thomas Marshall was convicted and suffered the same penalty as the Abbots of Reading and Colchester had a couple of weeks before him.

It was shortly after this that Thomas Leigh turned up in Durham once more, bringing with him this time not Richard Layton but Walter Henley, who had just succeeded Robert Southwell as an Augmentations solicitor, and William Blitheman, who had been a receiver since the office's inception.[2] We have what may well be an eyewitness account of their visit; but, if it is not that, then it must be a version written down verbatim from a description by somebody who was actually present when the Visitors arrived.[3] In the context of Hugh Whitehead's attempts to buy off Cromwell, and bearing in mind that Leigh and Layton had left Durham benignly after the earlier visitation, what happened next could only have been anticipated by the gloomiest pessimists, in spite of what had been taking place elsewhere in the realm.

It was certainly most shocking to the reporter, as it would have been to everyone else in the Priory and to all who heard about it throughout the region. For Leigh and his two aides coldly proceeded to desecrate St Cuthbert's shrine, one of the most venerated places in all England, 'where they found many worthy & goodly jewels, but especiallie one precious stone which by the estimate of those three visitors & and their skilful lapidaries (which they brought with them) it was of value sufficient to redeem a prince'. This was, of course, the great emerald which had been valued at £3,336 13s 4d at the beginning of the previous century, and which would never be heard of again after the desecration. The richly illuminated copy of the Gospels associated with Lindisfarne was despatched to London at the same time, probably for whatever price might be realised from its bejewelled golden binding rather

---

[2] A hundred years ago, it was supposed that this visitation took place either late in 1537 or early in 1538; but more recent scholarship has concluded that it occurred 'late in December 1539' (see essay by A.J. Piper in *St Cuthbert and Durham Cathedral: a Celebration*, Douglas Pocock, p. 102).

[3] The account appears in *Rites of Durham*, whose putative author (George Bates) was the last Registrar of Durham before the Dissolution, and Clerk of the Feretory. In his second capacity, if not in his first, it is almost inconceivable that he would not have been present during the activity he describes.

than for the intrinsic worth of its unrivalled decorations and superb calligraphy.[4] Also in the shrine was a great quantity of silks which had originated in Byzantium or Persia or Syria before being brought to the Feretory by wealthy and much-travelled pilgrims, or by pious people involved in commerce with the East. One of these was the so-called Nature Goddess Silk because its focal point was the upper half of a female figure with extended arms, surrounded by grapes and other fruit, fishes, ducks and other birds, which may have been brought to the tomb at the end of the seventh century. Fragments of this would survive the centuries, as would one much more precious thing in its entirety. For the Visitors overlooked Cuthbert's own pectoral cross, which remained hidden from them in the tumbled folds of the linen shroud which was originally wrapped round his body.

The most shocking thing was the violation of St Cuthbert himself. Thomas Leigh had evidently expected to find nothing but dust and bones lying in a grave cavity, but discovered an iron-bound coffin standing in its sarcophagus above ground instead. A blacksmith was summoned, with a sledgehammer, and when this had smashed open the chest 'they found him [Cuthbert] lying whole incorrupt with his face bare and his beard as if it had been a fortnight's growth, and all his vestments upon him as he was accustomed to say mass withal; and his meet wand of gold lying beside him there'.[5] The smith, up beside

---

[4] The *Lindisfarne Gospels*, unlike the great emerald, was not lost to us, however. Later in the sixteenth century the volume surfaced in the Tower of London's Jewel House, where much confiscated monastic wealth had been deposited. It was acquired in the seventeenth century by the bibliophile Sir Robert Cotton, whose heirs made it over to the nation in 1703; and fifty years later it formed part of the new British Museum's first collections. And when we consider what was lost at Durham, *pace* the great emerald, it is worth remembering that when the shrine of St Thomas à Becket was desecrated in Canterbury, the loot removed was reckoned to have filled twenty-six carts.

[5] We know much more than this about the appearance of the corpse, because a detailed examination was made by the medical Dr Selby W. Plummer when it was exhumed for the seventh time in its history in 1899. The body belonged to a long-headed man 'of considerable muscularity' about fifty-five years old at the time of his death and five foot eight or nine inches tall, whose teeth were in perfect condition, set beneath a prominent nose. Dr Plummer surmised that 'The interment within a stone coffin in the sandy soil of Lindisfarne may be a sufficient cause for mummification.'

the tomb, realised as soon as he exposed the corpse that the hammer had broken one of the saint's legs and he passed this information apologetically to the commissioners standing down below. At which 'Doctor Henley hearing him say so did call upon him & did bid him cast down his [Cuthbert's] bones, then he made answer again that he could not get them in sunder for the sinews and the skin held it that it would not come in sunder'. Thomas Leigh then climbed up to inspect the damage in person, and saw that what the man said was true, but Henley was still sceptical, until Leigh told him to come and see for himself if he still didn't believe what he was being told. Henley did so and was suitably impressed, too;

> then did he command them to take him [Cuthbert] down, and so it happened contrary to their expectations that not only his body was whole and uncorrupted, but the vestments wherein his body lay and wherewithal he was accustomed to say mass, was fresh safe and not consumed. Whereupon the visitors commanded that he should be carried into the Revestry where he was close and safely kept in the inner part of the Revestry till such time as they did further know the King's pleasure, what to do with him, and upon notice of the King's pleasure therein, the Prior and the monks buried him in the ground under the same place where his shrine was exalted

In fact, the body appears to have remained in the vestry for the next four years or so. At any rate, not until January 1542 were several craftsmen paid for their work in building a new tomb. 'Given to George Skeles ... for 2 days and a half concerned with making St Cuthbert's grave 15d. Again, given to the same man for John Paxton (at 3d), John Wyll'amson (3d), John Oxenett (3d) for two days and a half 22 ¹/2d. Again, given to the same man for William Tayller (at 3d) for 1 day and a half, 4 ¹/2d. Again, given to Cuthbert Jonson for 2 and a half days, 15d'. Jonson's wife earned herself 3d for sewing a sheet to wrap the saint's body in.

Bede was not spared that day, either. After exhuming Cuthbert, the visitors moved from the Feretory to the west end of the church:

There is two stones, that was of Saint Bede's shrine in the Galilee of blue marble, [one of] which after the defacing thereof was brought into the body of the church and lyeth now [in 1593, when the narrative was written] over against the eastmost tomb of the Neville ... And the other is a plain marble stone which was Lowest and did lie above a little marble tomb, whereon the lower end of it five small pillars of marble did stand, which pillars did also support the upmost stone, the said stone lyeth now both together (as is aforesaid) endway before where Jesus Altar did stand.[6]

The narrator of these events did not say anything about Bede's remains, but there certainly wasn't a complete corpse or even a skeleton there at the time, because many of his bones had been distributed elsewhere as sacred relics, and some had probably never left Jarrow in the first place.

It is believed that Hugh Whitehead was present when the two shrines were violated: there is certainly no record of his being away from his monastery, and if he was in Durham that day it is highly improbable that he would not have danced attendance upon the commissioners as a matter of normal courtesy, let alone as an act of solicitude consistent with his previous behaviour towards Cromwell and his men. William Wylam would certainly have been there in his capacity as Keeper of the Shrine, and we know that Cuthbert Tunstall's suffragan, Thomas Sparke, was present in place of the Bishop himself, who doubtless found it expedient to keep out of the way, even though his views on shrines and their sanctity had been on record for some years. 'The bodies of saints, and namely the relics of holy martyrs', according to a declaration made by Tunstall and three other bishops in *c.* 1536, 'are to be honoured most sincerely as the members of Christ. And churches builded in their names, deputed to the service of God, be to be gone unto with faithful and good devotion, and not to be contemned. And pilgrimage to the places where Almighty God

---

[6] The Neville chantry stood between two bays near the eastern end of the south aisle, the Jesus Altar at the east end of the nave, just before the transeptual crossing which separated the nave from the quire. What remains of the first has survived but nothing of the second has.

sheweth miracles may be done by them that have thereunto devotion.[7]
The Bishop of Durham was not an unprincipled man, but he loathed
confrontation and did everything possible to avoid it. And he knew
very well which side his bread was buttered on.

As did the Prior of Durham who, as a desperate year in the English
religious life drew to a close, carried on with his vocation as though
nothing untoward was happening. He made no protest against the
violations; or, if he did, it has gone unrecorded, which seems most
unlikely in the circumstances. In some ways, indeed, he flourished as
abundantly as he had ever done since being elected superior of his
community almost twenty years earlier. Throughout that time he had
regularly been recruited by the Crown for different forms of public
service. In 1528 he had been made a commissioner for Scotland, thereby
helping to negotiate a peace between the two countries at Edinburgh
six years later. Reporting from Durham directly to his sovereign on
the outcome of this parley on 9 July 1534, he wrote that after the treaty
was made 'there was a demonstration of melody and good cheer', and
said that he believed James V 'is wholly inclined to be the King's loving
nephew, well given to justice, and that his subjects are well ordered
and kept in obeisances'. When uncle and nephew fell out again in
1535, Whitehead was made Treasurer for the Border wars that swiftly
erupted across the Debatable Lands. These were high-profile positions
for any man to occupy in the service of his King, but for most of his
life as Prior, Hugh Whitehead had also been a Justice of the Peace, a
Crown appointment which had been renewed as recently as July 1539.
In that role he sat on a bench for the Liberty of Durham which was
also occupied by Thomas, Lord Audley, who was Lord Chancellor
and therefore a prime instrument of government policy, detested by
dissidents almost as much as Cromwell himself. Several peers of the
realm were also Whitehead's colleagues in the regional judiciary, as
was Cromwell's agent Richard Bellasis and Robert Bowes, who had,
during the Pilgrimage of Grace, been captain of the particularly belligerent host which ransacked the Bishop of Durham's palace and

---

[7] The other prelates were John Clerk, Bishop of Bath and Wells, John Stokesley,
Bishop of London, and John Longland, Bishop of Lincoln.

caused him to take refuge at Norham; but since then Bowes had been a rising star in government service, appointed to a place on the King's reconstituted Council in the North under its first President, who was none other than a distinctly uncomfortable Cuthbert Tunstall.

One of Hugh's final acts in 1539 was to present his nephew William Whitehead to the extremely profitable benefice of Heighington a few miles north-west of Darlington, whose vicar the younger man duly became. Then the Prior of Durham, on 31 December, took his brethren into the Priory cathedral for the last office of the old year, their breath puffing into small clouds of vapour in the frosty air. Beneath that sensational roof of symmetrically balanced stones, where everything dissolved mysteriously into the surrounding gloom of the evening time, they intoned their prayers and chanted their psalms in the thickening darkness of the quire, while the candle flames swayed and danced in the eddies of draught, and made great orbs of light where they were clustered on the high altar and behind it, near Cuthbert's shattered shrine. Little else, however, had changed in any particular for several hundred years; and if some stray jackdaw had been watching from the clerestory high above, it would perhaps have regarded the violation as no more than a new oddity in the mannerisms of these men, unknowing that it signified much more than that.

Compline ran its measured course, from the opening quietness of private prayer, from the general confession and the absolution that followed it, through the hallowed sequences of entreaty, devotion, submission, which these obedient men had uttered so many, many times before; until, with the final Amen said and the last office done, Hugh Whitehead led his brethren out of the church, leaving it to brood over itself in the great silence of that bleak and reluctant Wednesday night. A few hours earlier, the Prior of Durham and his monks had surrendered their monastery to King Henry VIII, just as so many had done before them by then.

'Know ye that we, the aforesaid Prior and Convent', the signed and sealed document said,

> of our unanimous agreement and consent and of our most deliberate
> intents, certain knowledge and mere impulse, for certain just and

reasonable causes that specially move us, our hearts and consciences, have voluntarily and of our own accord given and granted, and by these presents do give, grant, render, deliver and confirm to our most illustrious and unconquered Prince and Lord Henry the eighth, by the grace of God King of England and France, Defender of the Faith, Lord of Ireland, and on earth of the English Church supreme head, all our said Monastery, and also the whole site, ground, circuit and precinct and the Church of the same Monastery, with all our debts, chattels and movable goods to us or our said Monastery belonging or appertaining, as well those which we possess at this present, as those which by bond or for any other reason whatsoever, are in any way due to us or our said Monastery.

And also all and sundry our manors, lordships, messuages, gardens, curtilages, tofts, lands and tenements, meadows, grazings, pastures, woods and underwoods, rents, reversions and services, mills, passages, knight's fees, wardships, marriages, niefs, villeins with their families, commons, liberties, franchises, privileges, jurisdictions, offices, courts, leets, hundreds, views of frankpledge [corporate responsibility for behaviour or taxation within a tithing or similar community], fairs, markets, parks, warrens, fishponds, waters, fisheries, ways, roads, wharfs, void sites, advowsons, nominations, presentations and donations of churches, vicarages, chapels, chantries, hospitals, and of all other ecclesiastical benefices whatsoever, rectories, vicarages, chantries, pensions, portions, annuities, tithes, oblations and all other sundry our emoluments, profits, possessions, hereditaments and rights whatsoever, as well within the said County of Durham and in the Counties of York, Lincoln, Northampton, Nottingham, Stafford, Lancaster and Northumberland, as elsewhere in the realm of England, Wales and the marches of the same, to the same our Monastery aforesaid in any way belonging, appertaining, appendant or incumbent, and all and all manner of our charters, evidences, bonds, writings and muniments whatsoever to us or our said Monastery, our lands or tenements or other the premises with their appurtenances, or to any parcel thereof in any way belonging or appertaining, to have, hold and enjoy our said Monastery and the aforesaid site, ground, circuit and precinct, and our Church aforesaid with all debts, goods and chattels ...

The document continued in this windy fashion to bestow the monastery and its great multitude of possessions on 'our unconquered Prince and King aforesaid, his heirs and successors and assigns, to the use of the same the Lord King, his heirs and successors, for ever in this behalf . . .'.

This was surrender in a grand manner, both abject and comprehensive, leaving not the smallest loophole through which a lawyer might wriggle at any time in the future to argue and obtain alteration; but at least it did not also contain a repentance for the way the religious life had been practised there, as happened in the case of others faced with the same predicament. The surrender was made, the document was sealed and presented to Thomas Leigh, who received it in the name of the Crown in the chapter house of the monastery, with the entire community of monks there to witness their Prior handing over their inheritance, their present and their future, to a man they had every reason to loathe by then.

Only one significant figure was missing from the drama of that moment in the dying embers of 1539. Cuthbert Tunstall was in London that day, in the vast royal entourage which greeted Anne of Cleves at the foot of Shooter's Hill, at the end of her long and bewildering journey from Düsseldorf.

XII

A NEW ORDER

✠

'The monasteries, wonderful to relate, are all destroyed, or will be before Shrovetide.'

JOHN BUTLER TO JOHANN HEINRICH BULLINGER,
24 FEBRUARY 1540[1]

The surrender of the Priory produced no great spasm of either anguish or anger among the civilian population of Durham and its hinterland. Both might have been expected in the circumstances, given the devotion of everyone in the region to St Cuthbert and the fact that northern people had so far largely shunned Protestantism, which was gaining more than a foothold in other parts of the realm[2]. The popular inertia of the North after the surrender, and especially after the desecration of Cuthbert's shrine, seems particularly odd when the Pilgrimage of Grace had been such a northern rebellion in defence of the old faith, for which several hundred people had impetuously given their lives. The rebellion and its aftermath, however, supplied a powerful reason for the quiescent response locally to the events of December 1539.

Though it is true that the north-eastern counties had yielded but a small handful of martyrs two years earlier, compared with Yorkshire, with Lincolnshire and with the north-western shires, Durham had

---

[1] Butler was a Royal chaplain and commissary in the English colony at Calais; Bullinger was a Swiss Reformer based in Zurich, not much less influential than was John Calvin himself in Geneva.
[2] 'In no county did the Reformation make slower progress than in Durham', according to a distinguished official history of the area.

'Half church of God, half castle 'gainst the Scot' was Sir Walter Scott's summary of Durham's Castle and Cathedral, dominating the skyline and surrounding country-side. Others have reckoned the Cathedral to be the finest Norman building in Britain and possibly in all Europe.

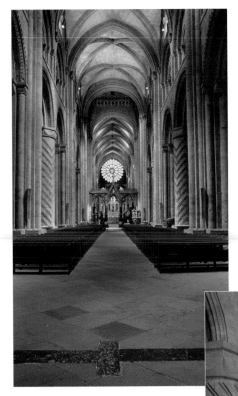

The view along the nave towards the east end of the cathedral. In the foreground is the blue marble line beyond which no woman was allowed to go towards the altar (or Cuthbert's shrine) in the Middle Ages; because, it was said, that was Cuthbert's will. The prohibition, in fact, probably had more to do with the long-standing misogyny of the Norman cathedral's founder, William of Calais.

The Bishop of Durham's throne is reckoned to be the highest in Christendom outside Rome. Underneath is the tomb of the fourteenth-century Bishop Thomas Hatfield, who was responsible for it.

The Feretory behind the Neville Screen separating it from the high altar. Cuthbert's remains lie under the stone slab: the tester above is twentieth-century work by Sir Ninian Comper.

Twelfth-century wall painting in the Galilee Chapel, at the cathedral's west end, of a bishop which some sources believe to be Cuthbert, but is more likely to have been the builder of the chapel, Hugh du Puiset.

Beside the altar of the Galilee is the table tomb of the Venerable Bede (*c.* 673–735), monk of Jarrow and the first English historian, whose shrine became a place of pilgrimage second only to Cuthbert's. Some have found the arrangement and decoration of the chapel's pillars oddly suggestive of the Alhambra at Granada.

LEFT: When the Deanery (formerly the Prior's Lodging) was being restored in 1974, workmen uncovered a wall painting in the hall, which in the sixteenth century was part of Hugh Whitehead's private chapel. This fragment pictures the Resurrection, but another part portrays the Nativity.

BELOW: An impression of Hugh Whitehead's study, drawn to illustrate *The Story of the Deanery, Durham 1070–1912* by G. W. Kitchen, who was Dean of Durham from 1894 to 1912.

The Prior's Study as before the Reformation. Deanery, Durham.

The monks' dormitory above the west cloister, the most complete example of its kind in England and with a superb hammerbeam ceiling, was built as the fourteenth century turned into the fifteenth. Unlike its predecessor, where the sleeping arrangements were open plan, it provided separate cubicles for each monk. It now houses the modern collections of the Dean and Chapter Library.

The northern side of Cathedral seen from the battlements of the Castle, looking across the Castle courtyard.

Clergy and other members of the Cathedral Chapter in procession along the cloisters on their way to the church for a celebration of Palm Sunday, 2006. Apart from the fact that two members of Chapter (one of them a priest) are women, the same ceremony, in much the same vestments, would have taken place at Eastertide in the sixteenth century.

just as much reason as anywhere else north of the Humber to be subdued by the retribution which followed the failure of the Pilgrimage. Durham Castle was where the Duke of Norfolk chose to set up an assize that tried and convicted many of the rebels in that superb and battlemented place, which Cuthbert Tunstall would shortly augment with a new private chapel and on which he eventually left his coat of arms graven in stone above a window; and it was in Durham (very probably in the market place, where there could be a more salutary public spectacle than would have been possible in the confined area of the Castle's courtyard) that more than a small handful of zealots were put to death by one of the most hideous forms of execution ever devised by some human beings for the punishment of others. The ruthless Norfolk had doubtless selected this venue very thoughtfully, in order to demonstrate that royal power was ultimately superior to all other forms of authority, including the virtual autonomy traditionally enjoyed by the Prince Bishops of Durham.

Therefore demoralising fear and the memory of recent terror inflicted by the state would alone have probably been enough to ensure that the citizens of Durham, at worst, went about their business sullenly in the wake of the violation and the capitulation of so much that was dear to them. But it has also been suggested that Cuthbert Tunstall's moderate disposition and apparent acceptance of everything that had happened since his sovereign decided to part company with Rome also played a significant part in quietening the populace. Certainly his behaviour after the surrender indicated an eagerness to soothe those who would be angry, while simultaneously doing his best to ensure a harmonious transition from the monastic state to whatever Henry VIII had in mind. The Bishop's local loyalty in the face of government pressure had been made very clear two years earlier, when Jervaulx Abbey was suppressed in the wake of the Pilgrimage, as a result of which the future of the grammar school and the song school on Palace Green in Durham seemed bleak: for more than two hundred years the wages of the teachers running them had been paid out of a Jervaulx endowment, which the suppression had promptly diverted into the royal treasury.

Tunstall had been so concerned about this that he wrote to

Cromwell, pointing out that the teachers were already owed a year's stipend and that unless something was done about the arrears 'the said two schools ... shall thereby be laid down, which were to the undoing of that poor country and the hindrance of youth in those parts'. The money was quickly paid, and the schools continued to function as before. Now, following the surrender by Hugh Whitehead and his monks, Tunstall may have intervened once more, this time to secure the future of the monastic library at Durham, which even in the fourteenth century had contained almost 900 volumes, and had been expanding ever since. It is thought that he had much to do with the strict regulations that were now imposed upon the Sacrist, who was expected 'to guard diligently in the book-cupboard or library the scholars' books, which he should exhibit yearly before ... others summoned for this purpose, so that none of them be either spoiled or lost'.[3]

The Bishop was on safer ground than usual in challenging the government in these two areas: as he would shrewdly have been well aware, Henry VIII did have, for all his manifold and usually monstrous faults, a high regard for education and anything to do with scholarship. While offering his protection to the monastic community in this limited but important fashion, however, Tunstall had no intention of being mistaken by the Crown for anyone other than a dutiful subject. At the time of the surrender, Hugh Whitehead and his senior brethren appear not to have declared to Thomas Leigh the full extent of their valuables, as they were bound to do by the Acts of Dissolution, and divided among themselves 'monastic vessels, valued at seventy pounds'. Being appraised of this sometime later, Tunstall insisted that the items should be returned, or else that 'these men, or their executors, shall make restitution within two years'. It is at least conceivable (and local opinion would later toy with the possibility) that the monks also secreted the 107 alabaster figures which had stood in niches upon the Neville screen behind the high altar; there is no evidence whatsoever for this, and a greater probability is perhaps that the figures finished

---

[3] As a result of this careful invigilation, the library at Durham was significantly preserved for posterity, its ancillary deposit of archives being justly regarded 'as one of the most important collections of medieval monastic records in Europe'.

up in the Tower of London with all the other monastic valuables taken by the Crown, to be disposed of piecemeal later on in the great trading of such things. But certainly they disappeared at the surrender and have not been seen since.

One other factor would have weighed powerfully with all those for whom Durham Priory and its Cathedral church had been such a dominant in their lives – it may well have been the most telling of all apart from the element of fear – and it was the example and recent history of Norwich, coupled with the gradual realisation that Henry had chosen not to destroy the Wearside community and its buildings, but to transform it and them into something different but still permanent. The East Anglian Benedictines had evidently adjusted to their new lives as a Dean and Chapter without too much agony or hardship, and their cathedral continued to be a focal point of the faithful for many miles beyond its close, its spire signalling a form of continuity that some had never dared hope to see in these disordered times.

Since their abbey's translation into a secular cathedral, moreover, it had become apparent that Henry's treatment of it was but the first step in his larger vision for the English Church, which retained some customs that were perversely but reassuringly traditional. A Bill had been presented to Parliament in May 1539 setting out his plans for a reorganisation of bishoprics. Although the technicalities were left to a committee of prelates to work out, Henry could not resist leaving his personal mark on the legislation, writing the preamble to the Bill himself, in which he loftily claimed that his redeployment of monastic wealth was intended to ensure that 'many of them might be turned to better use ... whereby God's word might be the better set forth, children brought up in learning, clerks nourished in the universities, old servants decayed to have living, almshouses for poor folk to be sustained in, readers of Greek, Hebrew and Latin to have good stipend, daily alms to be ministered, mending of highways, exhibition for ministers of the Church'.

To this end, he drew up a plan for endowing thirteen new sees with the revenues from twenty large abbeys, but this was subsequently abandoned for something less ambitious and only six newly founded dioceses were eventually set up, spreading out from the abbeys of Westminster, Gloucester, Bristol, Oseney (Oxfordshire), Peterborough and Chester, none of which had been a cathedral before. Of these, Westminster lost its bishop within a decade and its abbey was thereafter maintained simply as a college of secular priests led by a dean, something of a rarity which became known as a 'royal peculiar'. In addition to these substantially new creations, Henry proposed to retain eight of the old monastic cathedrals as the seats of their respective bishops, the already established Norwich being one of them. The other seven members of this re-foundation were Canterbury, Rochester, Winchester, Ely, Worcester, Carlisle – and Durham.

The fourteen monasteries and their churches which were thus rearranged in Henry's new order were the only houses (with the exception noted on p166) to survive the great purge that had been going on for four years when the Augustinian priory of the Holy Cross at Waltham in Essex was surrendered to the King's commissioners on 23 March 1540, thus bringing the Dissolution of the Monasteries to an end; and, with it, the biggest transfer of wealth from one section of the population to another that the country had ever known. No one has worked out precisely how much the plundering of the fallen houses and their properties was worth in hard cash, though in 1544 Sir John Williams, Treasurer of Augmentations, noted that 'Proceeds of sales of lands by commissioners' had brought in £164,495 os 7d, with another £22,616 13s 4d coming from the 'sale [mortgages] of lands to the citizens of London'; and one estimate made half a century ago put the figure loosely at something between £15 million and £20 million in current terms. We have a much better idea of the transactions which took place in the aftermath of a house's destruction. A total of 1,539 grants was made by the Crown, of which a mere forty-one were gifts from Henry to thirty-nine individuals, eight of whom were peers, fourteen courtiers, half a dozen Crown officials, three Augmentations officers and eight servants of the King, including his barber Edmund Harman, who was given the hospital maintained by Augustinians in Burford, Oxfordshire, for his deftness with the razor.

Otherwise, all the transactions of monastic property and other wealth were strictly a matter of business, with preferential terms offered to peers and other influential customers in a distinct pecking order which descended from the nobility through the ranks of courtiers, royal servants and Crown officials, down to a motley of knights, esquires and gentlemen who found themselves facing a bargain that hardened more, the longer it took to be made. Those at the lowest level bought half as much loot as the peers – but paid four times as much as their betters for it. Thomas Cromwell did very well for himself under this arrangement, being given (gratis and tax free) the abbeys of Lewes, St Osyth, Launde, Michelham, Modenham and Alcester; while his nephew Richard acquired five properties in Huntingdonshire and another lucrative holding in the City of London. Cromwell, however, did not live very long to enjoy the fruits of his assiduous labours on behalf of his sovereign. He was sent to the Tower on 10 June 1540, charged with treason and heresy, almost certainly trumped up by the Duke of Norfolk and others in high places who had always detested the Vicar-General; and on 28 July he was executed in the name of a King he had served well, who would not forgive what he perceived to be the bungling of his fourth marriage and his own consequent humiliation.

The royal wealth was increased not only by the cash realised from dealings in property, plate, jewellery and other marketable commodities, but also by raw materials which could be put to alternative uses by the Crown. Lead which had covered monastic roofs often finished up as bullets stockpiled in the royal armouries in the Tower and elsewhere, and bell metal came as manna from above to the King's gunfounders at Houndsditch: as when, in the wake of the Lincolnshire suppressions, the Privy Council authorised 'the conveyance hither of such bell-metal as lieth ready at Boston ... to be employed here about the affairs of the ordnance'. And then there was the timber, which Henry needed for the navy he was steadily building in order to maintain his reputation in northern Europe, and particularly in order to stay one step ahead of his greatest rival, Francis I of France. Every monastery owned many acres of woodland, and the Benedictine abbey of St Mary at Abingdon, Oxfordshire, was exceptional only insofar as it was the sixth wealthiest house of its Order, with an income of £1,876 per annum. When Cromwell's commissioners surveyed it in 1538, they carefully noted that on 1,197 acres there were 12,712 trees, which they valued at £2,948 15s 4d. A great deal of this was destined to be made into the hull planking and the futtocks and the knees and the other vital parts of the men o'war that sailed the Channel and the North Sea in Henry's quest for greater glory and the security of his realm.

What happened at Durham in the first few months after its surrender, we simply do not know. We can only surmise that Hugh Whitehead and his brethren quickly adapted to the new order, as had the Benedictines of Norwich, because documentary evidence has never surfaced to indicate anything more positive. Not until 12 May 1541 does the obscuring cloud of uncertainty lift, with letters patent being issued to mark the re-foundation of the Cathedral church of Christ and Blessed Mary the Virgin, as it was henceforth to be styled, Cuthbert being removed from the dedication in order to discourage what were deemed to be the superstitious practices of the Roman obedience. The reason for the seventeen-month delay in actually promulgating the new order in Durham is almost certainly related to an unusual turmoil in government at that time, and particularly to the fate of Thomas Cromwell.[4] For he had been so much in total control of events over the four years of monastic suppressions that his sudden removal from office must have produced stasis (if not chaos) among those who were responsible for drafting all forms of legislation, which was intricate and meticulous work that could not be hurried along, that required intensive preparation and attention to detail if it was to be legally watertight.

Legality was the key to the statutory obligations imposed in Henry's new order, and the element that distinguished most sharply the new rules and regulations under which cathedrals must now function from the ancient Rules of St Benedict, St Francis or St Augustine which had traditionally governed the behaviour of religious communities,

---

[4] All the re-foundations were variously delayed, for the same reason. Westminster Abbey did not become a cathedral church until 17 December 1540, with Winchester's modification not happening until 28 March 1541, followed by those of Canterbury (8 April), Carlisle and Durham (both in May), Rochester (18 June) and Ely (10 September). The new foundations were also affected, starting with Chester (4 August 1541) and finishing with Oseney (1 September 1542): but in November 1546, the see of Oseney was transferred to Christ Church, Oxford, where it has remained ever since.

whether or not they also provided a seat for their local bishops. Until the English monarch took it upon himself to meddle in such matters, a failure to live according to these Rules could only be corrected by the authority of whichever Order a deviant community belonged to, or by the episcopacy. But the Rule of St Benedict, which had been the only such reference point in the existence of Durham Priory, was made redundant from the moment Prior Castell's clock struck the midnight hour which separated 1539 from 1540. Henceforth, Durham Cathedral and its attendant corporation of clergy would operate only according to precepts laid down in documentary form and enforceable by the sovereign who had assumed total control of the English Church.

These were the statutes compiled for all the foundations on the King's behalf – but not completed until 1544 – by three prelates who had risen swiftly in the royal service, not least as commissioners in the long processes of altering the Church in England. Two of them were bishops, Nicholas Heath of Worcester and George Day of Chichester, the third being Richard Cox, Archdeacon of Ely.[5] Whether or not it was their responsibility alone, or whether the King's own hand can be seen interfering again, the model of Norwich was not repeated elsewhere. The distinction between its constitution and those now imposed on the other establishments mattered little to anyone but the clergy whose lives were affected by the change, and were otherwise of significant interest only to canon lawyers. The most important, in effect, was that at Norwich the new Dean's powers were unspecified, whereas he had enjoyed clearly prescribed autocratic rights when he had functioned as a Benedictine prior. Moreover, the Norwich monks who were now to serve as a Chapter of secular priests did so in their entirety, five of them being named as prebendaries (the suffragan Bishop of Thetford was added to this number), the other sixteen being defined as canons, who had a lesser influence in Chapter, and were to be paid smaller stipends.

---

[5] Heath had been Bishop of Rochester before being translated to Worcester in 1543, Day had been Master of St John's College, Cambridge and Provost of King's before reaching Chichester, and Archdeacon Cox held the immensely profitable prebend of Sutton-cum-Buckingham in Lincolnshire.

Neither of these examples was pursued in the other cathedrals. At Ely, three monks became prebendaries and only two or three minor canons; at Westminster the Abbot and six monks became prebendaries; at Chester four monks became prebendaries; at Worcester five monks (at least) became prebendaries; at Peterborough three monks became prebendaries and five became minor canons. Canterbury was exceptional because its Prior, Thomas Goldwell, did not become Dean at the refoundation but was pensioned off because he was disliked by his Archbishop (Cranmer), who thought that 'no-one has hindered the word of God as much as he, or maintained superstition more'; he was replaced as head of the new establishment by Nicholas Wotton, the Archdeacon of Gloucester, with twenty-six of Canterbury's fifty-two Benedictines being found positions in the revised order of things.

At Durham, where 'there shall be created, erected, founded and established a Cathedral Church of a Dean in priest's orders and twelve Prebendaries, priests, who shall in that place serve almighty God entirely and for ever ... with the other ministers needful for divine worship', the pecking order was limited to the seniors.[6] The King did

> make, prefer, appoint and by these presents ordain our beloved Hugh Whithed, Doctor of Divinity, the first, original and present Dean of the aforesaid Cathedral Church, and Edward Hyndmers, Doctor of Divinity, the first priest Prebendary, and Roger Watson, Doctor of Divinity, the second priest Prebendary, and Thomas Sparke, Suffragan of Berwick, Bachelor in Divinity, the third priest Prebendary, and William Bennett, Doctor of Divinity, the fourth priest Prebendary, and William Todde, Doctor of Divinity, the fifth priest Prebendary, and Stephen Marley, Bachelor in Divinity, the sixth priest Prebendary, and Robert Dalton, the seventh priest Prebendary, and John Towten, Bachelor in Divinity, the eighth priest Prebendary, and Nicholas Marley, Bachelor in Divinity, the ninth priest Prebendary, and Ralph Blakeston

---

[6] The quotation comes from Henry's letters patent for Durham, issued at Westminster on 12 May 1541. No copy of his statutes for Durham has ever been found, though we have a fair idea of their content by referring to statutes issued elsewhere that year and also to those issued later by Queen Mary (see Chapter XIV), which were a revision of her father's original document.

the tenth priest Prebendary, and Robert Bennett the eleventh priest Prebendary, and William Watson the twelfth priest Prebendary, of the aforesaid Cathedral Church.

These seniors were augmented as a Cathedral community by twelve minor canons: John Erysden, Henry Brown, William Hackforth, George Cornforth, William Smith, John Brown Jr, John Forster, Thomas Hawkwell, John Bynley, Robert Pearson, George Cuthbert and Richard Robson.

The seniors alone constituted the first Durham Chapter; and between them, they would govern Henry VIII's new founding on the banks of the River Wear after nomination by the Crown with no intervention by the Bishop: neither was there to be another election of superiors by their brethren, as had been the tradition until now. But while a great deal of that government would rest jointly in the hands of the new Dean and Chapter, it was made clear that Hugh Whitehead would have supervisory powers; so that

> for the time being [the Dean] shall from time to time for ever make, appoint, admit and accept all and sundry the inferior officers and ministers of the said Cathedral Church, and all other persons … as occasion or cause shall demand; and may have power and capacity not only for lawful reason to correct, but also to depose and to remove and expel from the same Cathedral Church those so admitted or any one so admitted of them; saving to us, our heirs and successors, the title, right and authority of nominating, appointing and preferring from time to time the Deans, Prebendaries and all the poor folk living of our bounty in the same place …

Numerous other responsibilities and certain restrictions fell upon the Dean's shoulders. When he made his annual survey of the former monastic estates, he had to account for them to Chapter within eight days of his return; and only with the consent of Chapter (which would meet at the very least once a fortnight) could he negotiate sales or leases of property. Moreover, although the Dean was the official guardian of all the Cathedral's valuables as well as its property, he could not open the treasury chest which contained them as well as the great seal of the foundation without the agreement of two prebendaries, the sub-Dean and the Treasurer, who also held keys necessary to unlock it. In these ways was the onus removed from the Dean of being regarded personally as the owner of property under his supervision, by which Henry had craftily acquired a number of monasteries when their superiors were held to have transgressed the law.

One other important relationship was singular to Wearside. If the see fell vacant, then until it was filled again by royal appointment, Dean Whitehead and his successors were to act as temporary Bishops of Durham. But in the corporation of clergy which constituted Chapter, the appointed bishop had no place and very little of the influence that had traditionally been enjoyed by the princely occupants of Durham Castle. He was to act as statutory Visitor at the request of Dean and Chapter and, apart from his right to hold a visitation every three years, he could intervene only at their invitation in matters of custom or of discipline. Nor could he preach in the Cathedral whenever he felt like it (nowhere except at Peterborough and Carlisle did the diocesans enjoy that privilege), but only when he was asked to.

The members of Chapter were to be well paid for their endeavours according to a diminishing scale which gave Whitehead an initial salary of £284 4s 8d, while the twelve prebendaries collected £32 5s 10d apiece, these incomes being enlarged (considerably in some cases) by the monies coming in from the various prebendal estates attached to each position.[8] Below these senior priests, the minor canons were awarded £10 each per annum, a Divinity reader £20, the schoolmaster £11, the Master of the Choristers £9 15s, eighteen almsmen £6 13s 4d, sixteen lay singing men and a deacon £6 6s 8d (a sub-deacon getting fourpence less), two vergers, two porters and two sacristaries £6, eighteen scholars and ten choristers £3 6s 8d, two cooks and two barbers £5 apiece. The graduations throw some light on Henry's notion of priorities, with the Divinity reader and

---

[8] The prebendal stalls were initially more or less equal in value, but over several generations discrepancies evolved, so that by the eighteenth century the eleventh stall had become known as the much coveted Golden Prebend, because it was worth several times more than any other.

the schoolmaster both being better paid than the minor canons.

So does his decision to dispose of the other monks with pensions; which meant that Thomas Holburn, Richard Crosby, Richard Johnson, John Swalwell, John Brown Sr, Henry Strother, Cuthbert Robinson, John Dove, Alexander Woodmans, John Duckett, John Todd, John Watson, Christopher Risely, John Scott, Christopher Robinson, Thomas Harper, Cuthbert Bailiff, Giles Preston, Thomas Robinson, Christopher Egglestone, John Robinson, Miles Swalwell, John Blithe, Robert Chilton, Roger Rawe, John Sotherán and Richard Forster returned to the world they had once renounced, as they thought, forever; the better equipped to do so, however, with an assured income from the Crown of between £5 and £6 13s 4d apiece.[9] This bounty was not peculiar to Durham: it had been the custom and was repeated every time a monastery was dissolved. Many such pensioners were still collecting their dues late in the sixteenth century, when Henry's daughter Elizabeth was on the throne. A Cistercian from Biddlesden Abbey, Buckinghamshire, which was suppressed in 1538, was still a monastic pensioner when he died as a parochial rector in 1601. He was but one of many former religious whose working lives continued as parish priests in the new Church of England.

The liberality which this capricious monarch could demonstrate in tandem with his more notorious vindictiveness and self-regard, was never shown more amply than in his endowment of Durham. Dean Whitehead and his Chapter were given and granted 'our manor of Bearpark in our County of Durham, with all its rights, members and appurtenances ...'; and this was only the first entry in a long list of benefactions which were all so meticulously itemised that the completed document was more than four times as long as the voluble letters patent. They referred to eighteen manors in County Durham, starting with Witton Gilbert and finishing with Shincliffe, 102 'towns, fields,

---

[9] These are the names officially calendered in LP XIV (2) 772, but they do not complete the full tally of Durham monks at that time. Young George Cliffe, for example, who was studying at Durham College on the day the mother house surrendered (and eventually became its Rector), would go on as a priest to occupy the twelfth prebendary's stall on Wearside from 1558 to 1596, when he died, leaving a widow and five sons.

parishes or hamlets' in the same area, together with many more in Northumberland and much further afield, including Frampton in Lincolnshire, Ruddington in Nottinghamshire, Fishlake, Bossal and Brantingham in the County of York.

The farm at Elvethall Manor thus remained in the re-formed community's possession, but now under the supervision of Prebendary Watson DD, instead of the monastery's Terrar that the reverend gentleman had been in the previous organisation. Its barley, its oats and its wheat would continue to be harvested as before with the assistance of Shincliffe men, who would also continue to earn a crust by carting manure as their forefathers had always done, by scouring the Elvethall ditches, repairing its hedges, mending its buildings and walls. To this extent, nothing at all would be changed in the foreseeable future from the habits and traditions of the past; and the same went for practices on all the old monastic lands.

The endowment carefully delineated areas that were usually more vaguely defined, like 'that close of pasture called Godriche close, containing by estimate sixteen acres' and 'all that close called Ox Close, and another close called Cow Close, and one other close called Pump Close, and all that water mill for corn lying next and near by the gate of the manor and cell aforesaid. And all that fishery and salmon-fishing, and free fishing in the water of Wear ... the which sometime were belonging and appertaining to the said late monastery, or were parcel of the possessions of the said late monastery.' It included 'all that site, enclosure, circuit, circumference and precinct of the late cell of Holy Island. And all the Church, bell-tower and churchyard of the same cell, with all the houses, buildings, pigeon-houses, orchard and soil, both with and without ... and fifteen cottages in that same place, two gardens, one called Bagotts, the other called Coldingham Walls. And thirteen little gardens in the same place ... And also all that our island of Farne within the sea in the same ...' Nothing at all was omitted; not messuages, grazings and underwoods, not wardships, marriages and escheats and heriots, not tithes and oblations, 'views of frankpledge and all things that to views of frankpledge appertain or can or ought hereafter to belong ...'; not even mere marshes and pools were excluded from this accountancy.

Tithes 'of corn and hay within' were granted to the Dean and Chapter up and down the North Country, and 'all that pension or annual rent of forty shillings, issuing and yearly to be received from the vicarage of Middleham', with other sums accruing elsewhere (53s 4d at Heighington); and 'the tithes of lambs, wool, flax, hemp, and tithes of fisheries, with the tithes of the Lenten Book in that place within the parish of Norham aforesaid'. The Dean and his colleagues were also granted 'all manner of advowsons, donations, nominations, collations, presentations, free disposals and rights of patronage'. They were, territorially at least, having restored to them what they had only just surrendered to the Crown, and in this respect Durham was not at all worse off than it had been before the Dissolution of the Monasteries began. Henry had simply taken over the title deeds and rearranged the working habits and timetable on Wearside.

He exacted a price, of course; and while the biggest part of that was total obedience to his will, there was also a fiscal element in the balance of payment he expected from Hugh Whitehead and the new prebendaries. They were now required, 'yearly thenceforth for ever', to pay the Court of Augmentations £218 'of lawful money of England, at the feast of St Michael the Archangel, in full recompense and satisfaction of all services . . .'. They were required to pay a further £3 19s 6d a year to Thomas Tempest, knight, Nicholas and Robert Tempest, 'jointly officers of the parkership of Bearpark'; 46s 4d to Thomas Forster, 'palliser of the said park'; £413s 4d to Jasper Horsley, 'bailiff itinerant or cursitor of the Exchequer of the said late Monastery'; 26s 4d to the bailiff of Shoreswood, 26s 8d to the bailiff of East Merrington, 33s 4d to the bailiff of Heworth, 53s 4d to the bailiff of South Shields, and other sums to a number of other such functionaries. The curate of St Margaret's chapel in the Durham parish of St Oswald could look forward to receiving £5 6s 8d in salary from the Dean and Chapter, but his colleague at the Cornhill chapel in the parish of Norham would only receive £5, and the incumbent at Muggleswick a mere £3 6s 8d on a sliding scale which saw the chaplain to the Hilton chapel pocket only 10s, twice as much as the chaplain of the chantry at Bradbury received. The Durham clergy also had to spend 13s 4d a year 'for bread and wine at Eastertide in the administration of the Body of Christ to the parishioners in the church of Norham', whose vicar earned £20 from the same source, and they were obliged to present the Master of the College of St Frideswide, Oxford, with 2s.

In return, they were excused some traditional payments to the Crown because 'we, our heirs and successors have not and will not demand, claim or assert our right to any first-fruits, revenues or profits or any sum of money whatsoever for ... the aforesaid manors and other the premises' and the taxation known as the tenth was henceforth also to be waived. Henry, however, was never at a loss for an excuse to impose upon his subjects whenever he ran short of ready cash. Within three years of the new establishment on Wearside, he had billed Dean Whitehead for £100 and Bishop Tunstall for £500 because 'Being entered into league with the Emperor and having covenanted to invade this year the realm of France ... having commenced the war with honour and likelihood of better success, he sees occasion for greater charge than was at the beginning considered, both for the tarrying longer than was determined and for the leaving money to furnish the strongholds already taken ... of such of his loving subjects as he knows will press themselves to satisfy his desire ...' Hugh Whitehead's share of the burden was no greater than that of nineteen other deans in the Church of England, but only the Archbishop of Canterbury and the Bishops of Lincoln and Winchester had to find more than Cuthbert Tunstall (twice as much each), while twenty other bishops paid a good deal less.

Although some corporate matters were superficially unchanged on Wearside after December 1539, a number of alterations were obviously made under the new dispensation. The most radical concerned the basic living arrangements of the incumbent clergy there. Hugh White-head remained in the mansion which had been his dwelling place for almost twenty years, but now the old Prior's Lodging was translated into the Deanery. Much more of an upheaval – and it must have been an agreeable one – came the way of the Chapter canons who, as Benedictine monks, had hitherto occupied nothing grander than a small room apiece within a common dormitory. Now each of the resident priests was given a home with many rooms to it in the garth which separated the Cathedral from the outer wall of the old monastery, and which would subsequently become known as the College.[10] Stephen Marley BD, formerly Hugh Whitehead's deputy as sub-Prior but now the sixth prebendary, was allotted what had lately been the refectory of the almonry children beside the gatehouse, which he proceeded to rebuild more comfortably, while Robert Dalton, who had never held any monastic office but was now the seventh prebendary, took over the old granary inside the southern wall; and their colleagues were similarly installed as next-door neighbours in old monastic buildings which had been superseded or otherwise made redundant. There they were expected to run a recognisable household in which hospitality was deemed to be an important element; and they were now (or very soon would be) at liberty to entertain guests with the companionship of a wife if they were so disposed. Only one of the first occupants (William Bennett) ever did get married, however, although their successors steadily became more and more attracted to the idea; conspicuously, as we already know, in the case of George Cliffe.[11]

The other noticeable change was liturgical. No more than very general directions about church services were given in the first statutes of the new order, for the great revision of liturgies was still some distance in the future; but one or two alterations were instantly made. The old monastic horarium was not totally eradicated and the offices continued to be said, though the habit of saying Matins at midnight was no longer regarded as essential or in keeping with the new times. But at the various altars still positioned around the Cathedral, Masses punctuated each day as in times past, and prayers were still offered up for the eternal repose of the Nevilles and the other benefactors. Feast days were still kept and all the principal services were still gorgeous with the colour of vestments, still mesmerising in their intricate harmonies, their movement, their stillnesses, still sonorous with great

---

[10] This usage was not quite unique to Durham in referring to the college of priests who dwelt there. Elsewhere, similar enclosures would be regarded as the cathedral close, except at Bristol and Ely, whose Chapters were also gathered into colleges.
[11] The habit of continuing celibacy as then practised in Durham was not always maintained by former religious, including the Cambridge Dominican prior who took a wife as well as an image of Our Lady with him when he was elevated by Henry to the Deanery of Exeter.

Latin periods, still melodious with the accompaniment of the organ and the human voice. John Brimley, secure in his new Music Master's emolument of £9 15s, continued to coax his choir (but ten choristers and sixteen singing men now) through the intricacies of plainsong and pricknote and chant, just as he had done before the break; though from 1544 he would be leading them through the Litany in English for the first time, on Rogation days, on St Mark's day and in times of national emergency caused by the elements or foreign powers. Even then, incense still drifted in pungent clouds from the high altar, scenting the now empty niches on the great stone screen as it rose towards the vaulting of the roof, just as it had always done, to the discomfiture of any jackdaw that might have strayed in.

In such relatively small, but nonetheless significant ways as this, the traumatic moment of a great monastery's surrender was eased into the future, where St Cuthbert, relegated though he was in official esteem, still lay venerated at rest, a thoroughly desiccated corpse by now. As for the past, the reality was that Henry had made only the beginning of an end.

XIII

THE END OF AN ERA

✠

'*So many as intende to bee partakers of the holy Communion, shall sygnifye their names to the Curate, ouer night; or els in the morning, afore the beginning of Matins, or Immediately after.*'

FIRST RUBRIC FOR 'THE SUPPER OF THE LORDE AND THE
HOLY COMMUNION, COMMONLY CALLED THE MASSE'
(FIRST PRAYER BOOK OF EDWARD VI, 1549)

For several years after the surrender, time might have stood still on Wearside in some respects, as the re-formed and much reduced community came to terms with and accommodated itself to the new regime. How much this novel corporation of Anglican clergymen missed the company of those of their old brethren who had been pensioned off into the world outside, with whom they had lived (in some cases for decades) closely, we have no means of knowing; but the emptiness of some places in the quire, the lack of general intercourse in the refectory and frater, the regularity with which all had gathered in the cemetery to remember those who had gone before, must have impinged upon all of them, quite painfully for some. We have only the sketchiest knowledge of what happened to most of the pensioners, and of some we know nothing further at all.

Of Richard Johnson, Henry Strother, Richard Crosby, Giles Preston, Thomas Robinson and John Watson, nothing more was heard after they were pensioned off. The same obscurity fell on John Dove, who had typified so many generations of Durham Benedictines in pursuing his vocation unobtrusively. No more than a novice when he attended Hugh Whitehead's election, not yet thirty at the time of the surrender, and never having been considered for promotion to the senior ranks of the obedientiaries, he had served as the priest at several chantries in the cathedral, had done his stint as a monk at the Finchale cell and later at Jarrow before returning to the mother house; until he collected his state pension as he was bidden to one day and effectively disappeared as anonymously as he had lived most of his life in obedience to the letter and the spirit of Benedict's Rule.

Of the rest, Thomas Holburn never strayed far from the Cathedral, and is said to have died at Durham in or about 1546, as did Cuthbert Robinson in 1549 and John Swalwell, not far away at Merrington, in 1547. John Brown died in January 1546, but where we do not know, as also did Christopher Egglestone in 1551. Some of the former monks could be tracked for a little while longer than that, though no more distinctly than the rest of the absentees: John Todd's pension was still being paid in 1552, likewise John Scott's, John Robinson's, John Blithe's, and Richard Forster's. Cuthbert Bailey was said to be living in Lancashire at the end of 1552, which was about the time that Thomas Harper died at Howden in the East Riding of Yorkshire.

Some of Durham's Benedictines lived on outside the cloister not only to enjoy their pensions but also to continue their vocations as priests. Alexander Woodmans's money was still being paid by the government in 1552 and he was employed as clerk of the Chapter's church of St Margaret's in Durham in 1568. John Duckett was priest of the chantry of the Virgin Mary at the same church in 1548 and twenty years later was curate of the Chapter's church at Whitworth; though not, perhaps, for very long because he made his will in that year. Christopher Risely was Cantor of the chantry at St Oswald's, Durham in 1548 and was still drawing his pension there in 1552. In 1548, Miles Swalwell was priest of the chantry of St Katherine in All Hallows, Newcastle, where he was said to have died in 1551, while Roger Rawe survived to become parson of the Chapter's church of Rounton in 1558, John Sotheran as priest of the chantry of St Katherine at Aycliffe in 1548, and Robert Chilton as curate of St Michael's, Stamford, in Lincolnshire, in 1554, for which he received an income of £4 to almost double what came to him annually from the royal exchequer.

One of the pensioners fared more spectacularly than the rest. Christopher Robinson, who had served as priest at the Neville and Hatfield chantries in his Priory days, was presented by Queen Mary to the chaplaincy of the chantry of the Twelve Apostles at Barnard Castle in 1554 and was curate of Gainford, Co. Durham, in 1570; by which time Mary's young sister Elizabeth was on the receiving end of a papal bull condemning her for having cruelly put down another northern rising in the name of the old faith. By then, five of the youngest monks at the time of the surrender, as well as George Cliffe, would be well into their clerical careers in the thoroughly Reformed Church of England. George Blount, John Matthew, Hugh Winter, Anthony Todd and James Gray were either studying at Durham College on the last day of 1539, or would shortly be bound for it, and they were among twelve Divinity students there supported by Henry's new foundation from 1541, by which time Cliffe had just become (or was about to become) the College's Rector. In another thirteen years, his charge would be known as Trinity College, Oxford, after the original buildings had been acquired by the lawyer Sir Thomas Pope, Treasurer of the Court of Augmentations by then and one of Henry's legal executors, who obtained a charter from Queen Mary and re-endowed the premises.

The residentiary priests now domiciled around the College can be more clearly accounted for, because the same documentary evidence that enables us to have a fair idea of the monastic life in Durham continues undiminished as the sixteenth century proceeded towards its halfway mark and beyond. It is, however, almost entirely evidence of a collective nature, as in the Benedictine time, with individuals rarely making a distinct appearance in the Household Book or the Bursar's Accounts or some other archive of the reshaped community: nobody wrote letters yet to flesh out the very bare bones of the invoice and the timetable; or, if they did, none have survived. A rare shaft of light falls on Prebendary Robert Bennett in June 1545, because in that month he set off for London and did not get home until 11 or 12 July, more than three weeks later. He travelled with at least one servant because 'at Durham the night before we took our journey' he and his companion(s) were at pains to make sure their three horses were properly fettled for the many miles ahead, spending 20d of the

Chapter's money on fodder and 2s on having them shod. The first stop came at Darlington, which cost 'drink at night 4d, in wine 2d, horse-meat 23d' and next day they paused at Northallerton for dinner before supping at Boroughbridge and spending 5s 3d in all. Down through Yorkshire they went by way of Ferrybridge, into Nottinghamshire at Tuxford, and Lincolnshire at Grantham, called at Stamford ('dinner 16d, wine 2d, horsemeat 2s, in ale 2d') before making Huntingdon on the 24th, Ware in Hertfordshire on 25th for dinner, and Stepney for that night.

Bennett was in London for a week, though what he was doing there we have no idea, while it cost him and the others 30s 11d to keep themselves and their animals. Then on 4 July they set off for home, but this time by way of High Wycombe and Oxford where, even if they did stay at Durham College (which seems logical, because they certainly visited it), it still cost them 'breakfast in the morning 8d, dinner 2s, supper 18d, in wine 4d, horsemeat 3s'. Before heading north-wards, 4d was spent on 'mending there master's saddle ... for 6 ells of canvas for packing up the stuff in the revestry ... for cord and twine to the same 2d and in rewards to the students one angel 8s'. Next day they were in Daventry, paused at Lutterworth, and enjoyed 'supper at Leicester 16d, in wine 4d, horsemeat 2s 2d, in butter and ale 2d, regards [tips] to the maidens 2d' (this was daring territory into which no Durham Benedictine had ever strayed so far as we know).

The 8 July saw them dining in Nottingham, supping at Mansfield; the next day they passed through Doncaster and Ferrybridge, before retracing their steps through Boroughbridge, Northallerton and Darlington. They then had to pause in Aycliffe for refreshment, to buy a saddlecloth and to receive some attention from the blacksmith again, before regaining the peninsula, the College and their beds on the 11th day of July. A puzzling pendant to this itinerary and its costing indicates that they had to take into account 'William Gamleston's expenses at Stepney by nine days keeping there the horses ...' and 'Item for one pair of stirrup leathers and 1 pair of girths to Thomas Watson 9d'. Who these two men were we do not know (though Watson was very probably a servant, Gamleston maybe an ostler); but the bigger question is what was the occupant of the eleventh stall doing in the capital for a whole week? Perhaps he was preparing the ground for another journey south only a few weeks later.

In October he was off on his travels to London again, following more or less the same route there and back, staying somewhere in the capital from the 10th to the 31st of that month, and incurring almost daily expenses in hiring a boat to ferry him to and fro between his lodgings and Westminster (the normal method of travel from one part of the metropolis to another, with scores of passenger wherries plying for hire along the Thames every day of the year) where we know exactly what his business was. The Dean and Chapter were in dispute with the Vicar of Northallerton over a pension, the matter had come to court, and Prebendary Bennett had been sent to Westminster to represent Durham's interests there before a judge. A reading of his expenses for this excursion makes it clear that he took a parcel of documents with him (at Newark, on the way down, he had to have mended a device attached to the saddle, which would bear a substantial load, and when he reached London he soon found it necessary to spend 3d on 'one canvas bag for carrying books'). We also know the name of the lawyer who acted on behalf of the Dean and Chapter because Bennett itemised 'to Master Gostall for retaining him of our counsel one angel 8s. Item the 16th day of October for entering and calling our matter against the vicar of Allerton 5s. Item to Master Manere, attorney in the same court 20d. Item the 17th day of October for entering the day of appearance of the said vicar or else attachment to Master White, Master Duke's clerk 8d ... Item to Master Gostall for drawing the replication to the answer of the vicar of Allerton 5s. Item to Gall his servant for writing the same in parchment. Item to Master Gostall for calling our matter and declaring the same 3s 4d ...'; and so on until, on 29 October, we read of the 'Item to the said White for the copies of the injunction and the act in the court against the said vicar 12d' with further sums paid for the sealing of the document and enrolling it. Robert Bennett spent a total of £12 13s 7d in going to London and representing his Chapter there; of which his learned friend Master Gostall pocketed £13s plus expenses and other legal costs.

The Dean and Chapter would never be slow in going to law when they were in dispute with outsiders about something, and they assiduously guarded their income when they felt it threatened by anyone, highborn and lowly alike. In November 1546, one Ellin Layton, a widow, petitioned them from Middleton St George, near Darlington, asking not to be taken to court ('I marvel much that you are so extreme against me to sue me before the King's Majesty's Council') when she was doing her best to pay the £7 she owed them before the Michaelmas which followed the one that had just passed; that is, in eleven months' time. She had clearly got herself into difficulties after the death of 'my bedfellow, God pardon his soul' and was obviously having to juggle her resources to see her through and out of the bailiff's hands. It would be good to think she was treated generously by the reverend gentlemen inhabiting the College in Durham, but that we do not know.

Such personal glimpses are rare, though we can see rather more clearly how the fledgling community as a whole was getting on in the first exploratory years of the new order on Wearside. The household records of the Cathedral and its ancillary parts might have been lifted from the old monastic accounts, so small are the differences between the two. Between Michaelmas 1540 and 24 June 1541, for instance, a total of £561 5s 4d was expended on foodstuffs, paid for in the name of Robert Bennett, who had retained his old obedientiary role as Bursar (whatever his other responsibilities, implicit in the October expedition, may have been) in charge of the accounts. Of this sum, £92 13s was spent on corn, £157 11s on brewing and barley, £55 16s on beef, £47 4s 8d on heifers and 60s 11d on pigs. Lambs could be had for a few pence that year, and it may be that Hugh Whitehead and Bennett were in some sort of rivalry to live up to the new provisions for providing hospitality, because the kitchens dealt with a total of 154 carcasses in that period 'of which by Master Bennett 75 at 12d, and 99 at 12d by the lord warden [i.e. the Dean]'. It is clear that Whitehead was still relishing his role as host, just as he had done when he was Prior: between Michaelmas and 12 December, when a total of £30 14s 10d was spent on fish, the Deanery was down for £20 14s 8d worth of it.

There were seasonal expenses in Durham Cathedral's calendar, no different from those that had been incurred when it was the Priory church, which indicated scarcely any difference at all between the rituals of the Benedictines and those they now practised as secular

Anglicans. After Easter 1545, the Dean ('Hugo Whitehead', as he had been referred to in Latin documents ever since the days of his election) accounted for the 3s 4d which had been 'Paid to James Person and Cuthbert Johnson [for?] the erection of the paschal candlestick, with others helping, the Wednesday of Holy Week'; and, when the feast was over, Robert Dalton paid a similar sum 'to James Peyrson (*sic*) and his colleagues for taking down the paschal candlestick'. That same month, Dalton was again the paymaster, this time for 20s 4d which was 'handed over to Nicholas Turpyng for wine received for the celebration of masses from the feast of the Nativity of the Lord to the sixteenth day of April: five and six quarts and for Robert Haclit's wages'. More humdrum matters were attended to, as when, after Easter 1542, Prebendary Dalton accounted for £4 18s 11d which was spent on a miscellany of purposes: 'for his expenses towards Newcastle for the road etc ... to John Eland for riding towards Edmundbyers ... to Ralph Dalton [the prebendary's brother] for his journey to London ... to Ralph Fies for 1lb of wax and 1 quire of paper ... to George Skeles for half a day working on the clock ... to the same man for putting in place ... for 5 cart-loads of plaster ... to John Smyth for windows ... to the same man for 3lb of ironmongery ... to Cuthbert Johnson for 3½ days ... to James Loksmith for 2 berris [bars?] for windows ...' Cuthbert Johnson (or Jonson) had evidently made the transition from one ecclesiastical condition to another, but as the community's handyman, as easily as had his employers; and doubtless his wife sewed as carefully for the Dean and Chapter as she had threaded her needle at the behest of the Prior and his obedientiaries.

But some of the traces that have survived from those years are more opaque. On 19 February 1545, someone prepared to set off for London, buying a breast girth for the horse first, and having it shod. At Darlington next day he paused 'for dressing my boyth [boots?]', then at Wetherby a couple of days after that he needed a horse shoeing again and bought a pair of spurs for sixpence (both on a Sunday!). He appears to have reached the capital the following weekend and he was accompanied by servants, one of whom evidently needed a new coat which may have been bought down there. It is possible that one of the animals in this caravan had been so troublesome that it had been left en route in Lincolnshire because there was a payment of 6s 8d 'to Mother Baker of Stamford for the gray horse the space of three weeks ... to his keeper 12d'. That is approximately the time the traveller spent in London because the account refers to 'At my cost Langhams the space of three weeks 3s 4d, wine at diverse times 16d, for my bed 3s 4d, for washing of my clothes 8d, to the servants 12d'. But who was this hazy figure and what was the purpose of his journey? Was it Dean Whitehead attending a conclave of cathedral administrators at Westminster? Or the itinerant Prebendary Bennett again, on another of his litigious forays to the capital?

Sometimes, the records are tantalising because the gaps in them are quite patently wilful. Hugh Whitehead one day authorised the payment of £6 11s 8d for two excursions made from Durham. After the first, £4 6s 8d was 'paid to John Wille of Merrington for one horse bought from him for Master Tutyng [otherwise known as John Towten of the eighth stall] riding to London on the church's business'.[1] After the second, 45s was 'paid to Master Nicholas Merloe [Marley?] for two horses bought from him for Percival Elyson and another man riding with him to Lynne on the church's secret and private business'. No record appears ever to have revealed what this mysterious journey was about.

While this utterly unspectacular transition from one state of being to another was taking place on Wearside, events elsewhere were shaping the future of Durham and the entire Church of England. The contending forces that had been present within the English Reformation from the beginning never gave up their tussle for supremacy in Henry's lifetime, and the King's own responses to it were those of a man divided in his conviction of how the new religion should be practised in his realm. In 1541 he reminded his subjects that 'Perceiving sundry superstitions and abuses to be used and embraced by our people ... [we] commanded that no offering or setting up of lights or candles should be suffered in any church, but only to the blessed sacrament of

---

[1] A number of the former monks adopted different names – William Smith (Ditchburn) and John Porter (Smith) are examples – after the Dissolution, for reasons that are obscure; but very few were known by more than one name when they were professed Benedictines.

the altar' and on a visit to York that summer he ordered the Archbishop to have all the shrines in the northern Province dismantled, though at approximately the same time he announced the restoration of the feasts of St Luke, St Mark and St Mary Magdalene to the calendar. Yet by October he had declared that all cathedrals should be cleansed of 'any shrine, covering of shrine or other pilgrimage'.

An episcopal commission was simultaneously set up to examine the whole matter of traditional ceremonies, and one of its leading figures was Cuthbert Tunstall, who played his usually moderating role in aiming for a balance between tradition and wholesale change. The *Rationale of Ceremonial* concluded that, while emphasis should be placed on the symbolic meaning of rituals (the Mass being 'a remembrance of the passion of Christ, whose most blessed body and blood is there consecrated'), the English Church must not turn its back on the habit of praying to 'any saint particularly as our devotion doth serve us, so that it can be done without any superstition, as in esteeming one to be the patron for one thing and another saint for another, as St Appolonia for the toothache, St Legeard for the eyes, St Loye for horses, St Anthony for ... hogs, St Rooke for the plague, St Barbara for thunder and gunshot, and such other'. The commission's report, however, was never published.

What did make the public prints was what became known as *The King's Book* in 1543, which was a successor to *The Bishops' Book* of 1537. That had been compiled in the aftermath of the Pilgrimage of Grace and it, too, had Tunstall's fingerprints all over it, as it considered all the weighty matters exercising English divines since the break with Rome, from the Creed to the Lord's Prayer and the Ave Maria, from the doctrine of justification by faith to the one which defined and responded to the concept of purgatory; it has been seen as a first attempt to find the *via media* in matters theological and beyond which was subsequently to be one of the great glories of Anglicanism; but Henry had never given the document his *imprimatur* and so it was stillborn.

The King's Book was a revision of this to the extent that it, too, considered in detail the Ten Commandments and other crucial injunctions and intercessions, and in some passages repeated the original text verbatim. It opened defensively, arguing the need for reform and urgency

by which 'all men may be uniformly led and taught by the true understanding of that which is necessary for every christian man to know
. . . a perfect and sufficient doctrine, grounded and established in holy
scripture'. It made dismissive noises about monasticism and inveighed
with a now familiar fluency against the consumption of supposedly holy
water and other forms of 'superstition'. But at the same time it rejected
the essentials of Lutheranism (another of Henry's old bogies) by sug-
gesting, among other things, that there was nothing in Scripture or in
the ancient Christian authorities to warrant the doctrine that anyone
was predestined by belief to salvation. If there was a central passage in
The King's Book, it was the warning that no one should 'so preach the
grace of God that they take away thereby freewill, nor on the other side
so extol freewill that injury be done to the grace of God'.

Scholars have debated ever since whether or not this was principally
an anti-Protestant tract. What it was above all, perhaps, is an indication
of how uncertain everything had become in the English Church after
the self-assurance with which it had been separated by its sovereign
from Rome. Most importantly, it made a distinct gesture towards the
application of reason when considering the fundamentals of Christianity, a notion that would be comprehensively and splendidly worked
out by Richard Hooker at the end of the sixteenth century.

The sovereign himself continued to attend Mass in the Chapel Royal
at Windsor on holy days and feast days, and resisted any temptation he
might have felt to tamper significantly with the traditional liturgies;
but at the same time he acceded to Thomas Cranmer's request that
the more demonstrative Lenten and Easter rituals in 1546 should be
abolished, that veiling the Cross and prostration and all-night vigils
on Easter Eve must now be a thing of the past. This is perhaps further
evidence that here was a man in conflict with himself about what he
had done and where he should now turn. But by then, Henry was
coming to the end of his life, having made two more marriages since
the disastrous episode with Anne of Cleves and having executed his
penultimate wife, the Duke of Norfolk's niece, Catherine Howard. He
had led his invasion fleet across to France and had retaken Boulogne,
but then he had made his peace with Francis I, partly because he
was now so heavily in debt to the moneylenders of Antwerp (Hugh

Whitehead's £100 had never been enough, nor his Bishop's £500 either) that he could no longer afford to make war. His body was exhausted, too, worn out by his manic lusts of the flesh and his growing corpulence and the festering sore in his leg, which had plagued him for years after an accident in the tilting yard.

And when he died, in the New Year of 1547, they buried him in the quire at Windsor beside Jane Seymour, whose life had ended in giving him the son he had for so long obsessively craved. The Dean and Chapter there were given lands worth £600 a year, in exchange for which two priests were to say daily Masses for Henry in perpetuity, say a special Matins, a special Vespers for the dead and a special Mass for the dead four times a year, and preach a sermon every week in front of the local townsfolk. A Catholic in communion with Rome could scarcely have asked for more.

With the accession of Edward VI, the English Church was to proceed even further along the way it had travelled from Rome. Only nine years old when he inherited the Crown, the third Tudor King was not announced to his subjects for a couple of days, so that all the seaports of England could be sealed and other precautions be taken against a coup d'état when word was released of Henry's death; such was the precarious tension that had been reached in the religious power struggle behind the throne, in which Edward's eldest sister, Mary Tudor, long banished from court because of her devotion to Romish ways, was very obviously waiting in the wings. On account of his age, Edward had been placed by Henry's express order under the protection of a regency, a committee of trusties which included Thomas Cranmer and Cuthbert Tunstall, and was initially led by Edward Seymour, Duke of Somerset, who increasingly dominated affairs until he was deposed in 1549 by John Dudley, Earl of Warwick, later Duke of Northumberland. Both these men were Reformers, though Seymour could be uncommonly benevolent towards those who differed from him (as Dudley never was), most notably in the clemency he offered protesters in southern and eastern counties who demonstrated against a number of agrarian policies, though even this was not without a religious dimension. Very little had been, or would be in the sixteenth century, after Edward's father dispensed with the papacy.

The new era began with a series of declarations which made plain what was now in store for the nation. At the end of July 1547, thirty-six Injunctions devised by Somerset and Cranmer detailed the forms of worship and ecclesiastical behaviour that were to be followed henceforth; four months later the Sacrament Act was promulgated 'against Revilers and for Receiving in Both Kinds'; and before the year had ended there was also the Election of Bishops Act, which announced that 'the King may by his letters patent at all times when any archbishopric or bishopric be void, confer the same to any person whom the King shall think meet'. At the same time, an official visitation was launched in August to inspect and enquire into the country's spiritual health, William Benson (Dean of Westminster) and Nicholas Ridley (about to become Bishop of Rochester) being among those charged with visiting the dioceses of York, Durham, Carlisle and Chester. Ahead of them, each Deanery was sent the sort of questionnaire that Thomas Cromwell's commissioners would have recognised, but almost no documentary evidence in any part of the northern Province has survived. We know little apart from the fact that Hugh Whitehead and his Chapter spent £15 4s 8d on entertaining the Visitors, 10s going to their servants, 54s 8d 'in expenses of lunch and dinner provided for the visitors and in food for horses'; they also disbursed 'by arrangement to the Lord King 100s'. We know, too, that in the wake of the visitation, the old monastic Kepier Hospital in Durham was closed, and that the city's Corpus Christi guild was suppressed.

Edward Seymour's alliance with Cranmer set the course of the English Church for the rest of Edward's kingship and, in spite of a brief interruption while Mary Tudor reigned and another disruption during the Commonwealth, settled its future into our own time more than four hundred years later. From the outset it was ordained that the Epistles and Gospels must be read in English, followed within twelve months by the inclusion of some English prayers at Mass; and this licensed an alliance between full-blooded Reformers and printers to publish tracts against the Roman version of Holy Communion, which would have been unthinkable in Henry's time. The Protector and the Archbishop were also behind an Act of Parliament in 1549 which permitted clergy to wed, and which would have come as a relief to Cranmer more than anyone.

In his salad days at Cambridge, before he became a priest, he had married someone we know only as Joan and had lost his Fellowship of Jesus College as a result, making ends meet thereafter as a much more humble reader at the Benedictine Buckingham College (subsequently Magdalene) in the university. Within a year or so, Joan died giving birth to a child which didn't survive either, and the widower returned to Jesus to continue a career which would give him a leading role in the English Reformation. Some seventeen years later, in 1532, on the eve of succeeding William Warham in Lambeth Palace, the Archbishop-elect married Margarete, a relation of the Nuremberg theologian Andreas Osiander, with whom Cranmer had become friends.

It has been convincingly suggested that this second marriage, no less than his experience of Nuremberg generally, changed Cranmer's attitude crucially away from his Roman obedience to a belief that it was the monarch, not the Pope, 'who exercised supreme jurisdiction of all descriptions within his realm'. At any rate, the marriage prospered and produced children though, improbable as it now seems, the presence of Mistress Margaret Cranmer in the Primate's household remained an official secret; which may have meant that most of her life before 1549 was spent at the archiepiscopal Ford Palace in Kent, a prudent distance away from the sharp eyes and ears and chattering tongues of the capital. But Cranmer would have been relieved when the new measure became law, making him the only Archbishop of Canterbury who would ever spend years with a secret life before feeling able to come out of the closet.[2]

Quite as momentous as the law by which Margaret Cranmer was at last recognised for who she was, was the Act of Uniformity which followed it a few months later in 1549. For this abolished the newly modified Latin Mass and decreed that henceforth the legal form of worship would be that set down in *The Booke of the Common Prayer and Administracion of the Sacraments and other Rites and Ceremonies of*

---

[2] It was only after Cranmer was burned at the stake in 1556, a heretic in Mary Tudor's eyes, that a scurrilous rumour surfaced to the effect that during the seventeen years of his supposed celibacy, the Archbishop had kept Margaret hidden in a large box with breathing holes.

the Churche after the use of the Churche of England; whose very first words (in its Preface) were 'There was neuer any thing by the wit of man so well deuised, or so surely established, which (in continuance of time) hath not been corrupted ...'. The most beautiful and luminous language that the English-speaking world would ever employ for liturgical purposes, and (by the time it had evolved into the version of 1662) one of the supreme works of English literature, was initially composed by a committee of thirteen divines but Cranmer, who led them, was principally responsible for the unforgettable cadences, the flowing style, the perfect balance between the numinous and the heartfelt devotion of the very ordinary folk who apprehended it. His second marriage quite possibly had something to do with that, too, for the 1549 Prayer Book followed many Lutheran usages, and some of its most memorable phrases ('Whom God hath joined, let no man put asunder') are distinctly German in origin.

This harmony between Church and state was disturbed by the transfer of power from Seymour to Dudley, from a stance that was Reforming but tolerant to one that was much more adamantly evangelical. In the name of her young brother, the Princess Mary was forbidden to attend Mass, for the Communion which she had continued to receive privately in the Roman manner in spite of all that had happened since their father assumed the pontiff's role locally. Bonfires of books (ever a sign of something nasty on the march) flared up across the land, the more conservative bishops were replaced by men who rejoiced in the flames, and the diocese of Norwich, drawing much of its sustenance still from the former Benedictine occupants of the Cathedral close, was subjected to particular attention by Cranmer's officials, who came down heavily on the slightest trace of anything that might have represented a wistfulness for the old times. Among other things, this meant that stone altars were instantly dismantled throughout East Anglia, so that the Lord's Table became literally that, a still substanial piece of church furniture, but now made of wood.

Durham was not spared this wind of change, and Cuthbert Tunstall was the first person there to feel the draught. Always a moderate but invariably more attracted by tradition than by revolutionary dogma, he had opposed the marriage of priests, and had argued a Catholic case during the Parliamentary debates which preceded the arrival of the Prayer Book. His principal stumbling block was its treatment of the Sacramental elements as mere bread and wine which were taken 'in remembraunce of me', rather than accepted as the literal body and blood of Christ.[3] The balance of power in the episcopate that year is indicated by the fact that he was one of eight bishops who voted against the measure in the House of Lords, with ten of its supporters finally seeing it onto the statute book. Protector Somerset had not allowed this obstruction to damage his regard for Tunstall, however; but John Dudley was a harder, more ambitious and more dangerous man and he moved against the Bishop the moment he assumed power, deceptively at first.

At the beginning of Dudley's regime, Tunstall was restored to the leadership of the Council of the North after an absence of eleven years, and received smaller marks of the new Protector's favour. As President of the Council, he summoned the belligerent John Knox (fresh from his captivity on the rowing bench of a French naval galley) to Newcastle to answer for some of the inflammatory things he had been saying about traditional doctrines; which Knox seized as an excellent opportunity to repeat that the Mass was idolatry and an abomination before God (he later reckoned that he had also told 'the false Bishop of Durham, before his own face . . . [that he was a] murderer and thief'). Knox certainly had the approval of Dudley – he was invited to London, where he preached at court – and this may well have influenced the subsequent course of events, though there were also grounds for believing that the Duke of Northumberland (as Dudley was from 1551) coveted northern lands that had traditionally been held by local magnates like the Percys, the Nevilles – and the Prince Bishops of Durham. This, too, may have had a bearing on what followed. Certainly, Dudley wrote to the Principal Secretary, Sir William Cecil, saying that the Palatinate jurisdiction should be altered in the same way that Chester's had been once before, 'that is, not abolished, but annexed to the royal domain in perpetuity'.

---

[3] A crucial passage in the Prayer Book was the Exhortation of the Curate (but at Matins styled a priest, as though by a slip of the pen) that 'if, with a truly penitent heart and liuely faith ... we spiritually eate the fleshe of Christ, and drinke his bloude, then we dwell in Christ and Christ in us, wee bee made one with Christ, and Christ with us . . .'.

Tunstall was in his turn summoned to the capital, where 'he was required to sign certain ordinances made here respecting religion', according to the Emperor Charles's ambassador Jehan Scheyfve, one of the few sources of surviving information about what happened next. 'He had refused to do so several times already; and as he persisted in his refusal, he was ordered to withdraw to his house in London and not to stir abroad until further orders.' The Bishop was not only put under house arrest at Coldharbour on Thames Street; he was also charged with misprision, which was but marginally less serious than treason, because it meant deliberate concealment of the more capital offence: he was reckoned to have been aware of an incipient northern rising against the Crown, which he had failed to report in Council to the higher authority, supposedly to restore Edward Seymour to the Protectorship. Dudley interrogated Tunstall in person, then appeared for several months to have let the matter drop, though the Bishop was still confined to his London home.

In May 1551 he was re-examined before the Privy Council where, according to Scheyfve, 'he defended to the last the mystery of the Mass and the Holy Sacrament'. The house arrest continued, while efforts were made to find incriminating material about the rumoured rising, and Dudley moved against Seymour in a strategy that culminated in the latter's execution in January 1552. By then, just before Christmas, Tunstall had been brought before the Council again because the hostile evidence had apparently turned up, hidden in a casket. 'His own letter', the proceedings recorded, 'was produced against him, which he could not deny but to be of his own hand, and being unable to make farther answer than he had done before by writing, he was, for that same seemed not a sufficient answer, committed by the King's Majesty's commandment to ward to the Tower of London, to abide there such order as his doings by the course of the law shall appear to have deserved.' Whereupon, Tunstall's 'goods, chattels, money and other things' in Durham and in London were seized and he was deprived of his see, an action which Cranmer rather bravely opposed. Within weeks, Dudley had taken steps to ensure that he himself would alone control the Palatinate lands in future.

In October 1552, the Bishop of Durham was brought to trial on

Tower Hill in what had once been the house of Dominicans, and Jehan Scheyfve is our only source for an outline account of what happened at the hearing:

> He was accused of having received seditious letters, conducive to insurrection, two years ago from certain gentlemen in Norfolk, which letters he had not denounced to the King and his Council within twenty-four hours, as ordered by an Act of Parliament, but had kept them five days before giving information. He excused himself by saying he had intended to deliver the author of the letters over to Council, and had sent a message back by the bearer of the letters, saying he wished to speak to the said gentleman. He professed to be ignorant of the passing of the Act, and declared that there could be no room for suspecting him of treason or criminal intelligence, for he was an old servant of the King's progenitors. But he was sentenced as a perjurer, and for a breach of the said Act, and therefore as guilty of minor treason, as they call it, towards the King's majesty.

Whereupon the Bishop was returned to the Tower, though not for long before being removed to the King's Bench Prison in Southwark. There he started writing a book on the Sacramental element in the Eucharist. And there he remained for the next three years, until Mary Tudor succeeded to the throne, released him, and restored him to his see as a still active Bishop of Durham at the age of seventy-nine.

Cuthbert Tunstall's predicament involved Hugh Whitehead as well. The Dean and Chapter of Durham would have regarded the imposition of the new Prayer Book with very mixed feelings, especially with regret that the old Latin Mass was now well and truly buried in the past: every one of them, after all, had spent most of his life so far as a Benedictine monk. On the other hand, the new service book contained a number of things with a familiar ring to them, for Thomas Cranmer was devoted to the Sarum Use above all other medieval rites, such as those which were particularly attached to the cathedrals of Hereford, Bangor and York; he found the subtle variations which were traditionally practised in Salisbury more pleasing both to the ear and to his sense of devotion. Durham had always used an ancient rite that was common to many Benedictine houses, but its clergy would not have felt completely lost in the Anglicised prayer of consecration and other passages, which held closely to the old formularies; although there were sixty-seven collects now notably derived from Salisbury. Other things in the new pattern of worship had recognisable origins in the monastic past, too. 'An Order For Mattyns Dayly Through the Yere' ('The Priest beeying in the quier, shall begynne with a loude voyce the Lordes prayer, called the Pater noster') was but an amalgamation of the old offices of Mattins and Lauds, while its evening counterpart ('An Order for Euensong Throughout the Yeare') brought Vespers and Compline together in one.

The Cathedral clergy were, of their nature and their history, however, conservatives to a man, and as such they were bound to be more in sympathy with Cuthbert Tunstall than any body of wholehearted Reformers could possibly have been. Dean Whitehead, with a past spent notoriously in total harmony with his Bishop, certainly as far as Church order was concerned and doubtless theologically as well, was especially vulnerable to any suspicions that might be entertained about Tunstall. On 15 May 1551, William Paulet, Earl of Wiltshire and King Edward's Lord Treasurer, informed Sir William Cecil that 'I have written to [the Bishop of] Durham and the dean to be at court on Monday'. This might have meant an attendance for witness questioning about Tunstall's behaviour, and any whispers that might have reached the Deanery about a possible uprising in the North; but, in fact, it was much graver than that. For on the previous 15 August, the Privy Council had communicated with Sir Robert Bowes – sometime rebel himself, now a pillar of the northern establishment – 'declaring unto him that information was given to Sir Thomas Hilton of a great quantity of treasure conveyed into the Dean of Durham's chamber, wherefore he was required to confer thereupon with the same Sir Thomas at his coming down, and to proceed to the search of it or otherwise as they two should think good'. Hilton, another big figure in the Palatinate, had also been tainted by the Pilgrimage of Grace, on whose behalf he had negotiated with the Duke of Norfolk at Doncaster in October 1536, but he, too, had subsequently become a devoted government man.

Whitehead was cited in the warrant which despatched his Bishop to house arrest on 20 May but by 8 June he still hadn't turned up at Westminster, and he was sent a very sharp letter 'to answer in writing unto such matter as he was charged withall at his being before the Council, and to answer in such sort as he will stand to at his peril'. Over a month later, he was said to have acknowledged 'the said recognisance accordingly, and then to continue his attendance from time to time before their Lordships till they shall enlarge him'. It is not at all clear when he actually arrived in London to face whatever charges had been drawn up by then, but on 3 November the Privy Council – the Duke of Northumberland and Sir Robert Bowes being present – noted that 'The Dean of Durham doth knowledge to owe to the King's Majesty, our Sovereign Lord, two hundred marks of lawful money of England ... Upon condition that the said Dean shall appear before the Lords of his Majesty's Privy Council the first day of the next term, and in the mean season be always ready to appear upon reasonable warning given him by their Lordships unless it shall appear evidently that he be in such terms of sickness as conveniently he cannot make his appearance in that behalf.' He was, in short, bound over to appear before interrogators on the due date.

We have no idea what was the treasure that he had supposedly concealed in the Deanery and we can only speculate that it might just have included the 107 alabaster figures that had gone missing from the Neville screen at the surrender.[4] All would have been revealed in the next stage of these proceedings, but Hugh Whitehead never did appear at the new term of the Counsellors. He died in London within a few days of the Privy Council's order at the age of seventy-one or thereabouts, worn out by the anxious years and the manoeuvring necessary to ensure the survival at least in part of the ethos by which he had lived, and of the fabric of his old Priory church; disheartened, probably, by his failure to bring with him into the future his entire community of Benedictine brethren; and fearful, perhaps, of what the future might now hold for him personally.

---

[4] Patrick Mussett has put it to me that the alabaster figures may not have been removed until Edward's or even Elizabeth's time. The fact is that we simply do not know their fate.

He was buried not in the cemetery of the place which was dearest to him, where Thomas Swalwell and many of his old brethren lay, but near the old Jewish quarter of Houndsditch, in the faraway City, in the Minories church of the Holy Trinity, which had once belonged to the Poor Clares (or Minor canonesses) who had evolved from the Franciscan Order.[5] By the end of January, the Clerk of the King's Majesty's Larder had been instructed to hand over to Hugh's kinsmen, Christopher and Thomas Whitehead, 'all such goods and chatells as he hath in his custody belonging to Hugh Whitehed, late Dean of Duresme': most of them were probably books he had collected throughout his life, which certainly included a breviary which has survived to this day.

An obituary was written by some anonymous chronicler who may have been personally acquainted with the Dean.[6] Whose whole life, he said, 'was given up to the worship of God. He was in truth entirely given up to the love of God; he always maintained around him a large household, and in his lodging he had a very great number of gentlemen and lowly men, by whom he was served in an honourable manner. His table was liberal and generously provided. At Bearpark he repaired many buildings that were collapsing from age. He also at Pittington built a new hall, called "The Priors Halle", with other buildings attached to each end of this hall. His charity was abundant, and the purity of his life was worthy of praise ...'.

That does not read like hearsay. It has a ring of familiarity which suggests that Hugh Whitehead, once the Prior of a great Benedictine monastery, later an ecclesiastical functionary in fee to a Protestant government, was remembered with great and affectionate respect by someone who had known him well and had, perhaps, even supped at his table.

---

[5] It was destroyed during the London Blitz of 1940, and no trace of it has survived.
[6] The obituary has sometimes been erroneously attributed to William de Chambre, who was marshal of the Priory's guest hall in the fourteenth century. The confusion has arisen from the fact that the obituary was attached to something de Chambre may or may not have written, leading to a false assumption when the Durham chronicles were published in 1839.

XIV

THE ICONOCLAST

✠

*'There are also many secrets of Chapter which are to be revealed to no-one,
not even to an absent member upon his return to Chapter or the Church...'*

STATUTES AND ORDINANCES OF THE CATHEDRAL CHURCH OF
CHRIST AND THE BLESSED VIRGIN MARY OF DURHAM, MARCH 1554

Dean Whitehead's successor at Durham, appointed when November
1551 was scarcely halfway through, was a different sort of cleric. Robert
Horne was a Cumbrian and a Cambridge don, a Hebrew specialist
who had been made Fellow of St John's during the Pilgrimage of
Grace. One of his patrons then was Sir Richard Rich, Henry VIII's
Solicitor-General and subsequent Chancellor of Augmentations, a
man detested by the Pilgrims ever since his treatment of Bishop John
Fisher before the latter's trial and execution in 1535. Horne had also
been the Vicar of an Essex parish before he moved in 1550 to London,
where he quickly became known as a trenchant evangelical preacher, a
talent which led to his being chosen by Edward's government to argue
disputatiously against people like Cuthbert Tunstall on the subject of
the Eucharist in the preparatory stages of the new Prayer Book. He
also had a hand in devising the Forty-two Articles of Religion which
defined the most important tenets of English Protestantism.[1]

---

[1] These would within eleven years have been modified into the Thirty-nine Articles
which appear at the back of the Book of Common Prayer even now (with their
definitions Of the Sufficiency of the Holy Scriptures for Salvation, Of Original or
Birth-sin, Of Works of Supererogation, Of Predestination and Election, Of speaking
in the congregation in such a Tongue as the people understandeth etc. etc.)

It was this reputation that propelled Horne into the Durham Deanery with his wife Margery, a Calvinist. Almost at once there was discord in and around the College, where only one of the original prebendaries had died thus far, as Horne's philosophy collided abruptly with his new colleagues' traditional views, and the friction became so serious that in February 1552 the Privy Council felt obliged to order the Durham Chapter to accept his instructions on how the Cathedral services should be conducted, at the same time emphasising the need for them to behave more charitably towards their new Dean. But the abrasiveness was clearly not all one-sided and, even if the author of *Rites of Durham* was not only writing nostalgically but tendentiously as well nearly half a century later, it is clear that Horne himself had much to answer for.

In the cloister garth there had long been a statue of St Cuthbert, 'a goodlie & verie large & greate thick Imadge of stone ... verie fynely and curioslie pictured and wrowght in ye said stone with paintinge & gilktinge marvellous bewtifull & excellent to behold in forme & fashion as he was accustomed to saie masse wth his myter on his head & his croisier staff in his hand'; the monument marked the spot where the saint's body had lain when it first arrived at the Priory after the journey from the White Church in 995. Horne, this accuser declared, 'caused ye said monumt to be pulled down & converted ye lead & all to his own use', St Cuthbert's image being parked against a doorway leading into what had been the monks' cemetery. The cloister also contained stained glass which depicted 'ye hole storie & myricles of that holie man Sacte Cuthb; from ye daie of his Nativitie & birth vnto his dyinge daie' and 'this story was pulled downe by Deane Horne & broken all to peces, for he might neur abyde any auncient monumt, actes, or deades, that gave any light of godly Religion'. The now decidedly ex-patron saint's memorials weren't the only things to suffer from the new man's vigour. In the nearby church of St Nicholas there was a Corpus Christi shrine which this rampant cleric 'did treade and breake in pieces wth his feet wth many other ornamentt'.[2]

---

[2] Horne's iconoclasm was to continue after he left Durham. As Bishop of Winchester and Visitor of colleges in both Oxford and Cambridge many years later, he became a notorious smasher of images, windows, vestments and architectural features, silencer of organs and defiler of books.

Cuthbert Tunstall was another who was affronted by the Dean, regarding him with as much distaste as he did John Knox. The antipathy was mutual, and there has long been a suspicion, based on an entry in Edward VI's own Journal, that Horne laid information before the government eleven months after he had been installed in the Deanery, about a plot by the Earl of Westmorland in 1551 to raise popular support against the debasement of the currency; that this information encouraged the authorities to bring Tunstall to trial, and led to the offer that was made to Robert Horne shortly afterwards. For it was on 28 October 1552 that the Duke of Northumberland wrote to William Cecil, lobbying for Knox to be made Bishop of Rochester ('he would be a whetstone to sharpen the Archbishop of Canterbury and confound the Anabaptists lately sprung up in Kent') and making another suggestion, this one about a replacement for Tunstall. 'If the dean of Durham is appointed bishop with 1,000 marks or more than his deanery, the houses he now has in the city and country will serve honourably – so may the king receive the castle, which has a princely site, and the other stately houses the bishop had in the country.'

An extension of Dudley's proposal was to split the diocese in two so that henceforth there would be a Bishop Horne in Durham and some other placeman sitting as Bishop of a new see in Newcastle, who would be financed, in part, with revenues enjoyed by the suffragan Bishop of Berwick. As this was still the former Benedictine Thomas Sparke, who was also third prebendary in the Chapter, the proposal can be seen as another act to reduce the old order in Durham, which had become an increasing irritant to the government. The plan was never adopted, however, at least partly because the Dean declined to be made into a bishop: at which the equally vigorous and evangelical Nicholas Ridley, Bishop of London, was primed to take Tunstall's place in Durham, which was regarded as much the more important of the two sees. By May 1553, the traditional lands of the Prince Bishops had become the King's County Palatine of Durham, though the Duke of Northumberland never would get his hands on them more than nominally as their Steward.

John Dudley swiftly became disillusioned at the setback to his careful preparations for a transformation of the North, writing in a much different tone about Robert Horne in early December 1552. 'This peevish Dean', he told Cecil then, 'should not receive what is meet for as grave a man as may be found. I am credibly informed he is loose of tongue, and lets not to talk on his ale bench that if he may not have it after his own will he will refuse it.' Clearly, the terms offered with his promotion to the episcopacy had not been substantial enough for the iconoclast. A month later, and Horne had descended even further in Dudley's estimation. 'I have been much deceived by him' was the Duke's attitude now, 'he is greedy, malicious, and an open evil speaker of which enough now can report. Let not the see be so long destitute of some grave, good man that knows his duty to God and his king rather than one of these new obstinate doctors without humanity or honest conditions.' And then, in a swipe that probably nettled Thomas Cranmer when he heard of it, 'Most of those whom the king has lately preferred are so sotted with wives and children that they forget their poor neighbours and all else pertaining to their calling – so will they so long as his majesty allows them so great possessions to maintain their idle lives.'

The Dean and Chapter did not have to endure their mutual dislike for much longer by then because on 6 July 1553, Edward VI died at the age of sixteen, a sickly, consumptive lad from the day of his birth. At once the nation was thrown into disarray, such as it had not known when Henry's majesty passed to the boy King; the utterly Catholic Mary Tudor had always been the principal lady in waiting for the Crown, but the Duke of Northumberland was by now promoting his daughter-in-law and Edward's cousin Lady Jane Grey (as was) with the obvious intention of being the real power behind the throne. Although Mary's chances appeared to be the slimmer at the outset, and although England did have a nominal Queen Jane for nine days, Northumberland's plan was a family catastrophe, which ended with his being executed, together with his son and the utterly innocent Jane, while Nicholas Ridley, who had been a vociferous preacher in favour of the Protestant nominee, was deprived of his see; and within a couple of years he would be burned at the stake for heresy.

Mary Tudor had a great deal of anger, pent up since the day her mother was abandoned by her father and she herself was banished from his court, waiting to be released the moment she became Queen. Her reign would be remembered most for the number of people who went to the scaffold or the stake for professing Reformed Christianity, including Thomas Cranmer, Hugh Latimer (Bishop of Worcester) and John Hooper (Bishop of the amalgamated dioceses of Gloucester and Worcester), as well as Nicholas Ridley, who were all burned as heretics. She ruled a people with a congenital hostility to Spain and she lost their sympathy by marrying the Holy Roman Emperor's Spanish son Philip, who effectively abandoned her as soon as it became unlikely that she would produce a son, the Privy Council having insisted before the marriage took place that under no circumstances could Philip ever rule England alone if his wife predeceased him. Locked and lonely in a loveless union, detested by an increasing number of her subjects because of her cruelty, childless, and losing the last English enclave in France on top of everything else, Mary Tudor was ultimately a tragic figure, whose reign was even shorter than her brother's had been.

Her arrival had been a tonic to the Durham Chapter, however, for Robert Horne was another casualty of the change in sovereign and ecclesiastical power. Queen Mary, wishing to appear no less clement than her predecessors on reaching the throne, officially pardoned many Protestant clergy for their errant ways on condition that they amended their lives, but Horne was excluded from the list. He was summoned from Durham to appear before the Privy Council and answer a charge of heresy, and one of his accusers there was the newly appointed Cuthbert Tunstall, who declared that the Dean had 'infected his whole diocese with new learning', having arrogated to himself a quasi-episcopal role; much worse, he had brought a wife into Durham Cathedral, 'where never woman came before'. Another hostile inter-rogator, Stephen Gardiner, Bishop of Winchester, charged him with having failed to answer three letters summoning him to the Council, which was not true.

Horne, believing that he was about to be sent to the Tower, and hearing that his goods had been confiscated in Durham, wisely decided to get out of England fast. At the end of October he fled to Strasbourg, then went to Zurich before moving on to Frankfurt, to lecture to the expatriate English congregation there and to become its pastor. Bitterly he denounced what was happening back in the Palatine, where the new regime meant 'God's book containing the word of life taken forth of the churches of the bishopric of Durham, and a foul sort of idols called Laymen's Books brought in ... the Common Prayer in the vulgar tongue ... banished, and in place thereof a kind of prayer used, far dissonant from the example of the primitive church, in a strange tongue ...'. Abominably, the new order also meant 'the Lord's Table taken away ... and Baal's altars reared up'. His recent charge on Wearside had become 'devilish dreaming Durham' now.

For all but one of the canons residing in the College, Mary's accession also meant a welcome return to ways they had been forced to relinquish over thirteen years earlier, and was signalled almost at once by the appointment of Thomas Watson, the conservative Gardiner's chaplain, to succeed Robert Horne in the Deanery.[3] This meant, for a start, that they would once again say and sing the old monastic offices. On 18 January 1554, just over a fortnight before her marriage, Mary issued the letters patent which ratified the Henrician status quo in the Durham diocese, thereby ending any hopes Newcastle might have had of equal status. Tunstall was restored to his see, while 'the Dean and Prebendaries of the said Cathedral Church of Durham and their successors ... be and shall be in time to come for ever annexed, incorporated and united to the aforesaid Cuthbert ... and his successors ...'. Shortly afterwards, in the name of 'Philip and Mary, by the grace of God King and Queen (*sic*) of England, France, Naples, Jerusalem and Ireland, Defenders of the Faith, Princes of the Spains and of Sicily, Archdukes of Austria, Dukes of Milan, Burgundy and Brabant, Counts of Hapsburg, Flanders and Tyrol', the Dean and Chapter of Durham received their new statutes.

They came in a document of forty 'chapters' plus addenda, which had been composed in Latin by Nicholas Heath, Archbishop-elect

---

[3] The odd man out was the Reformer John Rudd, appointed to succeed Ralph Blakiston in the tenth prebend on the latter's death in 1550. He was deprived of his stall by Mary in 1554 and succeeded by George Bullock, who occupied it until 1559 when he was in his turn deprived by Elizabeth.

of York, Edmund Bonner, the restored Bishop of London, Thomas Thirlby, Bishop of Ely, and Cuthbert Tunstall, with the assistance of 'our faithful chaplain William Ermysted', who was also Master of the Temple and a canon residentiary of St Paul's. They were intended to regulate the whole existence of a quite considerable community gathered up to the Cathedral: one Dean and twelve canons, twelve minor canons, one Deacon, one sub-Deacon, ten clerks 'who may be either laymen or priests', one Master of the Choristers, ten choristers, two instructors of the boys in grammar, 'of whom one shall be Preceptor, the other Under-preceptor', eighteen boys to be instructed in grammar, eight poor men, two sub-Sacrists 'who shall also be Vergers', two ministers 'who shall ring the bells and look to the clock', two porters, one of them the barber, another butler, another under-butler, one cook, one under-cook. 'Who shall all diligently do service in the same Church . . .'.

The statutes were a revision of the ones bestowed by Mary's father and one of the two most significant changes was that she dropped his possessive references to the Cathedral (*ecclesia nostra* – 'our church') and instead spoke of it impersonally. The other amendment of moment was part of the Dean's new job description. As before, he was required to be 'not only learned, but also distinguished by a title in learning, that is, a Doctor or Bachelor of Divinity, or a Doctor of Law' who had lived a previously unblemished life, but this was no longer enough: from now on he must also be 'of sound and Catholic faith and free from any suspicion of heresy', which was not a qualification that Henry VIII had thought it necessary to emphasise. Provided a candidate measured up to these standards, he was to swear on oath that 'according to my manhood' he would 'bear rule and governance in this Church well and faithfully . . .'. The prebendaries, too, had to meet similar requirements, though in their case being merely a Bachelor of Law would see them through. That much was revision, but the first four chapters of the Marian statutes were entirely new, with a preamble justifying the changes now made, a definition of the Bishop's role, which gave him precedence over the Dean and Chapter and allowed him to preach in the Cathedral whenever he chose, an order for the installation and admission of the Dean and a definition of his powers, and a similar treatment 'Of the Entry and Installation of the Canons'.

There were other rules that Hugh Whitehead would instantly have recognised from his own reinstallation in the 1540s. The Dean must be vigilant 'even as the eye in the body'. He must admonish and beseech the canons and all other ministers when the occasion demanded it, 'chide and rebuke them, and be instant in season and out of season, as keeping sleepless watch over the rest of the flock committed to his care'. The divine offices (still to be performed according to the Salisbury rite) must be celebrated with decency, the Dean must preach sermons on Easter Sunday, on Christmas day, at Corpus Christi and on other prescribed days, boys must be profitably trained, alms distributed to the poor. The Dean must maintain 'an honest household befitting his dignity', must behave honourably and thriftily (but 'A Dean who is mean and miserly shall be chastised by the Bishop of Durham; while Canons Resident who offend in like manner shall be chastised by the Dean'). He must, of course, keep his eye on all the treasure, jewels and ornaments of the Cathedral, all the lands, advowsons; also the appointment of minor canons, of boys learning grammar; and when visiting the manors and other properties in the line of duty, he was to be paid 6s 8d a day in expenses.

He must normally reside at home in the Deanery 'unless a lawful impediment prevent him', in which case he should still be counted as being present 'as regards the receipt of all profits and emoluments from the said Church' provided that, on his return, 'he shall prove before the Chapter the cause of his absence'. All the other Cathedral clergy had to do him reverence, 'obey, hearken to, assist and aid not only the Dean himself but also (in his absence) the Vice-dean or (in the absence of both) the senior Resident who is then present'. The canons must fulfil a minimal residential requirement, too, each being allowed eighty days in the year in which to visit their various benefices, and at least one third of them must be in the College at any time. The Dean was allowed one hundred days of absence to attend to 'his cures of souls and other benefices . . . and to despatch the rest of his private business'. He could also stay at Bearpark for another forty days, so long as he came into the Cathedral once a day for one of the hours or the High Mass, and attended all meetings of Chapter. Like all the other seniors, he took his place in a rota which saw everyone putting in stints of twenty-one days' uninterrupted residence.

He was to be paid £40 0s 15d 'as the bodily substance of his Deanery', every canon £8 4s 9 ¹/₂d, as the substance of his prebend, but these were only part of their emoluments. For every day the Dean appeared at Matins, the High Mass or at Vespers clad in his vestments, he was to receive another 12s 5d, while the canons who did likewise earned 16 ¹/₂d. The clergy had to be present from start to finish of these services, mind; there was to be no turning up and leaving again halfway through 'unless the constraint of nature without any feigning compel them, in which case let them leave the Church and return as quickly as they can'. On top of all that, each of them 'shall keep and retain all those lands, tenements, grazings, pastures or tithes ... for the provision and increase of hospitality'. There was a kitty (the common dividend) consisting of fines imposed for unauthorised absences from the Deanery or the College, and every Michaelmas it was shared between the clergy, the Dean collecting twice as much as any canon. There was also a system of fines for those lower down the order of precedence who didn't turn up for services: a penny in the case of minor canons and clerks who missed Matins or High Mass, a halfpenny for Vespers or Compline, a farthing for Prime, Terce, Sext or None.

The source of the additional territorial incomes were carefully set down in the statutes. The Dean's portion was 'the manor and park of Bearpark, with Arbour Close and three arable closes by Stotgate; Alansford with Shipley and Whitehall, North and South Ravensflat with Summer Pasture and Holme; the tithes of the Rectories of Billingham and of Merrington, and of all the towns appertaining to them'. The first canon had one half of Elvet Hall manor (Hallgarth), the second canon the other half. The third canon had the manor of Houghall, the fourth canon the manor house and farm of Witton Gilbert, Newhouse and Underside. The fifth, sixth and eighth canons each had a third of the manor house and park of Muggleswick, while the seventh canon enjoyed the house and demesne lands of the manor of Finchale with the mill and pond called the Dam. The ninth canon had the manor of Relley and Almoner's Barns, the tenth canon had the chief farm of the lands and tenements of South Pittington with the manor house, the orchard and the close called Pulterclose. The eleventh canon had the farm of the manor of Houghall, the twelfth canon the manor house of Bewley and its demesnes.

Property of one kind and another was considered in great detail, the whole of chapter 9 being devoted to the treatment of woodlands and everything that depended on them. The Dean was expressly forbidden to give anyone woods or trees 'fit for timber' or let anything without 'the counsel and consent of the Chapter', though he was allowed to give lessees timber for the repair of their premises without consulting his colleagues. Woodlands must be enclosed by a ditch or fences so that

> the beasts may not graze upon and pluck the tender woods and sprouting buds. And since in great part the principal treasure of this Church consists in woodland, we therefore appoint that, whensoever timber ought to be felled of thick oaks or other green trees for the necessary construction or repair of the Church, buildings, tenements or other matters ... nothing thereof shall be sold but the bark and tops which are useless for timber, and the felling of timber shall always be done at convenient seasons, so that the stumps may be able to shoot again, unless need require that it be done otherwise. Let tallies also or writings be made of the number of trees felled and for what purpose ... [4]

There was a great sense of hierarchy throughout the statutes and a number of roles were clearly defined. The vice-Dean sat next to the Dean in choir 'and higher in order than the rest, and accordingly more diligent and circumspect than the rest in the business of the Church'. The Receiver 'shall collect and receive all moneys, rents as well temporal as spiritual of lands tenements and churches' and pass them on to the Treasurer within twenty-eight days at most. The Treasurer's

---

[4] This reflected an attitude to conservation that Mary had inherited from her father, on whom it had dawned one day that the nation's timber resources were not inexhaustible, to the detriment of the navy he was carefully building at the time. Henry's discovery led to an Act for the Preservation of Woods in 1543, the very first piece of environmental legislation in English history.

responsibility was to pay all the stipends to the clergy and other monies that appeared in the accounts as outgoings; but he also had to repair 'the fabric of the temple and the houses of the ministers within the enclosure of the Church' except those of the Dean and Chapter, whose members were individually responsible for the upkeep of their dwellings. The twelve minor canons, the ten clerks, the Deacon and the sub-Deacon (the last two charged with singing the Gospel and the Epistle), had been appointed 'to chant the praises of God and the canonical hours continually in the temple of the Church ... fit to do service in Choir with voice and cunning'. One of the minor canons, 'of riper age and special distinction', was to be the Precentor, whose duty was 'to control with decorum them that make music in the Church, to stir up the careless to sing, to reprove with moderation and to keep quiet those that make disturbance and run about the Choir in disorder ...': he also had to oversee the music-making and 'finally to lead the rest with his voice in song and to be as it were the leader, that no discord may arise during the singing'.

The Sacrist had duties that any Benedictine would have recognised, to do with altars and chapels, vessels and books, relics and muniments, wax and wine; also custody of the book cupboard and the library. Under him was the Verger, whose job was 'to carry the verge in front of the cross, and in every procession to go in front of the Choir and the Dean, and to walk before the Bishop if he be present, or, if he be absent, before the Dean when he comes to the temple and when he leaves the same ...'. A couple of honest men, working under the Sacrist, had to open all the Cathedral doors before six o'clock every morning and close them after Compline in winter, after the ringing of curfew in the lighter months, which had been the custom back in the days when Hugh Whitehead was elected Prior. 'And after that time let not the doors be opened unless there be great and urgent need, lest (which God forbid) foul deeds be done in the privy places of the Church, or they who ponder ill deeds may be able to lurk in the same.' So the list went on, down to the inferior servants of the Church, who were the butler and the under-butler, the cook and the under-cook, and two porters to keep the keys of the Cathedral and watch the gates. 'And we will that one of them perform the office of barber, who shall shear and shave all the persons of this church for nothing.'

Nothing was left to chance or anybody's whim, which was more or less the prescription of St Benedict when he composed his Rule. The canons and the Dean took most of their meals separately in their homes, but the bachelor minor canons, the Deacon, sub-Deacon 'and as many of the Clerks as have not wives' messed together in a common hall. The Common Seal of the Dean and Chapter must never be applied to a blank charter or palimpsest, or to any piece of writing without the Dean's consent. Chapter had to meet at least once a fortnight for the regular management of things, with two general Chapters a year (20 November and 20 July) when more weighty matters were reviewed. Prayers were to be said in the grammar school at six every morning, while the Poor Men (old pensioners on the establishment, as during the monastic years) had to say every morning, noon and eventide, the Lord's Prayer, the Angelic Salutation, the Apostles' Creed, the Ten Commandments and a special prayer for the sovereign.

These were the ordinances by which the Dean and Chapter of Durham were officially expected to regulate their lives for the foreseeable future, though it is perhaps unlikely that the incumbents of the Deanery and the College in 1554 supposed that they would be observed indefinitely, given the twists and turns and reversals in the Cathedral's recent history. But not only did the statutes outlast the Queen who had begotten them: they were to remain the framework within which the community functioned for the next four hundred years and more.

XV

A GREAT VILLAIN

✠

'*Christopher Neville, Cuthbert Neville, uncles of the said Earl of West-morland, and Thomas Markynfield, with others to the number of three score horsemen, armed in corselets and coats of plate, with spears, arquebuses and dagger ... entered the minster there and there took all the books but one, and them and the communion table defaced, rent and broke in pieces ...* '

SIR GEORGE BOWES TO THE EARL OF SUSSEX, 15 NOVEMBER 1569

The departure of Robert Horne and the arrival of Thomas Watson inevitably lightened the atmosphere in the Cathedral community, with an instant celebration in the Deanery, where a feast was laid, minstrels played and a bonfire was lit in the garden; this, however, can be seen as delight that traditional ways of worship, traditional spirituality, were to be restored rather more than enthusiasm for a renewed attachment to Rome. All would be benign again around the Cathedral, and the terror that swept other parts of the country, as Mary settled old scores and cleansed her realm of heretics, might have been on another planet as far as Durham was concerned. Throughout her reign, as the punitive fires blazed and executions were a regular and widespread occurrence which took almost three hundred lives, there was only one burning in the entire northern Province, at Chester in 1555.

Cuthbert Tunstall, close enough to the Crown again to be in the party which welcomed Cardinal Reginald Pole from Rome, sailed with him up the Thames from Gravesend and saw him installed in Lambeth Palace, was silent in the House of Lords when it debated a reimposition of the heresy laws, and passed the necessary legislation without a division. It is unlikely that he thought the pyre a very Christian way of dealing with recalcitrants, but the courage to disagree with his sovereign, which had enabled him to challenge Henry VIII as a young bishop, had quite deserted him now. His appearances in London quietly dwindled, and he busied himself in his diocese with obligations which fell upon him in his role as northern administrator for the government, examining the state of Hartlepool, settling aldermanic disputes in Newcastle, and dealing with the fallout from Border skirmishes.

Then everything was turned upside down yet again when Mary, never a well woman and further reduced by increasing alienation from her absentee husband as well as by the humiliating loss of Calais, died in November 1558 at the age of forty-two, only a few hours after Cardinal Pole had preceded her to the grave. Her whole life had been a struggle and she had put her half-sister Elizabeth in the Tower as a reflex move to survive part of it, though she gave the new Queen a half-blessing before she died, even though it was inevitable that her co-religionists would now suffer from a purge similar to the one she had inflicted on Protestants. Although Elizabeth's faith was not the thing above all else which drove her on (the need to survive in an extremely hostile world had always been and would remain the gal-vanising force in her life), she was a cradle Anglican, begotten of Anne Boleyn, who had caused Henry to break with Rome and re-form the English Church.

In a perpetual atmosphere of plots and counter-plots against the Crown, it was inevitable that Elizabeth would react in much the same way as her sister had, and that most of those who now fell foul of her and were executed in their turn, would be remembered as people who had died for their Catholic faith. The bloodshed wasn't quite as high as Mary had caused (some 250 had been executed by the time Elizabeth was finished), but more lasting damage was done by the exile enforced on all priests and Jesuits, and by the other penal laws that were passed. The perceived threat from Spain and its allies was fundamentally responsible for almost all of them.

There was a less savage form of turmoil in Durham, which saw three different occupants of the Deanery in little over twelve months, as Thomas Watson resigned in July 1558 in order to become Bishop of Lincoln, to be succeeded by Thomas Robertson, who was out again in September of the following year; at which point Robert Horne reappeared to take possession of his old domicile. Robertson's brief tenure ended as a result of a government visitation of the diocese, whose object was to see what damage had been done during the five years since Edward VI died. It was conducted by Edwin Sandys, a Cambridge theologian who had only just himself emerged from exile in Strasbourg, by Henry Harvey, a lawyer who had kept his beliefs so quiet that he had managed to serve both Edward and Mary, and by Edmund Scambler, who had bravely eschewed exile while Mary was Queen so as to minister secretly to English Protestant congregations.

One of their principal tasks in the North was to extract oaths in support of Elizabeth's position as Supreme Head of the Church of England. This Robertson refused to take, as did every member of Chapter except Roger Watson, who had been a monastic student at Oxford when Hugh Whitehead was elected Prior, and was subsequently the last of the Priory's Terrars: Watson's reward for complaisance was to be incorporated into the team conducting the visitation. Another canon, John Crawford, who had succeeded one of the old Benedictines (Edward Hyndmers) on the latter's death in 1542, took the oath of Supremacy but jibbed at the Articles of Inquiry which were attached to it. Of the twelve minor canons, two-thirds took the oath, the other four being penalised along with the rest of the malcontents.

The penalties were not, in fact, as severe as they might have been, hitting each canon in the pocket instead of dealing with him more crudely. The obdurates were deprived of their supporting benefices, though not of their stalls in the Cathedral, which meant that they could remain in the College on their basic incomes and whatever came to them from the common dividend. George Cliffe was one of the deprived, having become the twelfth prebendary only in September of the previous year. On the same day as the canons were disciplined, Cuthbert Tunstall was deprived of his see by Elizabeth, because he, too, refused to take the oath of Supremacy. She had wanted him on her side because of his enormous prestige as a prelate who, for all his ability to keep his head carefully below the parapet when danger threatened, was a man well known to have remained steadfast in his deepest beliefs about the Sacramental nature of the Eucharist and much else. He tried to argue her out of raising the issue of Royal Supremacy, in a supreme example of what was to become a notably Anglican way of dealing with awkward situations: the belief that if you patiently tried not to force a potentially divisive issue it just might run out of energy and cease to be troublesome. But Elizabeth would not budge, as adamantly as he, too, remained immovable. She dealt gently with him, however, handing him over to the custodial hospitality of the newly consecrated Archbishop Matthew Parker at Lambeth Palace, where the once Prince Bishop of Durham died a couple of months later at the age of eighty-five.

Robert Horne returned to the Durham Deanery, had his confiscated goods restored to him, and was given the arrears of pay that would have come to him had he never had to fly abroad six years earlier. He started again much as he had left off, naming replacements for the defective canons and now having some support in Chapter, but he did not stay long enough in his second term to make much of an impact again: just over twelve months after arriving he was promoted to the see of Winchester, whose Bishop he remained until his death in 1579. His successor at Durham was Ralph Skinner, who had just spent three years as the Master of Sherburn Hospital, which he finally restored to the stability it had known before Thomas Leigh begged the position from Cromwell and then, essentially, plundered it; but Skinner's tenure of the Deanery was cut short by his death early in 1563. The man who followed him was to lead the Cathedral community for much longer than that and, before he himself died in 1579, he would have left a memory (detestable to some) more indelible perhaps than that of any man who had held his position either as Prior or as Dean of Durham.

He was William Whittingham, of Lancashire and Cheshire parentage, an Oxford man who spoke French and German fluently and had studied in Continental universities. Briefly he had acted as interpreter to the English ambassador to France, and he had also served as chaplain with the English army that embarked on the ill-advised Le Havre expedition to succour the Huguenots against French Catholics in 1562, when he often preached to Elizabeth's troops wearing armour like theirs. From 1554 he had become deeply involved in Protestant politics, first in Frankfurt, then in Geneva, where he soon aligned himself with John Knox's Calvinists in the internecine disputes over the revised Prayer Book of 1552. It was in Switzerland that he translated the New Testament in the English version of what became known as the Geneva Bible and had a hand in many other books that were shaping the direction of Protestantism. He translated a number of psalms for a new English edition there, one of which was the 23rd:

> The Lord is only my support
> And he that doth me feed;
> How can I then lack any thing
> Whereof I stand in need?
> In pastures green he feedeth me
> Where I do safely lie,
> And after leads me to the streams
> Which run most pleasantly

It was in Geneva, too, that he met and married the Huguenot Katherine Jaqueman of Orleans, who was to have almost as great an impact on Durham as her husband, with whom she would bring up six children in the Deanery in defiance of anything the late Duke of Northumberland might have preferred. They arrived in their new home six months after Ralph Skinner died, to a more congenial situation than Robert Horne had known when he first appeared in 1551. A thoroughly Protestant Bishop, James Pilkington, had succeeded Cuthbert Tunstall in 1560, and he was not only from the same part of the country as Whittingham, but he also had spent time on the Continent. Even more helpfully, only four of the original Benedictine Canons (Thomas Sparke, William Bennett, William Todd and Stephen Marley) now remained in their prebendal stalls, the rest having either died or left on the sequestration of their prebends; George Cliffe, who had not become canon of the twelfth stall until 1558, was one of the old guard, too. The seven other replacements were in greater or lesser degree Reformers to a man, at which Whittingham's heart doubtless rejoiced as much as at his preferment to one of the most lucrative posts the Church had to offer. His principal allies in Chapter were to be Robert Swift, who had held the first prebend since 1560, and the Bishop's brothers John and Leonard Pilkington, the second and seventh canons, who came to their stalls in 1561 and 1567 respectively.

At once, Whittingham began to impose his own notions of ecclesiastical propriety on the Cathedral and its Chapter, quickly establishing regular Prayer Book services with morning and afternoon sermons on Sundays, with another sermon on Wednesdays to emphasise the point of the fast the new Dean ordered for that day in every week. He cared about music and acquired highfalutin' anthems and services by Thomas Tallis and other composers now fashionable at the Chapel Royal, to encourage John Brimley and his charges in Durham to extend their range. He was quite prepared to labour beyond the cloister, too, teaching in the grammar school every day. From the outset, William Whittingham was a very industrious Dean. As important as anything he did was the vigour with which he applied himself to sorting out the Chapter's finances, which seem to have been in some disarray by the time he stepped in. He started going to law to obtain redress from incumbents and tenants who had not been paying their tithes or other monies the Dean felt was owing to the Cathedral community, and he was quite prepared to tackle the big fish as well as the small fry: from Charles Neville, Earl of Westmorland, he once claimed twenty years of arrears in rent. He paid particular attention to the situation with regard to lands which produced the revenues that supported the Dean and the prebendaries, and discovered that most of them were leased to families or friends of earlier incumbents of the College, who were reluctant to surrender these benefits to a collective of now mainly Protestant clergy.

A man who applies himself as vigorously as that to all points of the compass and cares not whose toes he steps on in the process is bound to make enemies, and Whittingham did. His first provocative act was to flaunt his puritan beliefs as ostentatiously as possible by walking the streets of Durham in a round cap and black gown, in the manner of Geneva, and by refusing to wear traditional vestments at the Cathedral services; in particular, by refusing to wear the cope and surplice at celebrations of Communion. For this offence, he was hauled before an ecclesiastical court in York, where the examining commissioners included none other than John Pilkington, Archdeacon of Durham as well as occupant of the second prebend's stall, who agreed with his colleagues that Whittingham must conform with the appropriate dress code like everybody else. The Dean's response was to take a year before signing the necessary document of compliance – and then never to celebrate Communion in the Cathedral again.

He was to be accused of much worse than that, though. The author of *Rites of Durham* pictured him as nothing less than an iconoclast with even more to answer for than had been the case with Robert Horne. For Whittingham added the east end of the refectory to the Deanery, making a profit of £20 after selling the lead, and he had a couple of the old stoups for holy water removed to his kitchen where henceforth they were used for salting beef and fish. He was a man 'who could not abyde anye auncyent monumt, nor nothing that appteyned to any godlie Religiousnes of monasticall liffe'. He had some grave slabs taken up from the old cemetery and recycled for building works. Worst of all (and it may have been at the bottom of all the antipathy) he was 'religiously loath (as it should seeme) that any monument of St Cuthbert, or of any man (who formerly had beene famous in this church and great benefactors thereunto, as the priors his predecessors were) should bee left whole and undefaced, in memorye or token of that holy man St Cuthbert . . .'. He was also supposed to have smashed more stained glass windows than his destructive predecessor, though the Joseph Window (in the Chapel of the Nine Altars), the Te Deum Window (south transept), the Window of the Four Doctors (north transept), and the Jesse Window (at the west end) somehow managed to survive his efforts, until they were vandalised by other hands in the seventeenth century. Other things also escaped his attention, or were deliberately spared. When Bishop Pilkington made a visitation in 1567, four years after the Dean's installation, he said there were some images in the Cathedral that ought to have been destroyed.

The reputation William Whittingham created during his time in the Durham Deanery was still anathema as late as 1776, when someone scrawled against his name in a copy of *Rites* that this was 'A Great

Villain of the Geneva Gang'. It was a reputation that his wife shared, for the same people who recalled the iniquities of the Dean also peddled memories of Katherine Whittingham using gravestones to make door lintels for the house she built for herself in the Bailey alongside the Cathedral after she had been widowed, and removing the aforesaid holy water stoups from the Deanery so that they could be used for culinary purposes in her new kitchen. Most dreadful of all, it was reckoned that she 'did most iniuriously burne & consume' Cuthbert's banner 'in hir fire in the notable contempt & disgrace for all auncyent & goodly Reliques'. But as the banner was supposed to have gone missing after rebels seized it in 1536 for service in the Pilgrimage of Grace, it is difficult to see how it could have been destroyed a generation later by a French pyromaniac. Had Mme Whittingham been English, the stories might have read otherwise.

There is evidence, in fact, that Dean Whittingham's puritanical zeal mellowed after he had been in Durham a few years. It is significant that when another royal visitation was conducted the year before he died, he was condemned not for any damage he might have done to the fabric of the Cathedral or for the doctrines he had imported from Switzerland, but for misappropriating Chapter funds, for immoral and drunken behaviour (which sounds improbably hedonistic) and – most seriously – for not being a properly ordained minister: he had taken holy orders in Geneva, and this whole area of authority consecrated in Switzerland was a matter of controversy in the Church of England.

Some influential people were gunning for Whittingham by then, one of whom was a new Bishop of Durham, Richard Barnes, who had been prevented from entering the chapter house in 1577 because he appeared as the northern Primate's representative rather than in his own right, thus overstepping a territorial boundary in the three-hundred-year-old dispute between Durham and York. Another man with a grievance was the new Secretary of State, Sir Thomas Wilson, who had been expecting promotion to the Durham Deanery years earlier, but saw Whittingham acquire it instead. The third figure who had it in for the Dean was one of the Durham prebends, Ralph Lever, who had not done as well as he had hoped in the rearrangement of Chapter revenues, and was clearly the shady inside man who discredited his superior before the authorities. Whittingham's health finally broke under the pressure even though he retained his position until he died at the Deanery in June 1579, leaving his wife and six children well provided for in his will.

By then, however, Durham had endured and survived another commotion, which contained some of the elements that had characterised the Pilgrimage of Grace. In May 1568, Mary Stuart had crossed the Border after being deposed as Scottish Queen, and among the northern English magnates who waited on her in Carlisle was the 7th Earl of Northumberland, Thomas Percy, whose father had been executed for his part in the Pilgrimage. Percy was a devout Catholic, as was Charles Neville, 6th Earl of Westmorland, and the pair of them – Neville with rather more enthusiasm than Percy – became involved in a plot to reactivate the Catholic cause in the North, with Mary as its figurehead.

By November 1569 things were so advanced that the church bells in Topcliffe (part of Percy's estates) were being rung backwards to signal open rebellion, while attempts were being made by Sir George Bowes, one of the Queen's Council in the North, to raise 1,500 foot soldiers in Darlington to repulse it. There is reason to believe that a number of the deprived Durham canons, former Benedictines, played their part in fomenting discontent; for while some of them had left England for the sweeter air of Catholic lands, others had attached themselves to (and were supported economically by) Catholic gentry still scattered around the Palatinate, such as the Salvins and the Tempests. One of these ex-monks was William Todd, who was deprived in 1567 after one complaint too many by his Reformed colleagues in Chapter that he continued to wear forbidden vestments and muttered proscribed prayers for the papacy.

The northern rising burst into flame in Durham Cathedral on 14 November, when the Nevilles and their tenants – with grievances against Dean Whittingham in particular for having billed the Earl of Westmorland for arrears in rent – and an assortment of other rebels entered the building, smashed the Lord's Table, and destroyed every book except the Bible. They then held a High Mass, with all the old Catholic ritual and colour, in which the celebrant was one of the minor canons, Robert Pearson, with four of his colleagues also taking prominent parts in the service, as well as nine of the ten lay clerks (singing men) on the Cathedral's choral strength. Conscious that something like this might be in the offing, Whittingham had made some preparations beforehand, urging Bishop Pilkington to muster all his tenants and arm them in Durham Castle, thus possibly deterring the insurgents from any aggression; when Pilkington demurred, the Dean rode hard to Newcastle to alert the burgesses of impending danger and, drawing on the expertise he had acquired at Le Havre, instructed them how to make the municipal defences ready to repel an attack. He then moved on to York and joined the Earl of Sussex, who had been given local command of the government forces. In mid-December he returned to Durham with troops loyal to Elizabeth, accompanied by a number of Reforming colleagues who had also fled at the prospect of trouble, to find that the Deanery and several homes around the College had been ransacked in their absence.

For a month the rising maintained a momentum, with large numbers joining the Earls' forces around Richmond in the North Riding, which had been a focal point of Catholic rebellion during the Pilgrimage of Grace. Barnard Castle, where Sir George Bowes had entrenched himself, was besieged by 3,200 foot soldiers and 1,500 of horse; and in the vicinity of York the position became so uncertain that Sussex stopped sending messages to London, in case they were intercepted. But support for the rising that had been expected from Lancashire and Cheshire never materialised and nowhere else was likely to provide it; so the northern rebels retreated to their estates and their tenancies, their forces disbanded, just as the Pilgrims had done thirty-three years earlier. The Earls themselves had fled to Hexham by 16 December, moving on shortly afterwards to the sanctuary of Scotland, beyond Elizabeth's reach. Charles Neville finally made his way to Spain, but Thomas Percy was eventually betrayed by the Scots, who handed him over to the English for execution at York in 1572. By then, the feudal power of the northern barons, which had staggered to its feet again after tumult before, had been extinguished once and for all.

There was a reckoning around Durham Cathedral, too, though it came much earlier than for the Earl of Northumberland. The four minor canons who had participated in the Mass, as well as Pearson, were expelled at once. George Cliffe, who occupied the twelfth stall in the Cathedral although his prebend had been sequestrated in 1559, was charged in the aftermath of the rising with certain offences committed at that time; specifically, that on 30 November 1569 he had attended sung Mass in the Cathedral, that on 3 December he had been present when Evensong was said in Latin, that on the following morning he had appeared at Matins in his monastic habit, while at Evensong that day, which he also attended, an anthem to Mary had been sung. It's not very clear what immediately happened to Cliffe as a result of these charges, but in March 1571 he was presented as Rector of Brancepeth by one of the Nevilles, the exiled Earl of Westmorland's sister, Lady Adeline.

Others got into hot water, too. John Brimley, sixty-seven years old by now and Choirmaster for the past thirty-four years, was brought before the ecclesiastical authorities in York. There he admitted that 'he was twice at mass when Robert Pearson, William Holmes, sang the same within the said Cathedral Church; but he sang not himself at them, but played at organs and did divers times help to sing *salvaes* [Hail Marys] at matins and even song; and played on the organs and went in procession, as others did, after the Cross'. He also heard 'a piece of William Holmes' sermon, wherein he spoke much in commendation of the Pope'. Other things Brimley couldn't remember, except that he knelt when bidden to, and 'received holy water, but no holy bread'; and he attested that 'the priests that sang mass … rather did by commandment of Mr Cuthbert Neville and the Earl of Northumberland'. Having confessed to everything he could recall, 'he trusteth that he is pardoned by the Queen's Majesty's free pardon'. And so he was, continuing as Choirmaster and organist in Durham until he died in 1576; at which he was buried in the Galilee beneath a stone on which were set the words:

> John Brimleis body here doth ly,
> Who praysed God with hand and voice;
> By music's heavenly harmonie
> Dull myndes he maid in God rejoice.

His soul into the Heavens is lyft,
To prayse Him still that gave the gyft.[1]

The lay clerks were similarly examined and added more jigsaws of testimony to what had taken place in the Cathedral during that very brief resurrection of its Catholic past. William Syme remembered three Masses being sung, with William Holmes celebrating at two of them and giving the blessing in Latin, as in the old days. John Clark said that John Robson, priest, celebrated at one of the Masses, that Holmes 'had spoken much against the religion now established in England and ... wished and charged each man to acknowledge his former faults in falling to the schism from the Catholic religion, as he termed it'. Thomas Harrison allowed that he had knelt with everyone else when Holmes pronounced the blessing in Latin, but had 'not been willing to set forward the popish religion, or willing to receive the Pope's absolution', nor was he in favour of such rites. Miles White had attended three or four Masses, hearing Holmes say that 'them that were not willing to submit themselves to the Catholic religion ... to depart thence'. Others made similar statements which sometimes contradicted each other in details, sounded confused or simply alarmed, all said they were sorry and hoped to be pardoned for their offence: as they were without repercussion, it seems. A sympathetic monarch may have understood that, however receptive to the old ways the singing men might have been, they had probably been coerced by the unpleasant power of a mob.

That was the last time Durham Cathedral echoed to the sounds of ritual which endorsed the authority of the Popes. And three of the men (just possibly four) who had served at its altars as Benedictine monks, were there to witness the final throes of the old religion to which they had once, long ago, dedicated their lives. Apart from George Cliffe, there was certainly Stephen Marley, sometime Prior of the dependent cell at Stamford, later Chamberlain at the mother

---

[1] Brimley also composed music, some of which is still heard from time to time in Durham Cathedral, whose choir (directed by James Lancelot) recorded his Responses to the Commandments on Priory PRCD 562 in 1996.

house, then Hugh Whitehead's deputy as sub-Prior at the surrender in 1539, subsequently canon of Durham occupying the sixth prebendary's stall: he was deprived of his position by August 1572, and thereafter we lose sight of him. Another, certainly, was William Bennett (brother of Durham's last Bursar), who had been present at Hugh Whitehead's election in 1520, and had acted as Steward of the Prior's Household in the 1530s before becoming Prior of Finchale until it was closed down by Henry VIII. In the new order of things he had been appointed canon of the fourth prebend, and had married Anne Thompson, with whom he fathered three boys and a girl, before eventually resigning his position in 1579, dying sometime before February 1584. The fourth ex-monk, possibly present at the last Roman offices, was Thomas Sparke, who had been Chamberlain and Prior of Lindisfarne before becoming suffragan Bishop of Berwick in 1537, a position which he would hold until his death in 1572. Although, since the rearrangement of things in 1541, he had simultaneously occupied the third prebend's stall in the Cathedral, it is possible, perhaps even likely, that he was otherwise engaged on his diocesan duties in November 1569.

But these four, and John Brimley, were Durham's last link with the olden times. Their memories of the Benedictine days were very distant now, but still vivid in their recollection of themselves as they had been long ago, and of these surroundings which had been at the very heart of almost all their lives. That is why they would have responded as they did, when the Latin words were spoken and sung again.

EPILOGUE

✝

'The Cathedral is so beautiful that it makes me want to cry.'

A SOUTH AFRICAN WOMAN IN DURHAM, 20 APRIL 2006

And the memories of Benedictine Durham are still there, stirred up the moment you enter the cloister on your way to Evensong, or come through the doorway with the sanctuary knocker at the north-western end of the nave to gape, open-mouthed, at the massiveness of this church, at the astonishing enclosure of sheer space, at the integrity of it all. But a certain amount has changed across the intervening centuries. The canons' stalls in the quire did not appear until 1665, in spite of some deceptively monastic misericords, and the huge and intricate canopy above the marble font comes from the same decade as them. The Miners' Memorial, with its poignant Davy lamp nearby, is a twentieth-century tribute to an industry that was linked inextricably with this city and this church. There is much fine modern sculpture and modern stained glass, including a window that was presented by the Durham branch of Marks and Spencer to celebrate its centenary in 1984. There is a deal of nineteenth-century work, not all of it good. George Gilbert Scott added the Choir screen in the 1870s, to strike the only conspicuously jarring note in the entire building: not because the screen is neo-Gothic in an essentially Norman context (the magnificent Neville screen, authentically Perpendicular from the fourteenth century, harmonises perfectly) but because its shining Frosterley marble columns are at odds with the rough stonework above it and on all sides; and, more than anything else, because it is half-hearted, tentative, in a cathedral where everything else is committed and bold.

Look at the roof, one of the most daring things that was ever attempted in the history of architecture, because logic said that it was impossible to carry such a weight of masonry as that supported by the vaulting and its ribs, whose stones are so delicately poised and balanced that they interlock and hold fast – but so easily might not have done: might, instead, have given way under the strain to bring the whole construction crashing to the ground. Then let the eye travel down any one of the colossal piers that uphold everything along the length of the nave and the transepts, and sense the monumental power inherent in each, emphasised by the great gashes of zig-zag and spiral and lozenges running up and down the huge blocks of stone. The Normans couldn't have done anything half-heartedly if they had tried. The men who assembled the Neville screen after its multitude of parts had travelled in bits and pieces from London, would have been very conscious of the fact that they were putting the finishing touches to a great work of art that could hold its own in any company, however domineering that might be.

Everybody who had anything at all to do with building this wonder of medieval craftsmanship and faith would have been in no doubt at all that they were engaged in holy work. Durham Cathedral feels as if it has known a lot of holiness and prayer since then. Candles flare perpetually in great banks of light from sconces framed in rows beside the crossing piers. Close by are the slips of paper with scribbled petitions on behalf of people who never needed intercession more: remember A and B, one says, whose marriage is in difficulties; pray for Mary, says another, who is fighting to beat cancer; be merciful to John, says a third, who is dying and afraid.

And those who enter the church today are often quite overcome by the sensations it produces, whether they are Christians or not. A small boy declares that when he looks up he wonders if the building will fall on him, and many people say that it makes them feel very small or very calm or overwhelmed by its palpable holiness. A woman steps over the threshold of the Galilee and, stopping in her tracks, lets out a great sigh. Sometimes, people are so moved by everything they see and otherwise sense here, that they do extraordinary and quite unforgettable things. A group of Africans from KwaZulu had finished praying in the Feretory, where Cuthbert lies beneath a gilded Ninian Comper tester now, when one of them, a woman, broke the silence and began to sing in her native tongue, her companions taking up a refrain at the end of each line; and people within earshot shivered at the thrill of it, were brought very close to tears by something they instinctively understood, though they couldn't comprehend a single word. Muslims have been observed unrolling their prayer mats in the Galilee, and falling to their knees. Cuthbert's shrine is very seldom without its quota of reverent onlookers, lighting candles at the tomb and saying their prayers, for the memory of him is still a powerful presence here, though children can sometimes put uncomfortably penetrating questions to the Cathedral stewards and guides. One boy wondered whether those who prayed to him in the Feretory were not making an idol of the saint.

People who normally try to control their emotions find that tears come all too easily in these surroundings. Michael Ramsey − saintly scholar and one of the greatest Bishops Wearside has ever known − wept unashamedly when he left Durham to become Primate of England in York, in the penultimate step towards St Augustine's throne in Canterbury. Ramsey, with the famously oscillating eyebrows and a lurching ploughman's gait, also endeared himself to the diocese because of his serene eccentricity. Durham has never lacked figures who would always be remembered for singular behaviour. In the nineteenth century there was the bachelor George Waddington, who had explored the upper reaches of the Nile and ventured to Greece during its War of Independence, who solaced himself in the Deanery by bottling his own ale, and patronised the boxing booths at Durham Fair (inside as well as outside the ring, according to some). In the twentieth there was Henley Henson, first as Dean, later as Bishop, who opposed the teetotal movement that was supposed to stimulate a correctly patriotic attitude during the Great War, and was obsessed with those who coughed during services (especially during his sermons), when he loudly asked the culprits to leave.

Even people who simply drop by the Cathedral sometimes do something which is inexplicably odd: like the young man who strode into the Galilee, ignored a group of people who were standing round Bede's tomb, threw a rosary onto its black marble top, stood still for a moment, then scooped up his beads and strode away again without a word. Then there are those who are moved to great happiness or to fond remembrance by something that happens to them here. Young people propose marriage to each other when they have been strolling around for a little while, and ask the Verger if he could possibly take their photograph as a memento of the event. Someone leaves a red rose in the Gregory Chapel with a note saying that another year has passed but love has not grown less. Few people can leave without feeling that some vital part of themselves has, in some way or other, been touched.

Other changes have occurred around the Cathedral in what was once the monastery. The fourteenth-century great kitchen has been transformed into a splendid bookshop, almost certainly the only one in the country with octagonal stone vaulting around an aperture that was designed as a ventilator; and where the Cellarer stored his wine has appropriately become a licensed restaurant under French management. The refectory was translated into the Dean and Chapter Library at the end of the eighteenth century and now houses some of the older books in the collection, though the bulk of that is lodged in the old dormitory running along the west side of the cloister, beneath one of the finest timber roofs ever constructed in England, and with small windows overlooking the cloister garth, to indicate the position of each monk's cell when the sleeping arrangements changed from the communal to the individual at the beginning of the fifteenth century.

The most precious things of all, however, Durham's unrivalled mass of archives, are housed in one of the former prebendal dwellings in the College, specially fortified and fireproofed for security; or else they are in the Spendiment beside the cloister, where the greatest literary treasures of all are kept under the protection of high technology. As for the old Prior's Lodging, changes have been made to it periodically ever since William Whittingham decided to improve his Deanery's amenities, so that very little above ground remains as it was in the Benedictine days (though its crypt is another matter). In 1974, however, a priceless discovery was made by workmen who, on removing old plaster in the Dean's hallway, revealed part of a fifteenth-century mural, picturing fragments of the Nativity and the Resurrection, which had decorated the wall when it belonged to Hugh Whitehead's private chapel.

In spite of the changes, there is a continuity here that stretches back to the sixteenth century and beyond and has nothing to do with buildings and their contents. The Dean and Chapter still functioned according to the Marian statutes with Elizabethan amendments until these were modified to take account of the passage of time in 2001; but plenty of the Tudor elements still regulate life here, such as the installation of the Bishop by the Dean, and the ceremony by which the Dean is himself installed, culminating in a communal acknowledgement and reception of the new man in the chapter house, before the Bishop sitting on 'the ancient Stone Chair'. Four years after the constitution and statutes were altered came another shift of emphasis, when Cuthbert's name was restored to the dedication, so that 464 years after he was dismissed by Henry VIII, this again became the Cathedral church of Christ, Blessed Mary the Virgin and St Cuthbert of Durham. That mattered a great deal to the people of the North, to the ones who worship here regularly, to those who attend services infrequently, to the many who enter this Cathedral only a handful of times in the whole of their lives but still feel that it belongs to them, to the voluntary workers who sometimes come by bus from as far away as Hartlepool several times a week, in order to serve their turn at stewarding and making strangers feel at home in a place and an atmosphere that might easily fill them with a nervous awe, and do nothing else at all for them. Instead, as things are, this church and its ambience makes them laugh and cry and sing, feel calmer and stronger and welcome. Quite often it makes them want to fall to their knees or simply sit silently to reflect on the most important things. Some feel impelled to receive the Communion which is offered every day of the week at half past noon, except on Sunday, when it can be received twice. At the Sung Eucharist that morning, the Dean and the attending canons move from their stalls to the high altar for the Dismissal and the Blessing; and they do so in line ahead, in order of precedence behind the Dean until they reach the altar steps, where the canons change formation to line abreast. Just so was it done in the monastic time.

The best way to catch a flavour of the past here, as well as the whole purpose of everything that happens, is to attend one of the services. There is nothing more in tune with Durham Cathedral's origins than the celebration of key moments in the Church's calendar, at Christmas and Easter and on a handful of great festivals. Most memorable of all, for anyone with a sense of history, is the Festal Evensong held every 20 March to mark St Cuthbert's day, when the Dean and Chapter enter the Cathedral richly robed in vestments that have changed but little down the ages, when the congregation joins in a long procession round the church, when Latin is sung by everyone, when Cuthbert's life is extolled, when incense adds its fragrance to the colour, the light and the great leaping harmonies.

But any Choral Evensong will serve, where the vestments are generally (except on feast days) muted into black cassock, white surplice and coloured hood, very Anglican in style and origin, but where the occasion is still such that even the ineffable Richard Dawkins might enjoy it without reservation as pure theatre of an exceedingly high order, accompanied by incomparable music in a sensational setting. Psalms from the Book of Common Prayer are sung, whose language is that of Thomas Cranmer and the other Tudor divines. And there are two moments in the ritual which do not imitate or modify but are in direct descent from the rites that the Priors of Durham observed. The first comes at the beginning of Evensong when a verger, bearing his wand with great dignity, precedes and conducts the Dean to his stall, where each bows gravely to the other in acknowledgement and courtesy; the second when the verger appears again at the end of the service, bows to the Dean as before, and leads him back through the south transept to the vestry.

The continuity of Durham was part of Henry VIII's master plan for the alteration of the Church in England. Even so, all this magnificence, this perfection of many things, might not have survived to our own time, if a sixteenth-century Benedictine Prior and his brethren had not obediently bent to a powerful wind of change that came rushing through the Church and across the land. They were not brave men, as some others most certainly were in accepting a hideous death with fortitude instead of compromising their belief in the way Almighty God should be worshipped and interpreted. Such men left behind them a wreckage of memorials, at Whalley and Sawley, at Jervaulx and Glastonbury and elsewhere, gaunt and broken reminders of what had so splendidly stood for enduring faith. That was not the way of the Durham monks, however; and we can be grateful for their obedience today.

Hugh Whitehead might have been puzzled by some of the things that have happened in his old Priory and its Cathedral since his time here as Dean. But he would still have felt at home in this place.

BIBLIOGRAPHY

✠

ABBREVIATIONS
AA *Archaeologia Aeliana*
CS Camden Society
CWAAS *Transactions of the Cumberland and Westmorland Antiquarian and Archaeological Society*
D & C Muniments of the Dean and Chapter, Durham
DUJ *The Durham University Journal*
EcHR *Economic History Review*
EHR *English Historical Review*
LP *Letters and Papers, Foreign and Domestic, of the Reign of Henry VIII*
NH *Northern History*
PBS Prayer Book Society
RHS *Transactions of the Royal Historical Society*
SHS Stamford Historical Society
SS Surtees Society

Barlow, F., *Durham Jurisdictional Peculiars* (Oxford, 1950)
Barrow, G.W.S., 'Scottish Rulers and the Religious Orders 1070–1153' (RHS 5th series Vol. 3, 1953)
Baskerville, G., *English Monks and the Suppression of the Monasteries* (London, 1937)
Bernard, G.W., *The King's Reformation: Henry VIII and the Remaking of the English Church* (New Haven and London, 2005)
Blake, J.B., 'The Medieval Coal Trade of North-east England: some fourteenth-century evidence' (NH Vol. 2, 1967)
Bonner, G., Rollason, D. and Stancliffe, C. (eds), *St Cuthbert, his cult and his community to* AD 1200 (Woodbridge, 1995)

Bonney, M., *Lordship and the urban community: Durham and its overlords 1250–1540* (Cambridge, 1990)

Bray, G. (ed.), *Documents of the English Reformation* (Cambridge, 1994)

Brewer J.S., Gairdner, J. and Brodie, R.H. (eds), *Letters and Papers, Foreign and Domestic, of the Reign of Henry VIII* 1509–1547 (21 Vols in 33 parts, London, 1862–1910)

Cambridge, E., 'The Masons and Building Works of Durham Priory 1339–1539' (Durham thesis, 1992)

Chambers, E.K., *The Mediaeval Stage*, Vol. II (Oxford, 1963)

Colgrave, B. (ed. and tr.), *Two Lives of Saint Cuthbert* (Cambridge, 1985)

Craster, H.H.E., 'The Red Book of Durham' (EHR Vol. 40, 1925)

Crosby, B., *Come on Choristers!: A History of the Chorister School, Durham* (private, 1999)

Dasent, J.R. (ed.), *Acts of the Privy Council of England*, new series Vols I–III, 1542–52 (London, 1891)

Dobson, R.B., *Durham Priory 1400–1450* (Cambridge, 1973)

Dodds, M.H., 'The Northern Stage' (AA 3rd series Vol. XL, 1914) 'Northern Minstrels and Folk Drama' (AA 4th series Vol. I, 1925)

Donaldson, R., 'Sponsors, Patrons and Presentations to Benefices in the Gift of the Priors of Durham during the later Middle Ages' (AA 4th series Vol. XXXVIII, 1960)

Duffy, E., *The Stripping of the Altars* (New Haven and London, 1992)

Emsley, K. and Fraser, C.M., *The Courts of the County Palatine of Durham from Earliest Times to 1971* (Durham, 1984)

Field, J., *Durham Cathedral: Light of the North* (London, 2006)

Fletcher, A. and MacCulloch, D., *Tudor Rebellions* (London, 1997)

Fowler, J.T. (ed.), *Extracts from the Account Rolls of the Abbey of Durham* (SS Vols 99, 100, 103, 1898–1900)
Rites of Durham (SS Vol. 107, 1903)

Fraser, C.M., *Durham Quarter Session Rolls 1471–1625* (SS Vol. 199, 1991)

Green, M.A.E. (ed.), 'Life of Mr William Whittingham, Dean of Durham' (*The Camden Miscellany* Vol. 6, CS 1st series Vol. 104, 1871)

Greenslade, S.L., 'The Last Monks of Durham Cathedral Priory' (DUJ new series Vol. X, 1948–9)

Greenway, D.E., comp. of John Le Neve's *Fasti Ecclesiae Anglicanae 1066–1300: Vol. II, Monastic Cathedrals* (London, 1971)

Greenwell, W. (ed.), *Boldon Buke: A Survey of the Possessions of the See of Durham* (SS Vol. 25, 1852)
Feodarium Prioratus Dunelmensis (SS Vol. 58, 1872)

Halcrow, E.M., 'The Decline of Demesne Farming on the Estates of Durham Cathedral Priory' (EcHR 2nd series Vol. 7 No. 3, 1955)
'The Social Position and the Influence of the Priors of Durham, as Illustrated by their Correspondence' (AA 4th series Vol. XXXIII, 1955)
'Obedientiaries and Counsellors in Monastic Administration at Durham' (AA 4th series Vol. XXXV, 1957)

Harrison, F.L., *Music in Medieval Britain* (London, 1958)

Hay, D., 'The Dissolution of the Monasteries in the Diocese of Durham' (AA 4th series Vol. 15, 1938)

Hinde, G. (ed.), *The Registers of Cuthbert Tunstall Bishop of Durham 1530–59 and James Pilkington Bishop of Durham 1561–76* (SS Vol. 161, 1946)

Horn, J.M., Smith, D.M. and Mussett, P., comps of John Le Neve's *Fasti Ecclesiae Anglicanae 1541–1857: Vol. XI, Carlisle, Chester, Durham, Manchester, Ripon and Sodor and Man Dioceses* (London, 2004)

Hughes, P., *The Reformation in England* (3 Vols, London, 1954)

Hutchinson, W., *The History and Antiquities of the County Palatine of Durham* (3 Vols, Newcastle-upon-Tyne, 1785–94)

Jones, B., comp. of John Le Neve's *Fasti Ecclesiae Anglicanae 1300–1541: Vol. VI, Northern Province* (London, 1963)

Kitchin, G.W. (ed.), *The Records of the Northern Convocation* (SS Vol. 113, 1907)

Kitching, C.J. (ed.), *The Royal Visitation of 1559: Act Book for the Northern Province* (SS Vol. 187, 1975)

Knighton, C.S. (ed.), *Calendar of State Papers Domestic Series of the Reign of Edward VI 1547–1553* (London, 1992)

Knowles, Dom D., *The Monastic Order in England 940–1216* (Cambridge, 1963)
The Religious Orders in England Vol. I, 1216–1340 (Cambridge, 1948)
The Religious Orders in England Vol. II. The End of the Middle Ages (Cambridge, 1955)
The Religious Orders in England Vol. III, The Tudor Age (Cambridge, 1959)

Lapsley, G.T., *The County Palatine of Durham: A Study in Constitutional History* (New York, 1900)

Loades, D.M., 'The Last Years of Cuthbert Tunstall 1547–1559 (DUJ new series Vol. XXXV, December 1973)
'The Dissolution of the Diocese of Durham, 1553–54' in Marcombe (ed.), *The Last Principality . . .*.
John Dudley Duke of Northumberland 1504–1553 (Oxford, 1996)
'Durham: the Reformation and the Prayer Book' (PBS Review No. 58, 2006)

Lomas, R.A., 'Durham Cathedral Priory as a Landowner and a Landlord 1290–1540 (Durham thesis, 1973) 'Developments in Land Tenure on the Prior of Durham's Estate in the later Middle Ages' (NH Vol. 13, 1977) 'A Northern farm at the end of the Middle Ages: Elvethall Manor, Durham 1443/4–1513/14' (NH Vol. 18, 1982)

Lomas, R.A. and Piper, A.J. (eds), *Durham Cathedral Priory Rentals; Vol. I, Bursar's Rentals* (SS Vol. 198, 1989)

MacCulloch, D., *Thomas Cranmer: A Life* (New Haven and London, 1996)
Tudor Church Militant: Edward VI and the Protestant Reformation (London, 1999)

Marcombe, D., 'The Durham dean and chapter: old abbey writ large?' in R. O'Day and F. Heal (eds), *Continuity and Change: Personnel and Administration of the Church in England 1500–1642* (Leicester, 1976). 'A Rude and Heady People: The Local Community and the Rebellion of the Northern Earls' in D. Marcombe (ed.), *The Last Principality: Politics, Religion and Society of the Bishopric of Durham 1494–1660* (Nottingham, 1987)
A Great Villain of the Geneva Gang? 'William Whittingham, Dean

of Durham: a reassessment in Conflict and Disaster at Durham' (Marcombe et al., Durham, 2002)

McCann, Abbot J. (tr. and ed.), *The Rule of St Benedict* (London, 1952)

Merriman, R.B., *Life & Letters of Thomas Cromwell* (2 Vols, Oxford, 1968, reprint of 1902)

Mussett, P., *Lists of Deans and Major Canons of Durham 1541–1900* (Durham, 1974)

Neville, C.J., 'The Courts of the Prior and the Bishop of Durham in the Later Middle Ages' (*History* Vol. 85 No. 278, April 2000)

Newman, C.M., 'Employment on the Estates of the Priory of Durham 1494–1519: The Priory as an Employer' (NH 36, May 2000)

Pantin, W.A., 'English Monastic Letter-books' in J.G. Edwards et al. (eds), *Historical Essays in Honour of James Tait* (Manchester, 1933)

Pevsner, N.B.L., *The Buildings of England: County Durham* (New Haven and London, 2002)

Piper, A.J., 'The Libraries of the Monks of Durham' in M.B. Parker and A.B. Watson (eds), *Medieval Scribes, Manuscripts and Libraries* (London, 1978)

'St Leonards Priory, Stamford' (*The Stamford Historian* Nos 5 and 6, SHS September 1980 and 1981)

'The Durham monks at Jarrow' (Jarrow Lecture, Durham, 1986)

'Dr Thomas Swalwell, Monk of Durham, Archivist and Bibliophile (d. 1539)' in J.P. Carley and C.G.C. Tite (eds), *Books and Collectors 1200–1700* (London, 1997)

Plummer, S.W., 'St Cuthbert: Notes on the Examination of his Remains' (*Northumberland and Durham Medical Journal*, March 1899)

Raine, J. (ed.), *Historiae Dunelmensis Scriptores Tres* (SS Vol. 9, 1839)

Sanctuarium Dunelmense et Sanctuarium Beverlacense (SS Vol. 5, 1837)

The Durham Household Book; or The Accounts of the Bursar of the Monastery of Durham from Pentecost 1530 to Pentecost 1534 (SS Vol. 18, 1844)

Depositions and other Ecclesiastical Proceedings from the Courts of Durham (SS Vol. 21, 1845)

Rex, R., *Henry VIII and the English Reformation* (Basingstoke, 1993)

Richardson, W.C., *History of the Court of Augmentations 1536–1554* (Baton Rouge, 1961)

Rollason, D. and L., Piper, A.J. and Harvey, M., *The Durham Liber Vitae and its Context* (Woodbridge, 2003)

Rollason, D. and L. (eds), *The Durham Liber Vitae* (forthcoming)

Savine, A., 'English Monasteries on the Eve of the Dissolution' in P. Vinogradoff (ed.), *Oxford Studies in Social and Legal History* Vol. I (Oxford, 1909)

Scammell, G.V., *Hugh du Puiset, Bishop of Durham* (Cambridge, 1956)

Scammell, J., 'The Origin and Limitations of the Liberty of Durham' (EHR Vol. 320, July 1966)

Scarisbrick, J., *Henry VIII* (New Haven and London, 1997)

Stevenson, J. (tr.), *Simeon's History of the Church of Durham* (Felinfach, 1993)

Stranks, C.J., *This Sumptuous Church: The Story of Durham Cathedral* (London, 1973)

Sturge, C., *Cuthbert Tunstal: Churchman, Scholar, Statesman, Administrator* (London, 1938)

Tanner, J.R., *Tudor Historical Documents* AD 1485–1603 (Cambridge, 1940)

Thompson, A.H. and Falkner, J.M. (eds), *The Statutes of the Cathedral Church of Durham* (SS Vol. 143, 1929)

Threlfall-Holmes, M. *Monks and Markets: Durham Cathedral Priory 1460–1530* (Oxford, 2005)

Tolhurst, J.B.L. (ed.), *Introduction to the English Monastic Breviaries* (Henry Bradshaw Society, Woodbridge, 1993)

Tudor, V., 'The Misogyny of St Cuthbert' (AA 5th series Vol. 12, 1984)

Williams, C.H. (ed.), *English Historical Documents 1485–1558* (London, 1967)

Wilson, J., 'The passage of the Border by Aeneas Sylvius in the winter of 1435–6' (CWAAS new series Vol. 23, 1923)

Wright, T. (ed.), *Letters Relating to the Suppression of Monasteries* (CS 26, 1843)

SOURCES

✠

(In quotations from *Letters and Papers* and other state papers, the figures refer
to documents, not pages, except where indicated otherwise.)

FOREWORD

xviii 'Durham is one of the great' Pevsner, p.159

CHAPTER I The End of an Era

6 'a man of exceptionally broad' Piper, 'Dr Thomas Swalwell, p. 71
7 'to go every night' Fowler, *Rites*, p. 93
8 'figs and raisins' ibid., p. 89
9 'And if the Master' ibid., p. 97
11 'When anyone newly cometh' McCann, Chapter 58
11 'I, brother M' Fowler, SS Vol. 103, p. xix note 2
11 'a marvelous fair book' Fowler, *Rites*, pp. 8–9
12 'with all his appurtenances' ibid., p. 51
12 'where he might have' ibid.

CHAPTER II The Reason Why

17 'although naturally strong' Stevenson, p. 673
17 'Oh holy Bishop' quoted Colgrave, p. 65
17 'a magnificently caparisoned' ibid., p. 69
18 'forthwith delivered' ibid., p. 167
19 'When they had taken' ibid., p. 263
19 'Within the monastery' Bonner et al., p. 33
19 'with angelic aid' Colgrave, p.217
19 'but when the soldier of Christ' ibid., p. 215
20 'knowing in his spirit' ibid., p. 267
21 'so that, freed' ibid., p. 261

21 'I think' Raine, *Sanctuarium Dunelmense*, p. xii

22 'opening the sepulchre' Colgrave, p.293

23 'more English' Dobson, pp. 18–19 footnote

24 'the vehicle on which' Stevenson, p. 671

24 'when Lent was nigh' ibid., p. 687

26 'placed on a censer' ibid., p. 678

26 'it could not be consumed' Bonner et al., p. 466

26 'some money and a jewel' Wilson, p. 18

27 'with his surplice' Fowler, *Rites*, p. xlix

28 'accounted to be' Fowler, SS Vol. 100 (1898), p. 454

28 'who wished to hear' Stevenson, p. 658

30 'adjoined it for Mass' Fowler, *Rites*, p. 4

31 'the only teacher of' Knowles, *The Monastic Order*, p. 24

32 'all finely gilded' Fowler, *Rites*, p. 107

32 'elaborate cycles' Dodds, 'Northern Stage', p. 34

35 'I will wash my hands' Psalm 26, v. 6

35 'a saint to be feared' Dobson, p. 13

CHAPTER III A Prince Among Bishops

37 'There are two kings' quoted Emsley and Fraser, p. 1

39 'it was through the negligence' *Victoria County History of Durham* Vol. 2, p. 156

39 'has been wrought by' LP I (2) 2283

40 'that the slayer might' *Deuteronomy* 15, vss 41–3

42 'Being found unable' Emsley and Fraser, pp. 33–4

43 'such times as' Fowler, *Rites*, p. 19

44 'the first bishop' ibid., p. 2

44 'His position' Thompson and Falkner, p. xxiii

46 'such as cooks and grooms' quoted Sturge, p. 121

47 'their singular protector' *Oxford History of England: The Early Tudors*, p. 354

47 'that the King is after Christ' Kitchin, pp. 217–20

47 'Why do you not' LP V Appendix 9

48 'where his chief abode was' ibid., 986

48 'of no great importance' LP XIII (1) 987

49 'sore grieved me' quoted Hutchinson Vol. I, p. 405

49 'Asks him to show' LP X 202
51 'spoiled the bishop' LP XIII (1) 708
51 'ungodly handled' LP XII (1) 50
52 'only to preach' quoted Sturge, p. 160

CHAPTER IV The Thirtieth Prior

53 'the most considerable ecclesiastic' Knowles, *Religious Orders* Vol. II, p. 324
54 'the Lord Prior' Fowler, *Rites*, p. 102
57 'the comprehensive and' Neville, p. 221
57 'he saw the monks' ibid., p. 222
58 'if a robber shall be taken' quoted Neville, p. 223
59 'took the sheriff to task' ibid., p. 244
60 'the election appears' Knowles, *Monastic Order*, p. 628
60 'Richard Bury had been' Dobson, p. 228 footnote
62 'certain poor children' Fowler, *Rites*, p. 91
63 'or annual rent of £5' D & C *Register V*, 265 r–v
64 'I and my brethren' quoted Dobson, p. 172
64 'the office of keeper' quoted Halcrow, 'The Social Position', p. 79
65 'a style of living' Dobson, p. 102
68 'of learning and good' LP IV (2) 3478
69 'leaving us destitute' Raine, *Historiae Dunelmensis Scriptores Tres* p. ccccxix
69 'I not only understand' ibid., p. ccccxx
71 'certain monitions and protestations' D & C *Register* V, 184v–186r
72 'the stall on the north side' ibid., 186r–189v

CHAPTER V Substantial Poverty

75 'one dispersed in the' Lomas and Piper, *Bursar's Rentals*, p. 209
76 'was held by them' ibid., p. 211
77 'was as ye go into the Guest Hall' Fowler, *Rites* p. 99
82 'the labour of the said office' quoted Dobson, p. 285
83 'In which situation' ibid., p. 286
83 'certain members of the convent' ibid., p. 289
84 'Distribution of napery' Raine, *Durham Household Book*, p. 69
84 'From the Hostillar' ibid., pp. 283–4

123 'down one side and' LP VIII 822

124 'I should advise you' ibid., 955

124 'I beg you will write' LP IX 632

CHAPTER VIII The Small Houses Fall

126 'The King and Council' LP X 601

126 'The silver plate' ibid.

127 'and bade theym loke' Wright, pp. 38–9

127 'There is a possibility' Knowles, *Religious Orders* Vol. III, p. 291

128 'Forasmuch as manifest sin' 27 Henry VIII c 28

130 'discreet persons' LP X 721

131 'of all ornaments, plate' ibid.

131 'of slender report' quoted Knowles, *Religious Orders* Vol. III, p. 307

132 'is a wise and discreet' ibid., p. 308

132 '& one anchoress' ibid., p. 309

133 'the King's Highness' 27 Henry VIII c 29 Clause XIII

134 'shall have their capacities' ibid.

136 'all such goods as' LP X 424

136 'his Majesty is pleased' 27 Henry VIII c 28

138 'The abbots and their' Merriman Vol. I, p. 183

138 'All these lords' LP X 601

139 'if it must go' ibid., 552

139 'not far from her' ibid., 385

139 'something out of Totnes' ibid., 551

139 'at a reasonable rent' ibid., 491

139 'beseeching you' ibid., 486

139 'Two gentlemen of substance' LP XII (2) 548

CHAPTER IX The Furness Example

142 'I thanked him' LP XII (2) 1030

142 'high judgement, Parliament matters' LP X 183

143 'no part of the realm' ibid., 182

144 '*Phillipus Dacre*' ibid., 364

145 'a Long bell' Fowler, *Rites*, p. 165

145 'wherein one of the monks' ibid., p. 38

145 'Where all the whole convent' ibid., p. 79

173 'the late abbot' ibid., 202

173 'I will say there is a pope' quoted Bernard, p. 469

173 'he had a relic' LP XIV (2) 256

174 'much grieved with' quoted Knowles, *Religious Orders* Vol. III, p. 347

175 'would not in any wise' LP XIII(1) 573

175 'I am a man' LP XIV (2) 185

175 'and examined him' ibid., 206

176 'and other secret places' ibid., 232

176 'the monks also' Wright, p. 258

177 'a book thereof' LP XIV (2) 272

177 'The plate from Glastonbury' ibid., 427

177 'on Thursday the xivth day' Wright, p.260

178 'asked God mercy' ibid., p. 261

179 'tyrants and bloodsuckers' quoted Bernard, p. 471

179 'the only supreme head' ibid., p. 472

179 'I would to Christ' ibid.

179 'the king shall never' ibid., p. 471

179 'I thought somewhat' LP XIV (2) 459

180 'where they found' Fowler, *Rites*, p. 102

181 'of considerable muscularity' Plummer, p. 3

181 'The interment within' ibid., p. 10

182 'Given to George Skeles' Fowler, SS Vol. 103, pp. 741–3

183 'The bodies of saints' quoted Sturge, p. 260

184 'there was a demonstration' LP VII 963

185 'Know ye that we' Thompson and Falkner, p. 65

CHAPTER XII A New Order

188 'The monasteries, wonderful to relate', LP XV 259

188 'In no country' *Victoria County History of Durham* Vol. 2, p. 101

190 'the said two schools' LP XII (2) 1083

190 'to guard diligently' quoted Sturge, p. 265

190 'as one of the most important' Threlfall-Holmes, p. 16

190 'monastic vessels' Sturge, p. 263

191 'many of them might be' LP XIV (1) 868

192 'Proceeds of sales' LP XIX (2) 328

222 'I have written to' Knighton, p. 515

222 'declaring unto him that information' Dasent Vol. III, p. 102

223 'to answer in writing' ibid., p. 314

223 'the said recognisance' ibid., p. 326

223 'The Dean of Durham doth' ibid., pp. 406–7

224 'all such goods and chatells' ibid., p. 468

CHAPTER XIV The Iconoclast

226 'a goodlie & verie large' Fowler, *Rites*, p. 68

226 'ye hole storie' ibid., pp. 76–7

226 'did treade and breake' ibid., p. 69

227 'If the Dean of Durham' Knighton, p. 747

228 'This peevish Dean' ibid., p. 774

228 'I have been much deceived' ibid., p. 799

229 'infected his whole diocese' quoted Sturge, p. 300

230 'God's book containing' ibid.

230 'the Dean and Prebendaries' Thompson and Falkner, p. 207

230 'Philip and Mary' ibid., p. 73

231 'our faithful chaplain' ibid., p. 85

231 'who may be either' ibid.

231 'not only learned' ibid., p. 87

232 'even as the eye in the body' ibid., p. 91

232 'unless a lawful impediment' ibid., p. 99

232 'obey, hearken to' ibid., p. 103

232 'his cures of souls' ibid., p. 101

233 'unless the constraint of nature' ibid., p. 117

233 'the manor and park' ibid., p. 121

234 'fit for timber' ibid., p. 95

234 'and higher in order' ibid., p. 125

234 'shall collect and receive' ibid., p. 127

235 'the fabric of the temple' ibid., p. 129

235 'to chant the praises' ibid., p. 131

235 'of riper age and' ibid., p. 135

235 'to carry the verge' ibid., p. 141

235 'And after that time' ibid., p. 149

236 'and as many of the' ibid., p. 151

INDEX

✠

Durham House, London 39, 143

Durham (later Trinity) College, Oxford 43–4, 62, 68, 69, 207

Durham Palatinate, the 37, 227

Durham peninsula, the 15

Easby 139

East Anglia 80, 137, 191, 218

Ecclesiastical History (Bede) 31

Ecclesiastical Licenses Act (1534) 106

Ecgbert, Bishop 31

Edgecumbe, Sir Piers 139

Edmundbyers 61

Edward the Confessor 23

Edward I, King 23

Edward II, King 39, 56

Edward III, King 38, 56

Edward IV, King 41

Edward VI, King 168, 215, 227, 228

Egglestone, Christopher 199, 206

Election of Bishops Act 216

Elfsige, Bishop 55

Elizabeth I, Queen 114, 238–40

Elstow 103

Elvet 17

Elvethall Manor 78–80, 200, 233

Ely Cathedral 54, 87, 192, 194, 196

entertainment 148–9

Erasmus 45, 46

Erysden, John 197

Eure, Sir Ralph 63

Evesham 29, 87

Evynwood, Richard 71

executions
    Durham 189
    under Elizabeth I 238
    Hugh Cooke 171–4
    John Forest 167
    objectors 109
    and the Pilgrimage of Grace 151, 152
    under Queen Mary 229, 237
    Thomas Cromwell 193
    Thomas Marshall 178–80

exempt orders 121

Eynon, Hugh 173

Farne Islands 19–20, 152

Farr, Walter 115

Felgild 21

Ferdinand of Aragon 91–2

Feretrar, the 7, 30

Ferrybridge 208

Ferryhill 76, 81

Field of the Cloth of Gold 96–7

Finchale Priory 6, 70, 81, 152–3, 233

first fruits 110, 136

Fish, Simon 105–6

Fishburn, John 7

Fisher, John, Bishop of Rochester 50, 94, 108, 109, 114, 120

fisheries 81, 200

Fishlake 200

Flambard, Ranulph, Bishop 25, 75

Flodden Field, battle of, 1513 27, 39, 45, 96

Foderley, Thomas 31

Folkstone 139

food 68, 104–5, 148, 210

Fordham, John, Bishop 38

Forest, John 167

forfeiture
    and the Act of Treasons 151–2
    by voluntary conveyance 154–6

Forster, John 197

Forster, Richard 199, 206

Forster, Thomas 201

Forster, William 8

Forty-two articles of Religion 225

Fossor, John 59, 67

Foster, Richard 6

Foster, Thomas 6

Fountains Abbey 80, 87, 136, 138

Fox, Edward 48

Frampton 200

France, threat of 95–6

Francis I, King of France 96

Francis of Assisi, St 109

Franciscans, the 125, 163

Freeman, John 140

friaries, suppression of 162–5

Friars Minor, the 109

Friars Observant, the 162

Fulwell Manor 76

Furness Priory 153–5

Gainford 207

Gamleston, William 208

Gardiner, Stephen, Bishop of Winchester 50, 229

Geneva Bible, the 241

Geoffrey of Burdon, Prior 16

Giggleswick 158, 159

Gilbertines, the 121, 135

Glastonbury Abbey 87, 174–8

Gloucester 87, 164, 192

Gloucestershire 131, 137

Godstow 102–3, 163–4

Goldwell, Thomas 196

Good Friday 146

Gostwick, Edward 120

Gotham 74

grain supplies 8

grammar school, the 189, 236

Granator, the 8, 83

Grantham 208

grants of sake and soke 58

Gray, James 207

'great matter', the 47
    the annulment 93–5
    background 91–3

Green, William 139

Greene, Richard 134

Grenewell, John 42

Hackforth, William 197

Hailes 160–1

halmote courts 39

Hampshire 131, 132, 137, 155

Harper, Thomas 199, 206

Harrison, Thomas 248

Harrow-on-the-Hill 120

Harvey, Henry 239

Hasard, William 164

Hatfield, Thomas, Bishop 43–4, 59, 68, 104

Hawkwell, Thomas 8–9, 197

Heath, Nicholas, Bishop of Worcester 195, 231

Hebburn 76

Heddon 139

Heighington 185

Helay, Henry 83

Hemingborough 61

Heneage, John 120

Henley, Walter 180–3

Henry II, King 38, 57

Henry III, King 148

Henry V, King 62

lead, roofing 193
Lee, Edward, Archbishop of
York 94
legality 194–5
Leicester 87, 208
Leicestershire 131, 132
Leigh, Thomas 118–19, 123–5,
142–4, 179, 180–3, 187
Leighs, Essex 114
Lent 145
lepers 61
Lever, Ralph 244–5
Lewes 87, 155–6, 193
Lincoln 60, 74, 102–3, 144, 146
Lincolnshire 74, 135, 137, 140,
151, 188, 193, 200
Lindisfarne 23, 24
Lindisfarne Gospels 180–1
Lindisfarne Priory 19, 20–1,
70, 152
Lisle, Lord 126, 139
liturgical plays 32–3
liturgical processions 32–4
livestock 79, 80
Lollards 86
London, John 172–3
London 207–9, 211–12
Durham House 39, 143
St John of Jerusalem 87
London, Dr John 163–4
Longland, John, Bishop of
Lincoln 93, 184
loot
disposition of 155–6, 192–3
Durham 180–1
Glastonbury Abbey 177
value of 192–4
Luther, Martin 46, 95
Lutterworth 208
Lynsdoe, William 41
Lytham Priory 70–1, 152
Lyttelworke, Edward 172

Mackerell, Matthew 151, 152
maintenance payments 110–11
Malmesbury 29
Malyvere, Ralph 134
Mansfield 208
Marches, the 38
Marham 121, 132
Marian statutes 230–6, 254
Marillac, Charles de 173
Marley, Nicholas 196
Marley, Stephen 7, 196, 202,
241, 248–9

Marrick Priory 125, 134
Marsh, Richard, Bishop 57–8
Marshall, Thomas 178–80
marshalsea court 58–9
martyrdom 167, 171, 188. *see
also* executions
Mary, Queen 92, 207, 215, 216,
218, 221, 228, 228–30, 237–8
Mary Rose (ship) 96
Mary Stuart, Queen of Scots
245
Mason, Barbara 121
Masses 34–5, 144, 172, 203, 216,
217, 245–6, 247–9
Master of the Galilee, the 8–9
Master of the Novices, the 9
Matthew, John 207
Matthew, William 164
Maundy Thursday 145–6
Maurice, William 8
Mayr, William 76
Melrose 18
Melsby 140
Melsonby, Thomas 148
Merrington 233
Merten 140
Merton 87
Michelham 193
Middleham, Roger 7
Middlesex 87
Miller, Thomas 51–2, 158
minstrels 148
Modenham Abbey 193
monasteries. *see also* small
houses
Cromwell's suppression of
99–100
definition 54
as depositories of wealth 62
expenses 113
holdings 60–1
and the Pilgrimage of
Grace 151
prisons 67
stewards 67
Monkwearmouth 10, 70, 76,
104–5
Monreale Cathedral, Sicily
54–5
Montague, Henry 172
Montague, Lord 64
More, Sir Thomas 45, 50, 105,
108, 109, 114, 120
Mount Grace Priory 135
Moyle, Thomas 173, 175–7

Muggleswick 79, 80, 233
Musard, John 119
Mussett, Patrick 223

Nature Goddess Silk, the 181
Neasham 152
Netley 132
Neville family 64
Neville, Henry, 5th Earl of
Westmorland 48, 138
Neville, Charles, 6th Earl of
Westmorland 227, 242, 245,
246
Neville, John, Lord 4
Neville, Robert, Bishop 59,
83
Neville's Cross, Battle of, 1346
16
New Testament, English
edition 105, 106
Newcastle-under-Lyme 163
Newcastle-upon-Tyne 42, 51,
142, 206
Newhouse 233
Norfolk 131, 137, 139, 155
Norfolk, Thomas Howard,
Duke of 27, 39, 51, 66, 67,
100, 138, 154, 156, 189, 193
Norham Castle 37, 38–9, 51,
59, 62
Normans, the 4, 5, 16, 24–5
Northallerton 208, 209
Northampton 133
Northamptonshire 133
Northern Rising, 1568 245–8
Northumberland 200
Northumberland, Earl of 63
Norwich, Bishop of 165–6
Norwich Cathedral 29, 54, 87,
165–7, 191, 192, 195, 218
Nottingham 74, 135, 208
Nottinghamshire 74, 139, 144,
200
nunneries 134
Nuthake, Thomas 179

objectors 108–9
Observants, the 109, 121, 127
Order of Canons Regular
(Black Canons) 130
Oseney (Oxfordshire) 192,
194
Owston 132
Oxford 208
Oxford, Lady 139